THE END OF THE Habsburgs
The Decline and Fall of the Austrian Monarchy

JOHN VAN DER KISTE

FONTHILL

Fonthill Media Language Policy

Fonthill Media publishes in the international English language market. One language edition is published worldwide. As there are minor differences in spelling and presentation, especially with regard to American English and British English, a policy is necessary to define which form of English to use. The Fonthill Policy is to use the form of English native to the author. John Van der Kiste was born and educated in England; therefore British English has been adopted in this publication.

Fonthill Media Limited
Fonthill Media LLC
www.fonthillmedia.com
office@fonthillmedia.com

First published in the United Kingdom and the United States of America 2019

British Library Cataloguing in Publication Data:
A catalogue record for this book is available from the British Library

Copyright © John Van der Kiste 2019

ISBN 978-1-78155-770-9

Typeset in 10.5pt on 13pt Sabon
Printed and bound in England

CONTENTS

The Habsburg Monarchy and the Holy Roman Empire

For several centuries, the House of Habsburg was almost synonymous with the Holy Roman Empire, the throne of which was occupied by Habsburgs between 1438 and 1740.

Only at the beginning of the nineteenth century did the terms 'Habsburg monarchy' and 'Austrian monarchy' become synonymous. Previously, the dynastic name had embraced a much wider territory. Historians had already applied the name 'Habsburg monarchy' to countries and provinces ruled by the junior Austrian branch of the House of Habsburg between 1521 and 1780, and subsequently by the branch of Habsburg-Lorraine until 1918, the senior line being the Spanish one that became extinct with the death of Charles II of Spain in 1700. Technically, the House of Habsburg became extinct in the eighteenth century, the remaining Austrian branch in the male line in 1740 with the death of Charles VI, Holy Roman Emperor in 1740, and completely in 1780 with the death of his eldest daughter, Maria Theresa. It was succeeded by the Vaudémont branch of the House of Lorraine, descended from Maria Theresa's marriage to Francis III, Duke of Lorraine, and henceforth formally styled itself as the House of Habsburg-Lorraine. Tradition was maintained in that the head of the Austrian branch of the House of Habsburg was elected Holy Roman Emperor, as he had been since 1415, with one exception, namely King Charles VII of Bavaria, elected in 1742 and holding the title until his death three years later. He was the only Holy Roman Emperor who was not Habsburg ruler of Austria.

For several centuries, the monarchy itself had been a group of territories within and outside the Holy Roman Empire, united in the person of the monarch with a dynastic capital at Vienna, apart from a brief period late in the sixteenth century. One of the first Habsburg emperors, Frederick III,

Holy Roman Emperor from 1452 until his death in 1493, was credited with coining the acronym A.E.I.O.U., or *Austriae Est Imperare Orbi Universo* ('It is Austria's destiny to rule the whole world'). From 1804, the Habsburg monarchy was formally unified as the Austrian Empire, and following the rapprochement with Hungary in 1867, it was known as the Austro-Hungarian Empire.

The title of Holy Roman Emperor of the German nation was held by successive monarchs since assumed by Charlemagne in AD 800. Named after Habsburg Castle, an eleventh-century fortress in present-day Switzerland, the domains of the dynasty were divided between the senior Spanish branch and the junior Austrian branch after the death of Charles V, ruler of the Holy Roman Empire and the Spanish Empire (as Charles I of Spain) in 1558. Fourteen monarchs in turn succeeded him as Holy Roman Emperor until the dissolution of the empire on 6 August 1806.

The one responsible for this change was Emperor Francis II. Two years earlier, he had founded the Austrian Empire and proclaimed himself Francis I of Austria, Apostolic King of Hungary and Bohemia. Having held two titles for two years, using the title 'by the Grace of God elected Roman Emperor, hereditary Emperor of Austria', and being the emperor of both the Holy Roman Empire and Austria, he was known as the only *Doppelkaiser* (double emperor) in history.

The purpose of this book is to tell the story from the end of the Holy Roman Empire and, more importantly, the emperors and their families— from the Napoleonic era to the end of the Austrian empire, from the life of the last Holy Roman Emperor to the lives of the last emperor, his widow, and their son and heir, and the end of the twentieth century. It was a turbulent age that began with the decline and fall of Napoleon Bonaparte and ended with the services rendered to the former empire, now a republic, by Otto von Habsburg, the last crown prince.

My particular thanks for help and advice during my writing and research are to Sue Woolmans and Mark Andersen, for the loan of pictures; to Ricardo Sainz de Medrano, for advice on various details; to Alan Sutton and Joshua Greenland at Fonthill Media; and, as ever, to my wife, Kim, for reading through the draft and for her support throughout.

1

Francis and Ferdinand

As head of the House of Habsburg, it was the misfortune of Emperor Francis to reign during the ascendancy of Napoleon Bonaparte. Born in Florence in February 1768, Francis was the eldest son of Leopold II, Archduke of Austria and Grand Duke of Tuscany from 1765 to 1790, Holy Roman Emperor and King of Hungary from 1790 until his death two years later. Leopold's predecessor and elder brother, Emperor Joseph II, had no surviving issue by either of his two marriages, both his daughters having died in infancy.

The family expected Francis would inherit the imperial throne in due course. In 1784, he was sent to the imperial court at Vienna on the orders of Emperor Joseph, in preparation for his future role. The emperor thought he had been grossly spoilt and indulged as a child, and that he needed a harsher regime to make him ready for the responsibilities that would one day be his. He was accordingly sent to join an army regiment in Hungary and, despite his pampered upbringing, settled easily into the routine of military life.

On his death in 1790, Joseph was succeeded on the throne by Leopold. He fell ill the following year and died in March 1792, at the early age of forty-four. Francis was now emperor, much sooner than anyone had expected. Now leader of the large multi-ethnic Habsburg Empire, he felt threatened by the ambitions and expansion of the First French Empire as engendered by Napoleon's social and political reforms. Austria had a dynastic connection with the deposed Bourbon dynasty, for Francis was the nephew of Marie Antoinette, wife of Louis XVI and Queen Consort of France, who was guillotined by the revolutionaries in 1793, not long after his accession. She was the younger sister of Emperor Leopold, but they had never been close, and he had little memory of her despite occasional meetings in his younger days. Georges Danton, one of the leading figures in the French revolution, offered to negotiate with Francis for her release, either by exchanging her for French prisoners of war or by payment of a ransom, but the latter was unwilling to make any concessions in return.

Francis's initial campaigns against Napoleon were unsuccessful. In 1794, he briefly commanded the allied forces during the campaigns in the Low Countries, a coalition of states also including Prussia, Hanover, Britain, and the Dutch Republic, and mobilised military forces along the French frontiers with the aim of invading revolutionary France. After a few months, he relinquished the command to his younger brother, Archduke Charles, Duke of Teschen, who was soon defeated by Napoleon. By the Treaty of Campo Formio, signed in October 1797, he ceded the left bank of the Rhine to France in exchange for Venice and Dalmatia. A few years later, he and his European allies were drawn into war against France again. The result was a major defeat at the Battle of Austerlitz in December 1805, in which, facing a numerically superior army of combined Austrian and Prussian forces, Napoleon achieved what was seen as the greatest victory of his career.

It brought that stage of the war to a close, and a treaty was signed between Napoleon and Emperor Francis at Pressburg at the end of the month. Austria was forced to withdraw from the Third Coalition made up of the allies fighting together against France, undertook to pay an indemnity of 40 million francs to France, and surrendered various territories to the French and their allies. Francis also recognised the kingly titles assumed by the Electors of Bavaria and Württemberg, foreshadowing the end of the Holy Roman Empire. Within months of the treaty being signed, as a reaction to Napoleon proclaiming himself emperor, and in recognition of the fact that his time-honoured position as Holy Roman Emperor was now untenable, on 6 August 1806, he abdicated the throne and declared the empire to be already dissolved.

For the rest of his life, he reigned as Francis I, Emperor of Austria. With it, he assumed a splendid array of additional titles, namely King of Jerusalem, Hungary, Bohemia, Dalmatia, Croatia, Slavonia, Galicia, and Lodomeria; Duke of Lorraine, Salzburg, Würzburg, Franconia, Styria, Carinthia, and Carniola; Grand Duke of Cracow; Grand Prince of Transylvania; Margrave of Moravia; Duke of Sadomir, Masovia, Lublin, Upper and Lower Silesia, Auschwitz and Zator, Teschen, and Friule; Prince of Berchtesgaden and Mergentheim; Princely Count of Habsburg, Gorizia, and Gradisca, and of the Tyrol; and Margrave of Upper and Lower Lusatia and in Istria. According to an old joke of the time, 'The King of Croatia declared war on the King of Hungary, and Austria's Emperor, who was both, remained benevolently neutral'.[1]

The main consequence for the map of Europe, albeit in the short term, was to weaken the Austrian Empire and reorganise Germany under a Napoleonic imprint, the Confederation of the Rhine. This grouping, which lasted from 1806 to 1813, comprised several German states allied to France, including the kingdoms of Saxony, Westphalia, and Bavaria and the Grand Duchy of Baden. The members of the confederation were German princes from the Holy Roman Empire. They were later joined by nineteen others, altogether ruling a total of over 15 million subjects. It provided a significant strategic advantage to the French Empire on its eastern front by forming a separation between France and the two largest German states, Austria and Prussia, to the east, which were not members of the Confederation. Napoleon sought to consolidate the modernising achievements of the revolution, but he needed the soldiers and supplies these subject states could provide for his wars. The success of the Confederation depended on victory, and his hopes collapsed with a humiliating defeat by the coalition armies of Russia, Austria, Prussia, and Sweden at the Battle of Leipzig, also known as the Battle of the Nations, in October 1813.

Francis was now the pre-eminent monarch in continental Europe of the opposition to Napoleonic France. In 1809, as part of the Fifth Coalition in which Austria and Britain fought as allies, he attacked France again, hoping to take advantage of the Peninsular War that was keeping the French forces occupied in Spain. Defeated once more, he had no alternative but to ally himself with Napoleon, ceding territory to the empire and agreeing to Napoleon's marriage with his daughter, Archduchess Marie-Louise. During fourteen years of Napoleon's first marriage, Josephine had been unable to bear him a child, and at the end of 1809, he told her of his intention to seek a divorce, remarry, and give France an heir. In January 1810, their union was dissolved, and two months later, he married Emperor Francis's daughter. This alliance did not prevent Austria from going to war against France for one last time in 1813 in alliance with Britain, Prussia, Russia, and Sweden. The War of the Sixth Coalition resulted in the defeat of France.

After his role in bringing Napoleon's years of invincibility to an end, Francis, represented by his foreign minister Clemens von Metternich, presided over the Congress of Vienna in 1815. Austria was a leading member of the Holy Alliance, a coalition created by the powers of Austria, Prussia, and Russia after the ultimate defeat of Napoleon on the initiative of Tsar Alexander I. Its purpose was to maintain the European status quo, and it succeeded in holding together until Britain and France jointly and victoriously went to war against Russia in the Crimea nearly forty years later.

The so-called Congress was not an orderly meeting of delegates, but a series of small and sometimes informal meetings between the Great Powers of Austria, Britain, Russia, sometimes Prussia, and post-Napoleonic France, with limited or no participation by other delegates. It was the first occasion in history where national representatives from different continental states came together to formulate treaties instead of relying largely on messages among the several capitals, and the resulting settlement formed a framework for European international politics that remained largely unaltered until the outbreak of the First World War in 1914.

Having won the war against Napoleon, after years of struggle, Francis was determined to maintain peace by keeping nationalist and liberal elements at bay, if not eliminating them altogether. As first president of the German Confederation, created in June 1815 at the Congress, he was theoretically the most powerful monarch among the thirty-nine states in central Europe, the post-Napoleonic equivalent of the old Holy Roman Empire. The verdict of historians would later be that this confederation was weak, ineffective, and the obstacle to the creation of a German nation state, but for Emperor Francis—and indeed for the next two emperors, for the next thirty years after his death—it served its purpose admirably.

The events of the French Revolution had made a deep impression on the mind of Francis as well as his main allies, the King of Prussia and the Tsar of Russia. As a result, he came to distrust radicalism in any form, seeing it as subversion and a threat to the established order, and he and Metternich jointly set up an extensive network of police spies and censors to monitor any sign of dissent. Even the emperor's own family were not excluded, and any meetings and activities of his brothers, Archdukes Charles and Johann, were likewise subject to surveillance. Despite this, he shrewdly presented himself as an open and approachable monarch. He regularly devoted two mornings each week to meeting his imperial subjects, regardless of status, by appointment in his office, even speaking to them in their own language, but his will was sovereign. It is said that a distinguished servant of the empire was once recommended to him for special notice on the grounds that he was a staunch and loyal patriot. His immediate reaction was, 'But is he a patriot for me?'[2]

His domestic policy was one of calm, orderliness, and lack of innovation. During his reign, agriculture remained the main industry of most of his subjects. He did nothing to promote or encourage trade in other areas, thus inadvertently allowing Prussia to preside over a more rapidly expanding economy and industry and pose an ever-increasing threat to Austria's leadership of the confederation. This, coupled with his neglect of increased spending on the army, would leave a legacy of problems that came to a head some forty years later, long after his death. Powerless to curb dissent in Hungary, after a meeting of the Central Hungarian Diet in 1825, he had to agree not to raise taxes without their consent.

Emperor Francis was married four times. His first wife was Princess Elizabeth of Württemberg, who died less than two years after their wedding in 1788 in childbirth, their baby daughter surviving her by only a few months. Later, in 1790, he married his first cousin, Princess Maria Theresa of Naples and Sicily. She bore him eight daughters and four sons before dying in 1807 at the age of thirty-four, following complications after the birth of her last child. The baby, a daughter, lived for only three days, and two of her elder sisters had likewise died in childhood, as had one of her brothers. The next year, the emperor married another first cousin, Princess Maria Ludovica of Austria-Este, who died in 1816, aged only twenty-eight. Soon after her death, he married Princess Caroline Augusta of Bavaria, who survived him. His third and fourth marriages were both childless.

Remaining in good health almost until the last, in February 1835, he celebrated his sixty-seventh birthday with a great court ball. One chilly evening soon afterwards, he and the empress went out to the theatre, and within a couple of days, he was confined to his bed with suspected pneumonia. Aware that he was dying, he added his signature to two testaments to his son and heir Ferdinand, which Metternich had prepared long before. One entrusted him with the duty of defending and upholding the free activity of the Roman Catholic Church; the other requested him not to take any decision on internal public affairs without consulting his uncle, Archduke Ludwig, or the ever-reliable Metternich, 'my most loyal servant and friend.'[3] Ludwig was charged with presiding over the council, whose members also included Metternich and Count Francis von Kolowrat-Liebsteinsky, chosen to govern in Ferdinand's name. Some of the ministers were surprised by this decision, for the emperor's other three surviving brothers were considered more capable. Charles was a proven military commander, Joseph a former governor of Hungary, and Johann a brave soldier and renowned patron of the arts. By choosing his least able brother, and one who could be guaranteed to support the 'most loyal servant and friend' without question, the emperor had assured Metternich would be emperor in all but name.

On 2 March, he breathed his last. At the funeral, his Viennese subjects respectfully filed past his coffin in the Hofburg Palace chapel for three days as he was laid to rest in the imperial crypt alongside the three wives who had predeceased him, and where his widow would join him almost thirty-eight years later.

Nobody had any great expectations of Emperor Ferdinand. The eldest son of Francis, aged forty-one at the time of his accession, he was a tragic victim of interbreeding. His parents had been first cousins, a consanguinity held responsible for his many chronic ailments and neurological disorders. He had epilepsy, a speech impediment that meant he could barely utter two connected sentences, and he could neither lift a glass with one hand nor descend a staircase without assistance. Nor was he the first of the Habsburg rulers to pay a price for having too few ancestors. The most unfortunate example had been King Charles II of Spain, born in 1661, the son of King Philip IV, whose wife, Princess Marina of Austria, was also his niece. Charles had what was known as the Habsburg jaw, with a huge tongue, a jutting lower jaw, and a thick lower lip. Severely developmentally delayed, he was unable to speak until four years of age, breastfed until five, and unable to walk until eight. Even in adult life, his communication was muffled and barely comprehensible. After a short life of constant ill-health, unable to consummate either of his two marriages, he died at the age of thirty-eight in 1700.

It was no secret in Vienna that 'Ferdinand the Good-Natured', as everyone called him, was feeble in body and mind. Metternich called him 'a lump of putty', and Lord Palmerston, successively British Foreign Secretary and Prime Minister, 'a perfect nullity; next thing to an idiot'.[4] Where truth ends and gossip or exaggeration takes over is uncertain. After meeting him, Empress Alexandra, consort of Tsar Nicholas I of Russia, wrote in her diary 'about his small ugly shrunken figure and his huge head void of any expression except that of stupidity—but the reality beggared all description'.[5] The duke of Reichstadt, son of Napoleon Bonaparte, judged him more kindly: '... a pathetic child, feeble-minded but fundamentally good at heart'.[6] It was said that his favourite amusements were to wedge himself into a large waste paper basket and roll around the floor in it, and to try and catch flies with his bare hands.

Even well into his adult life, there were doubts as to whether he would be able to take a bride, let alone become father of an heir to the throne. Eventually, when he was aged thirty-seven, he was betrothed to Princess Anna Maria of Savoy and they married in February 1831. The court physician thought it unlikely that he would or even could make any attempt to assert his marital rights. Apparently, Ferdinand did try one night, and suffered five epileptic seizures afterwards.

Fortunately, his brother had already helped to secure the imperial succession. In November 1824, Archduke Francis Charles married Princess Sophie of Bavaria, daughter of King Maximilian I Joseph of Bavaria. His contemporaries found him pleasant but unappealing, unambitious, clumsy, and rather stupid. He had no intellectual interests, no thirst for power or appetite for ruling, and his only passion was for hunting. Although not afflicted with his brother's sad deformities, he had a long thin face out of all proportion to his slight body. However, as the only surviving brother of Emperor Francis's physically handicapped heir, Ferdinand, the Bavarian royal family were sure their daughter would be empress one day. His mother-in-law damned him with the faintest of praise. While acknowledging that he was 'a good fellow and wants to do well', she thought him 'really terrible…. He would bore me to death. Every now and then I would want to hit him.'[7]

At first, there were fears that they might never have a family, for in their first five years of marriage, Sophie had two miscarriages. Nevertheless, she succeeded in producing four sons and a daughter. Francis Joseph ('Franzi') was born on 18 August 1830, Ferdinand Maximilian ('Max') on 6 July 1832, Charles Ludwig ('Karly') on 30 July 1833, Maria Anna on 27 October 1835, and, after an interval of nearly seven years, Ludwig Victor ('Bubi') on 15 May 1842. Maria Anna was epileptic and died at the age of four, but her brothers all reached adulthood. The three elder children were generally fit and healthy, but the delicate Ludwig Victor was often confined to bed with various infections, his family ever fearful that they might lose him as suddenly as they had his unfortunate sister.

Archduchess Sophie, a woman of character and the most resolute member of the imperial family, was sometimes known as 'the only man in the Hofburg'. While she had initially accepted Francis Charles as a husband without much enthusiasm, she gradually came to respect him and appreciate that despite his lack of personal qualities, he was a loyal, faithful, and attentive husband and a doting father. Nevertheless, the upbringing of their eldest son, who would undoubtedly be a future emperor, remained the main focus of her attention. Guided and moulded by her, he would be as conservative as any of his forebears, determined to hold on to the reins of power. She thought the revolutions of 1848 were the regrettable outcome of too much liberalism, telling a friend a year later that 'I could have borne the loss of one of my children more easily than the shame of submitting to a mess of students.'[8] She disliked Metternich as a man, but respected him as a statesman. Nevertheless, she never forgave him for having allowed Ferdinand to become emperor, believing he could have used his influence to have him passed over in the succession in favour of her husband. In his defence, Metternich claimed that he had done no more than honour the dying wishes of Emperor Francis, but Sophie knew he meant to be the real power behind the throne and was unwilling to relinquish such a status to her as the empress consort.

As Emperor Ferdinand was capable of reigning but not ruling, during his reign of thirteen years, the government was answerable not to him but to the council. Although physically handicapped, he was not the simpleton some people took him for. Mentally quite alert, he reportedly had a dry wit and kept a perfectly coherent and legible diary. Posterity credits him with having made some memorable remarks, not least during an argument with the imperial cook. When told he could not have apricot dumplings as apricots were out of season, he allegedly declared that 'I am the Emperor, and I want dumplings!'[9]

Once peace and order had been re-established at the Congress of Vienna, the reigns of Francis and Ferdinand were an era of reaction, with strict censorship and restrictions on the freedom of the press. Mounting social and political tensions gradually built up. The authorities were only partially successful in trying to control a flourishing liberal German culture, particularly among students who published pamphlets and newspapers discussing education, language, and the need for basic liberal reforms, including relaxations in censorship, and religious and economic freedom. Contemporary liberal clubs and associations in Vienna were part of a culture that freely criticised Metternich's government in the city's coffee houses, salons, and theatre stages, but their demands never extended to constitutional government, freedom of assembly, or even overthrow of the monarchy.

The younger Francis was a handsome, sturdy child, who had inherited neither of the less-becoming Habsburg characteristics—the protruding lip or the prominent nose of so many of his forebears. From early boyhood, he was destined to be a soldier. As a small child, he adored military ceremony, watched sentries pacing beneath the nursery window every day, and later loved to go and see soldiers at the barracks taking part in their drill on the parade ground. From the age of four, he enjoyed dressing up in uniform and playing with his toy soldiers, a collection eventually comprising every regiment of the Austrian army, with the details of each uniform perfectly reproduced. He took such care of them that none of the pieces were ever broken or lost.

Throughout childhood, the two elder brothers, Francis and Maximilian, both destined to be emperors, were devoted to each other despite their differences in character. Max was a dreamy, imaginative soul, with a fine singing voice, a gift for mimicry, a talent for taking part in tableaux and little theatrical productions for their parents and close relations, and a fascination with animals, birds, and flowers to be seen near the palace. Shortly before his birth, Sophie had been close friends with the duke of Reichstadt, briefly emperor of the French in name only after the fall of his father in 1815. He lived in the Schönbrunn Palace, but most of his short life was dominated by ill-health and he died of consumption in July 1832, aged twenty-one. Gossips at Vienna said that he was the father of Sophie's second son.

Max was the intellectual member of the family, and Francis had no time for reading or literature. He cared little for the visual arts, believing that painters should either be craftsmen or decorators, applying their skills to palace interiors, or else producers of meticulous landscapes and military scenes celebrating great victories. Both brothers regularly visited the theatre together and he enjoyed dancing, although apart from military marches, music did not interest him.

Francis's education began when he was six years old. Two close friends of Metternich, Count Heinrich Bombelles and Count Johann Coronini-Cromberg, were chosen as tutors. He was expected to spend eighteen hours a week studying from his books, increased to thirty-six hours at the age of eight, and forty-six hours at eleven. Two years later, he became seriously ill and had a brief respite after the physicians decided the regime was probably too much for him. Even so, after an interval, he was given further subjects to study, and at fifteen years old, he was working up to fifty-five hours a week. The importance of early rising and punctuality was impressed on him, particularly in summer, when lessons began at 6 a.m. and continued with short breaks until 9 p.m. Much emphasis was placed on learning by rote and little on how to think and solve problems for himself. By the age of eight, he was writing letters to his mother in French. Ironically, France was traditionally Austria's great enemy, particularly in the early years of the nineteenth century, while Britain was an ally, yet he never learnt English. It was important that he should also be taught the different languages of the empire, including Magyar and Czech, and lessons in these began for him when he was twelve.

Despite his fascination for the army and uniform, mounting a horse did not come easily to him. After his first attempts, he wept with fear, but he and his tutor persevered until he became a proficient rider. At the age of thirteen, he was appointed colonel-in-chief of the 3rd Dragoon Regiment, and in the next year, he was allowed to ride at the head of his regiment when participating in exercises. By then, the archdukes' parents and tutors were beginning to allow them their first taste of public life, and in 1845, the three elder brothers went on a semi-official tour of Lombardy-Venetia, under the supervision of Field Marshal Joseph Radetsky. Reviews, tours of various defence works, firework displays, and exhibitions of horsemanship were arranged for them. Francis had always enjoyed drawing, and during their travels in Italy, he made several sketches and drawings while staying in the towns, all showing technical skill and a sense of keen observation.[10]

Although the Italians resented Austrian rule in the provinces, their guests were enthusiastically cheered when they appeared on an excursion down the Grand Canal in Venice, escorted by a small fleet of gondolas. Soon Francis was appearing in public regularly at family funerals and various ceremonial occasions, including court receptions and field exercises in which he rode at the head of his regiment. Now almost an adult, he must have assumed that life would continue this way for many a year. His uncle was in good health, his father would presumably reign next, and he himself would become emperor in middle age. Only at eighteen did he realise he was about to enter on his inheritance with startling rapidity.

During the 1840s, economic unrest spread throughout Europe, with poor harvests, recession, and food shortages leading to radicalism and a desire for change. Trading competition from Britain and Prussia and increasing unemployment fuelled a depression from the poorer regions of Austria to the more prosperous areas of Vienna. By the end of 1847, Archduchess Sophie was in a state of gloom over the outlook for the empire. Her family connections included a half-brother on the throne of Bavaria, a twin sister as consort of the King of Saxony, and an elder sister married to King Frederick William IV of Prussia. As a regular reader of German newspapers and French periodicals, she was probably the best-informed member of the imperial family. While she might not agree with the new liberal ways of thinking, she was more aware than the others that younger politicians were impatient with the elderly Metternich's conservatism, and that within the Austrian Empire, the new linguistic and cultural nationalism was creating instability. Matters could not go on as they were.

The catalyst came early in the new year of 1848 with insurrection in Sicily, liberal agitation in Tuscany and the Papal States, and the granting of a constitution in Naples. At the end of February, demonstrations in Paris forced King Louis-Philippe of France to abdicate, prompting similar revolts elsewhere throughout Europe. In March, Lajos Kossuth, a Hungarian lawyer and journalist, made a speech to the Diet urging the establishment of a virtually autonomous Hungary with a responsible government elected on a broad franchise. While speaking respectfully of the Habsburg dynasty as a unifying force, he still considered it essential to change the character of government in the monarchy in order to safeguard their country's historic freedoms. When reports of his speech reached Vienna, they produced the response of a plea for civil rights and some form of parliamentary government.

As a senior figure in government as foreign minister since 1809 and chancellor since 1821, Metternich had successfully maintained the balance of power, largely through resisting Russian territorial ambitions in Central Europe and lands belonging to the Ottoman Empire. Like Emperor Francis, he was impatient with any talk of liberalism, and his objective was to prevent the disintegration of the Austrian Empire by ruthlessly crushing nationalist revolts in Austrian northern Italy and the German states. He gave his name to the 'Metternich era', when international diplomacy helped to prevent major wars in Europe, and the people of Austria and her neighbours could be grateful for three decades of European peace; but a period of political reaction and a faltering economic situation called for new ideas and younger men at the top. Now seventy-four, his grasp was loosening, and there were calls for his dismissal or retirement.

On 12 March, a petition was handed to Emperor Ferdinand, demanding the departure of Metternich and his hated minister of police, Joseph Sedlnitsky, and the removal of police surveillance. As revolutionaries marched on the palace and the chancellor explained what was happening, he looked surprised and asked if they were allowed to do such a thing. Early the next day, students marched to the Herrengasse, a major street in Vienna that was home to several palaces of the nobility. The army was sent to clear the streets, and in the ensuing affray, four men were killed and another was seriously wounded.

A meeting was convened at the Hofburg, where a garrison was keeping crowds at bay with some difficulty. The emperor's uncle, Archduke Ludwig, said at first that they should use force to put the rebellion down as firmly as possible, and proposed summoning Field Marshal Alfred, Prince von Windischgrätz, who had fought with distinction on several campaigns during the wars against France. His brother, Archduke Johann, argued that Metternich should be dismissed and the people of Vienna given an opportunity to voice their grievances. Archduke Francis Charles—the emperor's brother and heir—had no opinion. Archduke Albrecht, elder cousin of the emperor and commandant of Vienna, who had been slightly wounded in the street fighting, and Archduchess Sophie agreed Metternich must resign. They were kept informed of what was happening outside, and as reports of the unrest became more serious, everyone felt that their chancellor must go. On being summoned, he refused to leave office unless his sovereign and the archdukes in line of succession undertook to absolve him personally from the oath he had taken before the death of Emperor Francis that he would pledge his loyal support to his successor. He then addressed them at length, telling them to stand firm against mobs in the street without betraying any hint of weakness. When nobody agreed with him, he said he would resign, denying that his action was a generous one. Two days later, he left Vienna and fled to England.

With some prompting from Archduchess Sophie, Archduke Francis Charles emerged as chief spokesman for the government and urged the granting of an imperial constitution. Once this had been done, he said, all subsequent political reforms could follow in due course. The archduchess did not concur, as she knew there was a chance their son could succeed to the throne before long, and she did not want his powers limited by any concessions wrung from the imperial family at a time of crisis. She suggested they should wait until the agitation had died down. On the next day, Francis joined his father and the emperor on a carriage drive through Vienna to try and assess the public mood. There were some cheers for the emperor, but many sullen faces and apparently unmoved crowds as well.

To succeed Metternich, Count Franz Anton von Kolowrat-Liebsteinsky was appointed to the newly created post of minister-president. Regarded as a moderate liberal, he had previously been minister for the interior and finance under Emperor Francis in 1826. His frequent disagreements with Metternich during the years when both were two of the most senior politicians in Austria had meant an uncomfortable working relationship between them, but at first he was seen as the one most fitted to the task.

It was not good enough for those who demanded further reforms. Workers' and students' demonstrations, driven partly by sympathy for nationalist hopes in Hungary and the Italian territories, made the atmosphere in Vienna so strained that the imperial family decided to move under cover of darkness to Innsbruck and stay there for the next three months. Kolowrat-Liebsteinsky's period of office lasted barely four weeks before he resigned, ostensibly for reasons of health. His successor, Count Charles von Ficquelmont, a former staff chief of the imperial army, had been Metternich's right-hand man in government for a while. Tainted by association, he spent just a month in office. His three replacements lasted two months, ten days, and four months respectively.

In October, an army was assembled to leave for Hungary and fight the forces led by Kossuth. The grenadiers refused to go, joining the rioters instead. During the street fighting that followed, Theodore von Latour, the minister of war who had issued the order in Vienna for the troops to go, was dragged from his office and lynched. The revolution in Vienna was slow to subside, with tax boycotts, attempted murders of tax collectors, and assaults against soldiers. After several weeks of disorder and near-anarchy had threatened to escalate into a reign of terror, the citizens seemed weary of it all. At the end of October 1848, Windischgrätz ordered his army to surround Vienna and subjected it to a prolonged bombardment. The resistance of the more persistent radicals soon evaporated, and in the ensuing disturbances, over 2,000 protesters were killed. Within a few days, the city had capitulated to the imperial troops.

In November, the imperial family held a conference with the senior ministers. Prince Felix Schwarzenberg, the brother-in-law of Windischgrätz, a former adviser to Field Marshal Radetsky, who had been suppressing rebel forces in Milan, was the sixth man invited to become minister-president since the resignation of Metternich. He insisted that he would only accept office under a new emperor and demanded the abdication of Ferdinand as the price of his accepting office. Archduchess Sophie agreed with him. Although well-liked, Ferdinand was incapable of reigning, let alone ruling, and moreover he was ineradicably associated with the failed system against which the Viennese had been rebelling. In peacetime, Archduke Francis Charles would have made an adequate emperor, but he was regarded as indecisive and unintelligent. The only subject on which he held an opinion, it seemed, was that he had no desire to succeed his brother on the throne and was happy to renounce his place in the succession.

It was therefore decided that the next sovereign would be his eldest son, eighteen-year-old Archduke Francis. Untainted by any connection with the events of the last few months, he would serve as the symbol of a new, hopefully glorious era in Austrian imperial history. Much as Archduchess Sophie might have coveted the position of reigning empress, she realised that as the mother of the sovereign, she would be one of the powers behind the crown, not quite the reigning sovereign but the next best thing.

On 2 December, the family and ministers were bidden to appear before Emperor Ferdinand in the salon of the Prince-Bishop's palace at Olmütz. In his halting, hardly coherent voice, he read a declaration stating that he was laying down the crown in favour of his nephew. Embracing the young man tenderly, he assured him, 'Bear yourself bravely; it is all right'.[11] To Francis's baptismal name was added that of Joseph, and he was declared emperor by the Grace of God. At the end of the day, having laid down his burden, Ferdinand noted in his diary how the young new emperor knelt to his predecessor and asked for a blessing: '... which I gave by laying my hands upon his head and making the sign of the Holy Cross. Then I embraced him and he kissed my hand. And then my dear wife embraced and kissed our new master, and then we went away to our room'.[12]

2

'A young man of
great promise'

At the age of eighteen, the man who had until recently been just one of several archdukes in Austria, although admittedly one of the most important, was now the most powerful head of state in continental Europe—and next to Nicholas, Tsar of Russia, probably in the world. Emperor Francis Joseph was fully aware of his responsibilities, if not as yet his full authority. After returning from the accession ceremony, he reportedly burst into tears as he bid farewell to his youth.

One curiously uncharacteristic episode involving him occurred two weeks later. When six-year-old Ludwig Victor cracked a mirrored door in the episcopal palace while playing with a ball, he appealed to his eldest brother to defend him. Normally the personification of self-control, the emperor longed to revert for a moment to his carefree childhood. Asking their mother for permission, he joined his siblings as they proceeded to smash the door beyond repair. The archduchess noted in her diary that 'His Majesty went at it to his heart's content'.[1]

As for Ferdinand and Anna Maria, his uncle and aunt who had occupied the throne before him, they retained their titles of emperor and empress. Freed of their responsibilities, they spent the rest of their days in Hradschin Castle, Prague. Every day, the former sovereign took a stroll along the ramparts, as citizens respectfully saluted *der Praguer Majestàs*, the monarch who had never forfeited their affections as a man. He died in 1875 aged eighty-two, and his widow almost nine years later, at eighty. They were laid to rest next to each other in the imperial crypt at Vienna.

Meanwhile, a proclamation to the new ruler's subjects, probably drafted in advance by Schwarzenberg, took place outside the Rathaus in Vienna and subsequently on the cathedral steps. It included an assurance from the crown that they, rather than he, were 'convinced of the need and value of free institutions expressive of the age'. They were equally 'determined to maintain the splendour of the crown undimmed and the monarchy as a whole undiminished, but ready to share our rights with the representatives of our peoples', and counted on succeeding in uniting all the regions and races of the monarchy in one great state.[2]

One of the emperor's first priorities was to restore law and order throughout his empire by subduing the unrest in Hungary. By early January 1849, the Austrian forces under Windischgrätz were in control of the Hungarian capitals of Buda and Pest, but Kossuth's forces rallied, halted the Austrian advance, and retook the capitals. In April, Kossuth proclaimed that the House of Habsburg had been dispossessed by the republic of Hungary. Windischgrätz replied that there could be no negotiations with rebels, but having failed in his objective, the emperor relieved him of his command and replaced him with Baron Ludwig von Welden.

Despite his inexperience, the emperor was convinced it was his duty to preside over government meetings in person. In theory, he would not be a tool of anyone, be it his mother or his minister-president, although in practice, he still sought their advice and reassurance. In March 1849, he proclaimed a new imperial constitution that reclaimed Habsburg power after concessions made during the revolutions of the previous year. It also made provision for a two-chamber parliamentary system with elections, but with a limited franchise that favoured the more prosperous landowning classes, and for basic recognition of fundamental rights, including the freedom of assembly and association. While many of those in German-Austria responded to the law positively because bourgeois circles considered it a basis for further economic development, it was rejected by the Slavs and Hungarians. Within less than three years, the emperor had to conclude that Austria was not suited to government under the constitutional principle of England and France, and it was formally rescinded in December 1851.

Against the advice of Windischgrätz and Schwarzenberg, in April, the emperor asked Tsar Nicholas I of Russia if he would help Austria by despatching a Russian expeditionary force to help put down the Hungarian rebellion, writing that he had 'derived comfort and hope from the certainty that I can count on the unwavering friendship of Your Imperial Majesty'.[3] The tsar met the emperor in May and was very impressed, telling the tsarina that Austria was 'lucky to possess him'. Moreover, part of Russia's foreign policy was determined by her determination, or rather that of the tsar, to show solidarity with and uphold the cause of monarchism in Europe.

Some six weeks later, a Russian relief army was sent to Hungary. Meanwhile, General Julius Haynau, already there as commander-in-chief of the Austrian forces, was ordered to embark on a campaign of conquest. Although he might have won the war on his own, as he was convinced that his Austrian troops with reinforcements from Italy would have done, the Russian forces helped to inflict total defeat on Hungary by hastening the surrender of the revolutionary army under General Arthur von Görgei. It was a favour that would soon require Austrian repayment with interest.

The tsar advised Emperor Francis Joseph not to sentence any of the Hungarian rebels to death, on the grounds that showing mercy to the rebel leaders at this stage would help to secure Magyar goodwill in future years. Schwarzenberg, it is said, responded cynically that it was a good idea, 'but we must have some hanging first.'[4] In the name of the emperor, he and Haynau, who was notorious for his ruthlessness, had nine of the leaders sent to the gallows and another four shot. Almost 400 officers were sentenced to imprisonment and over 100 death sentences were passed. Against his better judgment, the young ruler was thus persuaded to begin his reign, not in a spirit of reconciliation, but with a display of ruthlessness. It did not escape the notice of posterity that between 1848 and 1853, he signed and confirmed more death sentences than any other European ruler during the nineteenth century.[5] Appeals for clemency from various quarters, notably his eldest brother, Maximilian, were in vain.

One execution that particularly shocked several countries outside the empire was that of Lajos Batthyány, the former Hungarian prime minister who had presided over the rebel government. After he was captured and imprisoned for several months, a military court found him guilty and recommended sentencing him to a further term of captivity, but under pressure from Schwarzenberg, the authorities decided to make an example of him and sentenced him to death. Hia wife wrote to Archduchess Sophie, begging for clemency; receiving no reply, she smuggled a knife into the prison, and he attempted suicide, but only wounded himself. The method of execution chosen for him was then altered from hanging to firing squad.

For a young ruler under twenty years old, Francis Joseph might appear to the outside world as harsh, if not tyrannical, and not someone to be trifled with. Those who knew him personally found him mild, polite, patient, and dignified, with a keen memory. Cautious and unimaginative, brought up with respect for tradition, he disliked change for its own sake, and appeared an old head on young shoulders. Meeting him for the first time in 1852, Ernest, Duke of Saxe-Coburg Gotha, the brother-in-law of Queen Victoria of England, thought him 'a young man of great promise' with a talent for organizing and a quick comprehension. He was, however, very insular, and if only he had had a wider education and been permitted to travel abroad, 'he would already through his own natural ability carry far more weight'.[6]

In April 1852, Schwarzenberg died suddenly after a stroke. The emperor then decided that he would assume a more direct role in overseeing cabinet affairs than before, and the post of minister-president was replaced by that of chairman of the Austrian ministers' conference, one that wielded less power and was more directly answerable to the sovereign. Count Ferdinand von Buol, formerly Austrian envoy to Britain who had worked closely with Schwarzenberg, was appointed to the post as well as that of foreign minister.

Although he was determined to rule and reign, Archduchess Sophie was still to some extent the power behind the court, if not the throne itself. His daily timetable was sent to her for approval, and she decided where and when meals were to be served, who was to be invited to the imperial table, and floral decorations for state and court balls at carnival time. She took responsibility for many of the trappings of royalty, such as ensuring that the emperor continued to uphold the prestige of the crown by riding in smartly refurbished carriages, with well-turned out coachmen and postilions resplendent in their royal livery. To her, it was vital that the people of Vienna should see that members of the imperial house were undertaking their rightful ceremonial functions and remained fully in the public eye.

While she intended her son to be a dutiful and model hardworking sovereign, she did not wish to commit him to a life of unremitting toil. It was only right, she knew, that he and his younger brothers should be allowed to relax when time allowed and, above all, to enjoy themselves at court balls, at which he always particularly enjoyed dancing. The time was coming when he needed to settle down with a wife and provide the empire with heirs. He had come to the throne at a turbulent time, and with war, uprisings, and scattered military campaigns, to say nothing of the threat of assassination, his life could not be guaranteed. Moreover, as his unexpected accession in early manhood had made him old and serious beyond his years, she knew the right companion and a family life might soften him and make his burden less onerous. Tentative plans were made with various possible brides in mind. There was briefly talk of a marriage with Princess Anna of Prussia, a niece of King Frederick William IV, and then with Princess Sidonia of Saxony, both of whom were rejected for various reasons.

At first, marriage was not considered urgent, until they were provided with a chilling reminder of mortality. On 18 February 1853, the emperor was strolling around Vienna when a man leapt at him from behind and stabbed him with a knife in the neck, leaving him bleeding profusely. Only the thick golden covering embroidered on the collar of his jacket had helped to lessen the impact of the blow. The assailant, Janos Libényi, a young tailor's apprentice from a Hungarian regiment that had fought during the rebellion of 1848, was condemned to death and executed eight days later. Francis Joseph made light of it and bravely told his mother that he had been wounded, 'along with [his] soldiers'. Nevertheless, he was confined to the Hofburg for three weeks, suffering from delayed shock and loss of blood. He resumed normal duties after a service of thanksgiving to celebrate his recovery in the middle of March.

This intensified the archduchess's determination to find a wife for her son, who would always have to live and reign with the threat of assassination. That summer, she invited her twin sister, Ludovica, Duchess in Bavaria, and her two elder daughters to stay with them in their summer palace at Ischl for a few days and celebrate the emperor's twenty-third birthday.

Ludovica's sisters had made excellent dynastic marriages. Apart from Sophie herself, there was Elizabeth, wife of King Frederick William IV of Prussia; Amalie, wife of King Johann of Saxony; and Marie, Archduchess Sophie's twin, who had been married to King Frederick Augustus II of Saxony, elder brother and predecessor of King Johann. She herself had found a less prestigious husband. Max, Duke in Bavaria, was a Bohemian-minded eccentric who loathed pomp and ceremony, and shunned all royal courts as far as possible, preferring to dress as a strolling minstrel, visiting fairs and peasant weddings, playing guitar and singing old folk songs. They had five sons (one stillborn) and five daughters, and sorely frustrated by his lack of ambition, she was determined to help their daughters make splendid marriages. Already she and Sophie had decided that the eldest daughter, nineteen-year-old Helene, would make an ideal empress of Austria. The lessons of dangers from too much interbreeding had not yet been learnt. It seemingly never troubled them that Francis Joseph and the Bavarian princesses were first cousins, or that all the latter were children of second cousins, both Wittelsbachs, whose ancestry included several marriages between uncles, aunts, nephews, and nieces.

The intelligent, well-educated young Helene had been groomed for such an eventuality. However, when the family arrived, she became embarrassed and tongue-tied. The second daughter, Elizabeth, known in the family as 'Sisi', who had no such expectations, whose education had been largely neglected, and whose main passion was for animals, made a much better impression on him. At their first family dinner together, he could hardly take his eyes off her. The archduchess assumed that her son was temporarily infatuated with the girl, but would soon realise that Helene, who had been so painstakingly prepared and educated for her position as his future wife, was the right one.

The shy but pretty Elizabeth was embarrassed to find out that he seemed smitten with her and not with her elder sister, but it was too late.

The emperor insisted that she was the one he would marry. Having been thwarted in her plan, the archduchess accepted it with good grace. It was a minor inconvenience that he had decided to pass over Helene and take her sister instead, but the latter was still young and presumably pliable enough to be suitably educated and trained for her position as first lady of the empire. The emperor duly asked Elizabeth's family for permission to propose, and she accepted him, although tradition has it that her immediate reaction was that she wished her handsome suitor was not an emperor.

After the return of his cousins to Bavaria, the husband-to-be was not only preoccupied with his forthcoming wedding but also with another crisis beyond the borders of the empire. It was one from which he would find it hard to stand aside. Earlier that year, in June, Tsar Nicholas had sent his army into the Balkan principalities of Moldavia and Wallachia, then part of the Turkish Empire, and Turkey accordingly declared war on Russia. Intent on keeping the Russians from Constantinople, England and France did likewise early in 1854.

Prussia remained neutral, while Austria hovered indecisively on the side-lines, a stance for which she would pay dearly in future. The government was subjected to pressure from both sides, and while the emperor recognised the need to safeguard commercial and strategic interests on the Danube, he did not want his empire involved in a potentially crippling conflict. Count Buol advised him not to commit himself or at least wait until a point when Austrian intervention would prove decisive and victory assured, while the pro-Russian element in the military thought it his duty to side with Russia as a bulwark against liberalism. After some hesitation, he agreed with Buol, and in April 1854, an offensive and defensive alliance was concluded between Austria and Prussia, with the aim of containing the Crimean War. The settlement suited Prussia, where the king and ministers feared being dragged against their better judgment into a war from which they would benefit but little.

That same month, Elizabeth arrived in Vienna for their wedding, which the emperor marked by announcing an amnesty for nearly 400 political prisoners. The ceremony took place in the Augustinerkirche next to the Hofburg. It was noticed that the bride, supported by her mother and mother-in-law, looked pale and nervous throughout, and at the altar, she whispered her vows almost inaudibly, unlike those of the groom which were bold and clearly spoken. After they had exchanged rings, the Cardinal-Prince Archbishop of Vienna delivered a long address on the virtues of family life, as he informed the bride that among other things, she would be to her husband 'an island of refuge amid the ranging billows, an island where roses and violets grow'.[7] Unlike her husband who had been well taught to endure such tedious public functions impassively and patiently, by this time, she looked bored and weary.

After a lengthy ceremonial procession and family dinner until late, the couple took their leave for an important traditional part of the wedding ceremony. Their mothers escorted the bride to the great chamber at the Hofburg with the marriage bed, and wished them both 'a good night'. The formerly high-spirited young princess, now an innocent bride, shrank at first from fulfilling her part in such a custom. Only after two nights could the emperor inform his mother, who insisted on being made aware of the necessary details, that 'Sisi had fulfilled his love'.[8]

It was not the most auspicious beginning to a marriage. However, for Elizabeth, there was at least one compensation. One of the next items on the programme for their festivities, much to her delight, was a command performance by the Circus Renz. With her love of horses and circuses, she was as enthralled by the displays of horsemanship and fireworks as her father, Duke Max, who found them a welcome contrast to the other boring spectacles and dinners to which he had been subjected. Having adored every moment of what she saw, she remarked afterwards to the emperor that she really must get to know Ernest Renz, the impresario responsible. Her mother-in-law was not impressed at the empress taking such an interest in trivialities of this nature.

The following day, Duke Max told Elizabeth that he had had enough of the stiff Viennese court etiquette, and he and the family were returning to Bavaria forthwith. Homesick, tired, and missing her family, she was now exhausted. While the emperor was normally content to be a willing slave to the traditional and ceremonial, he could see that the constant round of wedding festivities, receptions, and formality was not merely upsetting her, but proving more than she could tolerate. Notwithstanding Sophie's disapproval, out of deference to his wife, he cancelled them, warning his mother that she needed a rest. As court etiquette did not allow for a honeymoon, instead he took his bride to their countryside residence, Laxenburg Castle, 15 miles from Vienna. From here, he travelled back to the Hofburg each morning, leaving her to stay there and ride her horses, as well as enjoy the company of the dogs and parrots he had had sent from her childhood home at Possenhofen, Bavaria, and returning to her each evening.

For the emperor, the wedding and brief honeymoon were a much-needed interlude from pressing concerns for the empire—in particular, the worsening relationship with Russia. Some of the Viennese aristocracy and military thought they should intervene on the side of Russia in the coming conflict in the Crimea, as a gesture of solidarity with and gratitude to the tsar for having helped to put down the Hungarian rebellion. They were at odds with the emperor's ministers, who thought the tsar's ambitions should be held in check, especially as an alliance with the western powers would probably help to safeguard the empire's Italian provinces and also strengthen its position in the German Confederation against an increasingly mighty Prussia. Torn between both, the emperor decided to remain neutral, insisting in a letter to the tsar that his primary duty was 'to protect the dignity and the interests of Austria'.[9] This pleased nobody, least of all the tsar, who never forgave him. Austria had created for herself a powerful enemy, one that could cause considerable problems for Vienna if she should ever intervene with the Slavic communities in the southern and eastern parts of the empire.

Despite her dislike of court ceremonial and formality, the empress initially made a good impression on many of those around her with her approachable demeanour and simple manner. When she and her husband paid a state visit to Bohemia and Moravia in June 1854, she was much more her natural self, away from court life and the prying eyes of her mother-in-law. She was fascinated by the people and picturesque landscape of Bohemia, and at Prague, the kindly former Emperor Ferdinand and Empress Anna Maria treated her like the daughter they never had. She entered with enthusiasm into many of the ceremonial duties as empress, visiting churches and convents, alms-houses, hospitals, and orphanages, always ready with a friendly word.

After they returned, the emperor went on manoeuvres to Galicia, while she stayed behind at Laxenburg. Within weeks, the court physician confirmed that she was expecting a child. On 5 March 1855, she gave birth to a daughter, who was named Sophie without the mother being consulted. Archduchess Sophie was delighted at being a grandmother but intended to maintain control to the extent of selecting all the nursery staff, including a wet nurse and cook. The baby's quarters were set up next to her own rooms in the Hofburg, and every time Elizabeth wanted to come and visit her child, she had to climb a long staircase. When she reached the nursery, the archduchess was usually present, and she fiercely resented her mother-in-law's interference. Not maternal by nature, she resented the whole business of childbearing, the inconvenience and also the thought of what it would do to her good looks and beauty. However, she wanted to spend some time with her child herself, without so many barriers being put in her way.

After allied landings in the Crimea in 1854, the emperor signed a treaty of alliance with the western powers, worded ambiguously enough to give him and the empire ample opportunity to evade any obligations. By doing so, he alienated not only his uncle and hitherto firmest ally, King Frederick William IV of Prussia, but also forfeited for Austria the allegiance of the

Confederated German States, as most of the kings and grand dukes were related by marriage to the tsar. Nicholas of Russia died in March 1855, ostensibly of pneumonia, although some blamed a broken heart after Russian defeats. Despite ordering four weeks of court mourning and sending a letter of condolence to his successor, Tsar Alexander II, Francis Joseph received a withering reply, informing him bitterly that his father had loved the emperor like his own son, only to see him follow a political course that brought him ever closer to their enemies and would bring them inevitably to a fratricidal war, for which he would be 'accountable to God'. After Russia was defeated and had made peace with the victors, the Russian representative told the French envoy that, now they had finished tearing away at each other like the honest bulldogs they were, 'we have to work together to make sure that this mongrel Austria gains nothing from our quarrel.'[10]

The emperor was delighted at being a father, but the empress knew he wanted a son and heir as well. Later that year, she was expecting again, and on 12 July 1856, she had another daughter, whom they named Gisela. The birth of two girls was a disappointment to family and empire alike, and the archduchess redoubled her efforts to help find wives for her other sons. The next to marry would be Archduke Charles Ludwig, and in November 1856, he married a cousin, Princess Margaretha, daughter of King Johann of Saxony and Archduchess Sophie's sister, Queen Amalia. Max had fallen deeply in love with Princess Maria Amalia of Brazil, a sickly young woman who succumbed to consumption within less than two years.

Losing patience with her mother-in-law, Elizabeth insisted that her daughters must be moved to rooms adjacent to hers in the Hofburg, especially as Sophie was a delicate child who needed constant looking after. Every time the emperor took his mother's side in an argument, the empress would be 'indisposed' and retreat to the other side of a locked bedroom door. It did not stop the archduchess from insisting that Elizabeth was more interested in her horses than her children, and unfit to be in charge of them. When Elizabeth angrily threatened to leave the Hofburg altogether, the harassed emperor wrote firmly to his mother, deploring her habit of having the children confined to their own rooms most of the time, and begging her to be more understanding with Elizabeth.

Later that year, they visited Italy and stayed for about four months. For some time, there had been no love lost between the sovereign and the Italians, for he was determined not to cede any of his territory in Lombardy-Venetia, despite the nationalist aspirations of those who fiercely resented Austrian rule and Habsburg repression, and demanded a united Italy. A visit to the Provinces might improve Habsburg standing there, especially if the people could see and fall for the charms of their enchanting young empress and receive a friendly few words from her husband in person. Elizabeth welcomed the idea of such a journey, because it would remove them from her mother-in-law's all-pervading presence. She insisted that they take little Sophie, whom she said would benefit from the healthy mild Italian climate.

Arriving in Italy in November 1856, on the tour they were given a mixed reception, with sullen crowds in the streets and poorly attended public receptions. Many representatives of leading families who had been invited deliberately stayed away, and those who were attended were hissed by the crowds. Sometimes they were greeted with applause and friendliness, especially in Venice after the emperor announced an amnesty for a number of political prisoners. Part of the reason for their friendly reception was ascribed to the empress's charm and amiability. Milan proved less accommodating, with crowds bribed by the police to turn out on the streets and welcome the emperor and empress. They turned out, but their silence made their hostility plain. Some said the empress had only brought their infant daughter along in order to protect them from assassination attempts.

From one point of view, the visit to Italy had been a personal success for husband and wife. They found themselves closer than they had been on discovering a common purpose, showing themselves to the people and taking pleasure in meeting friendly faces and crowds, although some had been more welcoming than others. Above all, their time in Italy had been free from the all-pervading shadow of Archduchess Sophie. When they returned home early in March 1857, the empress found her husband the same remote character he had been before. Once again, he was a prisoner of court etiquette, inaccessible and undemonstrative. She was also distressed to find that baby Gisela, now aged eight months, hardly seemed to recognise her and had unsurprisingly bonded with her grandmother instead.

Feeling that for the emperor and empress to maintain a visible presence far beyond the capital of their empire would be good for public relations, the ministers sent them next on a royal progress through part of Hungary. Determined this time not to be a stranger to her youngest child during their absence, Elizabeth insisted on Gisela, not quite ten months old, joining them when they departed in the first week of May 1857, despite the archduchess's protests. Elizabeth loved her first sight of Magyar life and the picturesque aura of Budapest. The Hungarians realised that at last they had a strong and potentially influential ally at court. When she asked the emperor to give serious thought to making concessions to their constitution and national aspirations, he seemed hesitant, merely admitting that there were 'some good points' in what she said. Initially, he was inclined to agree with his mother that the only reason Elizabeth took an interest in them was because they appealed to her sense of the picturesque. Yet he was impressed with her rapid progress at learning Magyar, and at length, he would come to appreciate her point of view.

It augured well for a very successful few weeks abroad—until tragedy struck. Baby Gisela suddenly fell ill, but she was a healthy infant and soon recovered. Then Sophie started vomiting blood and bile. Despite the solicitous care of Dr Seeburger, her condition swiftly deteriorated, and on 28 May, the emperor telegraphed with a heavy heart to his parents that 'our little one is an angel in Heaven'. They were crushed, but 'Sisi is full of resignation to the will of the Lord'.[11] This was not strictly true. She was beside herself with grief, blaming herself bitterly for her daughter's death as she had insisted on bringing them both on the journey. To her relief, when they returned to Vienna, the archduchess was the soul of tact. Having lost an infant daughter herself, she realised what her daughter-in-law was going through.

After the funeral, Elizabeth spent much of the summer mourning her firstborn in the Habsburg crypt in the Church of the Capucines, Vienna. She wept and prayed by the tomb, and then returned to the palace, shutting herself away from everybody else, spending hours crying in her room or going for long solitary walks and rides, only allowing grooms and detectives to follow her at a distance. She blamed Gisela for passing on the virus to her sister, and throughout the girl's childhood, she rarely showed her any affection.

In August 1857, as court mourning for little Sophie came to an end, Maximilian returned to Vienna, bringing his bride, Princess Charlotte of the Belgians, daughter of King Leopold. They had married in Brussels on 27 July. Charlotte had once been considered as a possible bride for the emperor, and the archduchess may have thought that this lively, more outgoing Belgian princess would have made a far more suitable empress. She was delighted with this second daughter-in-law, whom she praised as 'charmingly pretty, intelligent and fascinating as well' and an asset to the family.[12] If the empress could not give the empire a crown prince, Max and Charlotte might succeed where their sister-in-law had so far failed.

Maximilian had recently been given a prestigious post within the empire. On his return to Vienna from Italy in March 1857, he had seen the wisdom of replacing a military dictatorship with benevolent civilian rule. The oppressive military regime in his Italian provinces had clearly failed, and it was apparent that only a more humane approach could prevent the threat of another revolution. The elderly Field Marshal Joseph Radetzky, who had been appointed Viceroy of Lombardy-Venetia in 1848, had just been persuaded to retire, and to replace him, Francis

Joseph appointed his brother. It did not bode well for his term of office that he was not granted full responsibility for military as well as civilian authority, as Radetsky had been. Command of the forces was entrusted to Count Gyulai, the senior officer in Italy and a noted reactionary who had no patience with any nationalist aspirations. While it was a sensible move in that the army would have probably not submitted with good grace to military leadership from the inexperienced and liberal emperor's brother, it was inevitable that Gyulai would have differences with the liberal archduke.

Maximilian, a fluent Italian speaker, had joined the Austrian navy as a young man, and was promoted to rear-admiral and commander-in-chief in 1854. His duties took him regularly to Venice and Trieste, letting him see for himself the results of Radetzsky's repression in Vienna and Lombardy that had brought Austria a reputation for cruelty throughout Europe. He had detested Russia ever since Tsar Nicholas assisted Austria in crushing Hungarian freedom, and if he had had his way, as an admirer of Britain and her navy, he would have liked to take part in naval engagements with the Anglo-French forces in the Crimea.

Although initially fearing he would be little more than a figurehead with no genuine political authority, he persuaded the emperor to pardon a large number of political prisoners and was instrumental in establishing a public works programme for Milan, along the lines of those recently undertaken for Vienna and other European capitals. He showed genuine interest in advocating home rule for Lombardy-Venetia with its own army and representative institutions, and major reforms in taxation, education, and other branches of local government. When severe floods in the Po Valley left thousands homeless, he was one of the first to come and see the devastation, and he made generous financial contributions from his own pocket to help those in need.

His period of office helped to win support for Austrian rule in Lombardy and Venetia, but in Vienna, the more conservative ministers thought such liberal measures would severely weaken Austria's hold on the provinces. One even suggested that Maximilian was seeking the crown of an independent state for himself. Persuaded that he was encouraging nationalist feeling and that it was only one step away from open revolution, the emperor was dismissive of many of his brother's schemes. Encouraged by Charlotte, who was very much her ambitious father's daughter and determined not to be a docile or merely decorative consort, Maximilian was inclined to be too impulsive and speak critically of the Austrian authorities, and in his frustration, he became less discreet. Some of his comments appeared in the press, and the emperor accused him of sympathizing with the opposition. In September 1858, Maximilian asked to be relieved of his duties and return to his old naval career, but the emperor refused, saying it would have a bad effect. Nevertheless, his position became untenable, and in April 1859, he was dismissed from his post and recalled to Vienna.

Any hopes that a son of Maximilian and Charlotte might succeed his uncle, Francis Joseph, on the throne faded when early in 1858 it was known that Elizabeth was expecting a third child. After a long and painful confinement at Laxenburg, on 21 August, a salute of 101 guns announced the birth of a crown prince. He was christened Rudolf in honour of Count Rudolf of Habsburg, the original founder of the dynasty. The emperor thought him very ugly, but 'magnificently built and very strong'. Like his sisters before him, he was soon taken from the arms of his mother to the nursery, where in accordance with court etiquette, she was not allowed to nurse him, much to her chagrin, and his upbringing was carefully supervised by Archduchess Sophie.

Meanwhile, a clash of arms was looming for the empire. Totally under the influence of the hawks in his government headed by Count Charles Grünne, head of the military chancellery, and Foreign Minister Count Buol, the emperor was persuaded that if Austria was to retain her sovereignty in Italy, the army had to be strengthened. Napoleon III, Emperor of the French, had recently made a secret agreement with Count Cavour, prime minister of Piedmont, that France would come to the aid of Piedmont if the latter was attacked by Austria, on condition that neither France nor Piedmont should appear to be the aggressor. Although Austrian diplomats later found out about the meeting, the emperor and ministers were convinced that the small Italian state would never dare to take up arms against Austria, or that Napoleon would honour his word. The Russians proposed that differences should be arbitrated by a conference involving all the European powers.

Insisting that Piedmont must disarm before Austria would participate, on 23 April, Francis Joseph sent an ultimatum to Cavour. When he told Metternich, who had returned to Vienna and was still a friend and valued adviser, the elderly statesman insisted that under no circumstances should there be an ultimatum. He was told it had been sent the day before. Buol resigned as foreign minister a few days later and was succeeded by Count Johann von Rechberg.

War was declared, and on 4 June, the numerically superior Austrian army under Gyulai met and attacked the French near the town of Magenta. In the indecisive battle that followed, the Austrians suffered over 10,000 casualties and conceded victory to the French. The emperor hurried to the front, relieving Gyulai of his command just in time for the decisive clash of arms on 24 June on a plain near Solferino. For the last time in

European history, three monarchs, the emperors of Austria and France, and Victor Emmanuel, King of Sardinia, faced each other on the battlefield at the head of their armies. At the end of several hours' bitter fighting, the defeated Austrian forces had suffered at least 20,000 casualties, and the victorious Franco-Italian armies around 17,000. Appalled at the sight of the slaughter and carnage, after the conflict, the Austrian and French emperors embraced each other with ill-concealed relief. From his headquarters in Verona, he wrote to the empress in the aftermath of 'a dreadful day', as a result of which he had 'learnt and experienced much and know what it feels like to be a beaten general'.[13]

An armistice was concluded at Villafranca the following month, at which Lombardy was ceded to the French, Austria retained Venetia, and the other Italian states formed a federation. Less than two years later, King Victor Emmanuel was proclaimed king of a united Italy.

In the shadow of defeat, Emperor Francis Joseph's stock had fallen heavily. General confidence in the army, the government, and the economy all slumped severely, and the Swiss ambassador in Vienna wrote that he believed the dynasty had never suffered a more severe blow than this.[14] The newspapers, prevented by censorship from criticising him in person, attacked his closest advisers. Rechberg lamented that they had allowed themselves to be drawn into 'a war for which we were neither diplomatically, financially, nor militarily prepared.'[15] When he next appeared at a military review in Vienna, crowds called for his abdication. Some thought that Maximilian, known for his more liberal views, would be a better emperor than his failed elder brother. There were rumours of a conspiracy by a footman at the Hofburg to assassinate the emperor and his mother. With discontent at home and pity for a once great but severely weakened nation throughout the rest of Europe, her sovereign recognised there were difficult times ahead.

'All power stays in my hands'

During this time, affairs had not improved within the family. In the emperor's absence, the atmosphere at home between his wife and his mother had deteriorated even further. The empress was thinner and more nervous still, sensitive to any criticism and seeing enemies everywhere. A further cause of friction was the upbringing of Crown Prince Rudolf who, like his sisters before him, had been taken as a baby from his mother's arms to the nursery, where the word of Archduchess Sophie was law. She chose Rudolf's nurse, the widowed Baroness Caroline von Welden. 'Wowo', as Rudolf soon named her, would be one of the very few steady influences in his childhood days. As a small child, whenever he was denied something he wanted and threw a tantrum, she was the only person who could calm him down.

By the time he was one year old, the attendants were sorely tried by contradictory orders from his mother and grandmother. Even if tradition had permitted, the neurotic, possessive empress was temperamentally unsuited to looking after the sickly infant on her own. The archduchess may have been domineering, but from experience, she knew better what was good for a child of that age and was genuinely upset by what seemed to her the younger woman's unreasonable behaviour. It was a difficult situation for both women. Count Eduard Paar, one of the emperor's adjutants, was sorry for the young empress, calling her mother-in-law 'a good old meddler'.[1] Elizabeth would sometimes try and wrest control of her children from their grandmother, but once she had done so, she was incapable of acting as an attentive parent and only appeared intermittently interested in them. She would suddenly come to the nursery and make a fuss of them, but when it came to supervising or taking part in the routine of their daily upbringing, she would leave most of the work to the nursery staff. Much as she resented comments from the children that Archduchess Sophie was their real mama, she lacked the determination to try and change the situation. For once, the emperor put head before heart, and despite his wife's protests, he allowed his mother to supervise his son's education, on the grounds that nobody was better qualified to do so than the person who had more than any other helped to prepare him for the throne.

Elizabeth was incapable of making a sustained effort. Her spontaneous generosity and affection one day could give way to paranoia and tantrums the next. She was too proud to admit that perhaps her mother-in-law was right, and that her advice about the younger woman's duties as a mother, wife, and empress was kindly meant, if perhaps clumsily given. Francis Joseph was a dedicated monarch who loved his wife deeply but failed to understand fully her sensitive and complex character or realise that there was something of value in her ideas, or that she found it hard to make an active contribution as his consort.

As a small boy, Crown Prince Rudolf rarely saw his parents, and even then only for about an hour at a time before he was taken back to the nursery. Elizabeth took little interest in him, while Francis Joseph treated him brusquely like a miniature cadet. At the age of four, the boy took fright when he thought a group of boisterous soldiers was coming towards him. Annoyed at this display of apparent cowardice, his father told him he had been 'a disgrace'. Fortunately, there were also happier glimpses of father and son together. Again, when he was four, he went with the emperor to inspect a military academy near Vienna. When the students called for three cheers for His Majesty, the boy waved his hat and joined them as he shouted 'hurrah!' His father almost wept with emotion and for some moments was lost for words.[2]

As a sovereign, Francis Joseph had been brought up to believe that his status would be compromised by allowing a more representative system of government in the empire to be adopted, and in June 1860, he had warned his council of ministers that he would not be party to any curtailment of monarchical power through a constitution. However, with his standing severely weakened by the loss of Italy, he was powerless to resist demands for modernisation. The result was the 'October Diploma', a fundamental law that strengthened provincial diets throughout the empire, giving them legislative authority over matters previously determined by ministers of the interior, and letting them send delegates to the parliament as the principal law-making body of the empire. With some hesitation, the emperor informed his mother that they would 'have a little parliamentarianism, but all power stays in my hands, and the general effect will suit Austrian circumstances very well indeed'.[3]

In the autumn of 1860, the emperor held a meeting at Warsaw with Tsar Alexander II of Russia and William, Prince Regent (and soon to be King) of Prussia. They aimed to restore mutual good relations after their differences over the Crimean War, and lay foundations for a new triple alliance and a united front against the Italian Risorgimento and other manifestations of national liberalism throughout Europe. The Austrian and German rulers hoped to align themselves against Napoleon III, a policy at odds with the tsar's hopes for a Franco-Russian alliance. Moreover, the Russian foreign minister, Count Alexander Gorchakov, was even less forgiving of Austria's recent neutrality than the tsar had been and was in no mood to be conciliatory to her emperor. A brief meeting at Weimar in the autumn of 1857 between Francis Joseph and Alexander had been cordial enough on the surface, but little more. The sudden death of the tsar's mother gave him an excuse to return to St Petersburg sooner than planned, and with no chance for agreement on anything, the meeting broke up with nothing to show for their efforts.

The emperor returned to Vienna to find his wife on the verge of a physical and mental breakdown. She was probably suffering from gonorrhoea or a similar contagious disease, the result of her husband having strayed. A combination of illness due to his infidelity, inability to take any more of the formality of court at Vienna, and her mother-in-law's presence had upset her so badly that she insisted she must leave the environment altogether and go as far away as possible for a while. The calming atmosphere of Madeira had been recommended to her by her own family.

Queen Victoria of England, who had been told about her problems, offered her temporary use of the royal yacht *Victoria and Albert*, and she sailed from Antwerp on 17 November. Although it proved a stormy voyage, she enjoyed the excitement of the rough seas, and by the time she and her suite arrived, she seemed in better spirits than she had been for a long time. For the next four months, she surrounded herself with her dogs, ponies, and books. Sometimes she would become melancholy, desperate to see her husband and children again, and issue orders to go home at once, only to cancel them moments later. Only five weeks after she arrived, she celebrated her twenty-third birthday. Among her gifts was a statuette of St George from her mother-in-law, but she did not take the trouble to write a letter of thanks. A letter to her youngest brother-in-law, Ludwig Victor, to whom she was quite attached, asked him to thank her and 'kiss her hands ... I do not write to her simply because I feel that my letters must bore her, for I have written so often to you and there is not much to say about this place'.[4]

In April 1861, she decided to return home, and the following month, husband and wife had an emotional reunion off the isle of Lacroma in the Adriatic Sea. After a brief visit to Maximilian and Charlotte at their home, Miramar, near Trieste, they went back to Vienna. It proved an unhappy homecoming. After a few days of giving interminable audiences and attending a state ball and dinner, the exhausted empress informed her husband that life in the Hofburg was impossible for her. She resented seeing the hand of Archduchess Sophie in everything, whether it was the drawing up of lists of ladies for presentation at court or the furnishing of her private apartments. Above all, it pained her to see how the much her children had fallen under their grandmother's influence. It probably never occurred to her that after her long absence she had nobody but herself to blame, with the archduchess being the obvious person to take charge of everything. Even so, Elizabeth told her husband she intended to retire to Laxenburg. The young couple spent a few days there, and all social functions and state dinners announced for the next few days were cancelled. Within two or three weeks, Elizabeth seemed in the throes of a rapid decline, with a severe cough, no appetite, and extreme weakness. Her physician allegedly said she might only have a few weeks to live. Some at court were sure she was malingering, and sympathised deeply with the harassed, worried, and desperately overworked young emperor.

In June, he escorted her back to Trieste, from whence she sailed for an indefinite stay at Corfu, where once again her physical and mental health soon improved. Rumours spread throughout Vienna of an indefinite break between husband and wife, and he sent Count Grünne to go and entreat her to return as soon as possible. She had always hated Grünne and initially refused to meet him at all. After relenting, she told him bitterly that he and the archduchess had been responsible for everything that had gone wrong, for making her life at court miserable, robbing her of her children, and, worst of all, introducing her husband to 'other women'. She then realised she had gone too far and offered him her apologies, but he recognised that any efforts to persuade her to do anything against her wishes would be wasted.

Back in Vienna, he reported to the emperor that the empress was mentally ill, the longer she stayed away from court the better, and that she was totally unsuited for her position. In Bavaria, her own mother, Duchess Ludovica, was appalled by everything she had heard, and sent Princess Helene, the woman who might have been empress of Austria herself and had recently married Maximilian, Prince of Thurn and Taxis, to Corfu. Helene was horrified by the change in her sister and her insistence on starving herself, as she was sure she was putting on weight. She persuaded her to eat sensibly for a change, kept her company, and managed to restore her to better spirits.

The emperor came to see her at Corfu in October and was relieved to find her greatly improved. He begged her to return home for his sake and for that of the children, the empire, and the dynasty. Once they were back, he promised he would take a more active role than before in matters concerning their upbringing and would stand up for her against his mother if necessary. She maintained that she would not yet return home as her health and nerves would not allow it, but she would go somewhere within the borders of the monarchy, and spend the winter in Venice, and he had no choice but to agree. For her to stay there during Christmas could have important political advantages, as he had refused to acknowledge the new kingdom of Venice and believed that Venetia was not irrevocably lost to the Austrian Empire. She arrived in the city at the end of October 1861 and did not return to Vienna until August 1862, in time for the emperor's thirty-second birthday and Rudolf's fourth later that week. The people welcomed her back, thanks largely to the more liberal newspapers giving the impression that their empress was at heart a progressive young woman who could bring some influence on their emperor and counteract that of his reactionary mother.

Elizabeth was home strictly on her own terms, including greater personal independence and minimum attendance at court functions and festivities. She was still clearly ill at ease on social occasions, and she made no great effort to give the impression that her marriage was idyllic. At a family dinner party in December 1862 attended by the crown prince and princess of Prussia, the latter was charmed by the empress, yet thought that her husband 'seems to *dote* on her—but I did not observe that she did on him.'[5] When she attended a court ball in January 1863, the foreign ambassadors were captivated by her appearance and thought she had completely recovered. She also insisted on having either her brother or one of her sisters constantly nearby to keep her company. The emperor spent what time he could spare from his work, accompanying her on walks and drives, with the archduchess tactfully keeping out of their way. As a devoted husband, he was eager to accommodate her every wish as if he was indebted to her for some reason. Whether it was the chivalry of a man who realised that she was temperamentally unsuited for her role, whether he feared that with her Wittelsbach inheritance too much stress might deprive her of her reason, or whether he felt a lifelong sense of guilt at infecting her venereally, one can only speculate.

Potential changes in Europe beyond the borders of Austria also occupied his mind for much of the time. He was aware that moderate change and reform were necessary for the empire's survival. At home, towards the end of 1862, he agreed to changes in imperial legislation regarding personal civil rights, freedom of the press, and local government administration, and further afield, he foresaw that the appointment of Otto von Bismarck as minister-president of Prussia in September 1862 might threaten Austria's position as leader of the German Confederation. Bismarck suggested to the Magyar ambassador in Berlin that the time had come for Austria to 'shift her centre of gravity' from Germany to Hungary. If the emperor of Austria was to comply, he could rely on Prussian support in Italy and south-eastern Europe as needed, but if Austria rejected his overtures, Prussia would side with France in any future European crisis.

In the summer of 1863, the emperor's ministers advised him to support a reform programme aimed at reasserting Habsburg leadership of a new German Confederation by bringing together delegates from the German and Austrian legislative bodies in a federal parliament. By taking the initiative, they might be able to curtail Bismarck's ambitions. The emperor was persuaded to invite the reigning monarchs of the German states to Frankfurt for a meeting to discuss the confederation's future. King William of Prussia felt obliged to attend alongside his fellow sovereigns and grand dukes. Bismarck, who was ready for a fight with Austria, put pressure on him to stay away as it would be an acknowledgement of Habsburg leadership in Germany, and also said that the invitation had arrived so late that it was an insult. Without Prussian participation, the conference achieved nothing. Presciently, the emperor agreed with the Duke of Saxe-Coburg that he feared it was the last time German princes would meet as friends and not foes.

At a short meeting with Queen Victoria, who had come on a private visit to Coburg, the emperor had a brief discussion about their future. He regretted King William's failure to appear at the conference and recognised that Bismarck was to blame. They agreed that it was important for Europe to 'keep the Emperor of the French quiet', but the emperor realised that the unpredictable Napoleon was probably less of a threat, at least to Austria, than Bismarck could ever be.

He was less aware of the poor state of the Austrian army. Despite his reservations about parliamentary interference in foreign and military affairs, he had already conceded some control to parliament over the military budget. At a time when Prussia was strengthening her army and equipping it with modern weaponry, Austria had to be prepared for war if she was to retain her supremacy in the German Confederation.

For the last few years, Maximilian and Charlotte had been living at their palace, Miramar, on the Adriatic. Since being removed from his position as Viceroy of Venetia-Lombardy by his brother in April 1859, he realised he would never be offered official responsibility again. However, Charlotte longed for a more important role, and there was every chance that if any vacant throne might be offered them, they would accept. In October 1861, he was asked by Napoleon if he would be interested in the crown of Mexico, a Spanish colony until 1821 and then briefly a constitutional monarchy for three years until the establishment of a republic. The country had been ravaged by civil war, leading to occupation by French troops brought in on the pretext of unpaid debts. By 1861, they had apparently succeeded in routing troops under General Juarez, and Napoleon planned to establish an empire under French patronage, with the continued presence of his army as a guarantee of security. Maximilian welcomed the prospect of independence from his brother, not to mention the chance to reign over an empire potentially greater than Austria, while the ambitious Charlotte was thrilled at the thought of becoming an empress.

Archduchess Sophie strongly opposed the whole idea. With the sickly Crown Prince Rudolf's survival to maturity looking less than assured, she thought Maximilian and Charlotte, and any children they might have, might still succeed Francis Joseph on the Austrian throne. The emperor himself distrusted 'that arch-rogue' Napoleon, and being cautious by nature, it was perhaps surprising that he did not veto such an idea outright. As head of the family, he could have forbidden his brother to accept. He did, however, feel duty-bound to warn him fully of the hazards and warn him that it could end badly, but allowed him the final choice. The chance of ridding himself of the popular brother and sister-in-law who seemed to be thirsting for power might have been too tempting. He let it be known that acceptance of the Mexican crown was out of the question unless it was clear that the people themselves really wanted him there, and if France, Great Britain, and Spain all pledged their unconditional support.

Another throne, in Europe, also became vacant at this time. In 1862, the Greeks deposed their unpopular and childless King Otho. Their first choice in a plebiscite to replace him was Prince Alfred, Queen Victoria's second son, but under the terms of a protocol signed in London, he was ineligible. Maximilian's father-in-law, King Leopold, who had also been offered the Greek throne in 1830 but declined it, urged him to accept, but he refused. Greece, he believed, was 'poor in men and money', while Mexico was a country of immense natural riches. Charlotte, the ambitious daughter of an ambitious father, was loath to let slip this opportunity of becoming empress instead of a mere archduchess, and she helped to stiffen her wavering husband's resolve. After almost five years of marriage, the couple still remained childless, and the lack of a child, particularly a son who might outlive his sickly cousin, Rudolf, and rule over the Austrian Empire one day, might have spurred her on to seek fulfilment outside motherhood.

By the beginning of 1864, Maximilian had formally accepted the throne. Most of his family, especially his parents and Emperor Ferdinand, and most other European sovereigns apart from Napoleon, tried to dissuade him and Charlotte, but in vain. Emperor Francis Joseph appeared impartial, but the formalities had to be observed. He presented Maximilian with an act of renunciation to sign, making his acceptance of the crown of Mexico conditional to his relinquishing for himself and any issue he might have any rights of succession and inheritance in Austria. If he did not, he would not receive the sanction of his sovereign to leave. Maximilian threatened to dispense with any such approval and sail away on a French boat instead. Should he do so, countered an angry Francis Joseph, he would be charged with disloyalty and formally deprived of all the rights he had refused to renounce.

When an angry Maximilian asked his mother to intervene, she begged the emperor not to take away his brother's birthright, but in vain. The most they could obtain from the emperor was a guarantee that should he be deprived of the Mexican throne and have to return to Austria, he would take all necessary measures to safeguard his position and presence in the Austrian empire as far as was compatible with the national interest. With reddened eyes and trembling hands, they added their signatures to the 'family pact' on 9 April 1864. As they embraced each other, witnesses looked away, for tears streamed down the brothers' faces, as if aware that they would never see each other again. Charlotte remained outwardly impassive as ever. Next day, a Mexican deputation came to Miramare and formally offered the crown to Maximilian and Carlota, her new Mexican name.

The Mexican Empire had been an unwelcome distraction for Emperor Francis Joseph from affairs closer to home. Early in 1864, Prussian and Austrian armies had fought side by side over ownership of the duchies of Schleswig and Holstein, as claimed by King Christian IX of Denmark on his accession in November 1863. The Danish army was soon defeated, and after the end of the war, at a conference in London, Prussia and Austria made a joint proposal that the duchies should become an independent state. Denmark refused to accept this, and the following year, it was decided that Schleswig should be administered by Prussia and Holstein by Austria. It could be no more than a temporary arrangement.

In January 1866, a telegram arrived in Vienna from Berlin accusing Austria of causing unrest in the duchies. Bismarck was seeking a pretext for declaring war on Austria, and relations with Prussia deteriorated steadily. War was declared and Prussia overran the smaller states allied to the Austrian Empire, emerging victorious from a decisive battle at Königgrätz on 4 July. The defeated Austrians and their allies had paid dearly for their poorly organised army, inferior artillery, and slow mobilization, in what proved an even worse blow to Austrian prestige than her defeat in Italy in 1859.

Habsburg power in Germany had been completely eclipsed by Prussia, and again there were calls for the emperor to abdicate. Peace was signed at Prague on 23 August, with the emperor ceding Venetia, the last Habsburg dominion in the Italian peninsula, to Italy. Most of the defeated German states were absorbed into Prussia, which henceforth assumed leadership of the new North German Confederation of states. Austrian humiliation was not absolute, for a Southern German Union was formed simultaneously, linked militarily and commercially to its northern neighbour, consisting of independent sovereign states. No territorial losses were suffered by the empire, apart from Venetia, which had been surrendered just before the war. Nevertheless, Lord Bloomfield, British Ambassador to Vienna, reported to Queen Victoria in December 1866 that Austria was 'in an almost hopeless condition', that the empire had been woefully unprepared yet still went to war, and, as a result, 'the Emperor had grown ten years older, & was terribly cast down'.[6]

Austrian defeat and loss of prestige after the war, combined with the empress's long-standing empathy with everything from Hungary, precipitated a rapprochement with the Magyars. She had initially become fluent in the language so that she could make herself understood by Rudolf's nurse, and later she appointed a Hungarian lady-in-waiting, Ida Ferenczy, in order to help her learn it better. After the war, the emperor asked her to spend some time visiting hospitals in Budapest, and also speak to some of the leading politicians so as to pave the way for a new climate of understanding. Among those she met were Francis Deák, a prominent Magyar lawyer, and Count Julius Andrassy, an aristocrat involved in the revolution of 1848, who had fled and returned after an amnesty. Both advised her to make a case with the emperor to give their country internal autonomy.

On her return to Vienna, the empress urged the emperor to visit Hungary with her and to appoint Andrassy minister for foreign affairs. Despite his initial objections, he was soon convinced that any settlement with Hungary would not necessarily weaken the Habsburg dynasty.

In February 1867, Andrassy was asked to form a Hungarian government, and in May, the *Ausgleich* or official compromise was agreed. The Austrian Empire, with Hungary as a subservient state, became the dual monarchy of Austria-Hungary, henceforth to be styled the Austro-Hungarian Empire. Both partners shared an army, a navy, and finance ministry, with the emperor as their supreme commander. German was still the official language of army and government officers, but military orders could be given in either tongue.

A coronation for the emperor and empress as king and queen of Hungary, the main event in six days of ceremonies to celebrate, was arranged for 8 June. The ceremony was held in St Matthew's Cathedral, Budapest, and in the procession, the emperor rode on horseback, attired in the uniform of a Hungarian marshal, while the empress wore national costume with a crown on her head as she drove in the state coach drawn by eight horses. At the ceremony, the empress was particularly moved as Count Andrassy and the Primate of the Catholic Church placed the Crown of St Stephen on her husband's head and laid the mantle of St Stephen on his shoulders. The crown was then held over her head to proclaim her as queen of Hungary. Despite her general antipathy to public appearances, on this occasion, she clearly revelled in the proceedings. Notwithstanding rumours of possible assassination threats, and subsequent strict security precautions, everything passed off without incident. For the emperor, the *Ausgleich* was a concession bordering on personal humiliation for Habsburg pride, which he accepted with grace for want of any alternative, while it was resented by Vienna and by minority groups such as the Slavs and Serbs within the dual monarchy's borders. For the Magyars and for the empress, it was a resounding success.

The creation of the dual monarchy had also been a severe blow to the pride of Archduchess Sophie. Her dreams of a greater Austria had been shattered by the Prussian defeat and the empire's exclusion from the German Confederation, and for it to be followed by the recognition of Hungary was to her a reward for the triumph of revolution and the work of the rebels who had been a thorn in the empire's side at the start of her son's reign. Almost everyone else was united in praise of the empress at the coronation, a perfect combination of beauty, grace, and reconciliation, but one of the archduchess's ladies-in-waiting, Helene Fürstenberg, noted somewhat acidly that Her Majesty 'looked quite supernaturally lovely during the solemn act, as moved and absorbed as a bride', adding that she felt as if, 'in one respect, she *did* interpret it in this sense'.[7]

Afterwards, the emperor and empress took a brief holiday with Gisela and Rudolf, but it was overshadowed by bad news. While there, they were told that the empress's brother-in-law, Maximilian, Prince of Thurn and Taxis and husband of her sister Helene, had died suddenly after a short illness, probably kidney failure, at the age of thirty-five. They cut short their holiday to attend the funeral, and then accompany her and her four small children, the youngest only six weeks old, back to the family home in Bavaria.

Far worse was about to come. Although Maximilian and Carlota had sailed for Mexico with the best of intentions, their stewardship of the empire had all too soon turned out to be the disaster that some had gloomily foreseen. They were appalled by the living conditions of the poor in contrast to the lifestyle of the well-to-do and initiated charitable ventures to raise money for those in need. Maximilian also oversaw legislation to restrict working hours, abolish child labour, restore communal property, and abolish corporal punishment. Yet it was not enough to overcome resentment at a European prince or archduke being chosen to rule the country. After the American Civil War ended in 1865, Napoleon was forced to withdraw all French troops and financial interests from Mexico. In desperation, Carlota returned to Europe to beg him for help, but he declared he could do nothing, and her pleas to the Pope to assist also fell on deaf ears. Months of tension and strain had left their mark on her, and her moods of increasing paranoia and irrational temper presaged a complete mental collapse, from which she would never fully recover during her remaining sixty years.

A brief civil war between loyalists and republicans, in support of President Juárez, ended in Maximilian's capture. Napoleon had assured Francis Joseph that his life was in no danger, as the Mexicans would never dare to kill a Habsburg archduke. Nevertheless, he was sentenced to death by a military court for crimes against the people. Appeals for clemency from several European heads of state went to Juárez, and Francis Joseph asked him to put his brother on board ship for Europe. Although he liked Maximilian as a person, the president refused to commute the sentence as some republicans had been killed in the fighting, and because he intended to make it clear that Mexico would never submit to government by a foreign power. Nevertheless, during the last two weeks of June 1867, unfounded reports from America reached Europe that the former emperor had been banished and was about to embark for Europe or had already done so, that America was about to intervene in Mexico to prevent anarchy and ensure that his life would be spared, and that whatever else might happen, the president would be afraid to shoot him.

Not until the beginning of July was it revealed that Maximilian had been dead for a fortnight. On 19 June, he and two officers who had remained loyal to him faced the firing squad. Just before the shots rang out, he stepped forward and said in Spanish: 'I forgive everybody. I pray that everybody may forgive me, and I wish that my blood, which is now to be shed, may be for the good of the country. Long live Mexico! Long live independence!'[8]

Full of remorse at not having tried harder to forbid his brother from going in the first place, Francis Joseph hurried to Vienna so he could tell their parents in person. Archduchess Sophie was shattered, weeping bitterly that savages had murdered him as if he was a common criminal. Juárez refused to release the body for another five months, and he could not be laid to rest until a state funeral in February 1868.

Although Napoleon had inadvertently been one of those most responsible for Maximilian's fate, Emperor Francis Joseph could not indefinitely put off a meeting with him. Like King William of Prussia and Tsar Alexander II, he had been among the crowned heads invited to attend the Great Exhibition in Paris that summer. The news from Mexico had initially ruled out any idea of his attending. Nevertheless, Napoleon wrote a letter of condolence, to which the emperor replied that he was sure he had done everything in his power to avert such an eventuality, adding that his words were proof of their close friendship. His sadness at losing the brother once close to him might have deeply distressed their parents, but it had also removed the man whose popularity had once briefly threatened his throne.

Moreover, the emperor was reminded by Count Beust—as if he needed reminding—that Austria needed France as an ally in Western Europe, and he agreed with some reservations to a meeting at Salzburg in August. Both sovereigns and their consort came face to face on 18 August, Francis Joseph's thirty-seventh birthday, amiably rather than cordially.[9] Beust told him that Austria and France were 'linked together but not bound together' and suggested that Francis Joseph should go to Paris in October, during the last weeks of the exhibition. Elizabeth was unwell, and possibly with child, so Francis Joseph went with his two surviving brothers. No longer a widower, Charles Ludwig had remarried in 1862, his bride being Princess Maria Annunziata of Naples, and they had two young sons, Archdukes Francis Ferdinand and Otto. To his surprise, he was overwhelmed by everything he saw and thoroughly enjoyed himself, even though he struggled to stay awake during performances at the opera and theatre.

The *Ausgleich* had brought Francis Joseph and Elizabeth closer again, if only for a while. He saw that she was justifiably proud of her role in helping to bring it about and was pleased that at last she seemed to have found a genuine purpose in the official life of the empire. It may have helped to console him for the fact that she was obviously much happier in Budapest than in Vienna. At court dinners in the Magyar capital, she was quite animated, quite unlike the bored, tongue-tied empress at the Hofburg.

By late autumn, her pregnancy was confirmed, and she decided the baby would be born in Hungary. Her success in and love for the country was resented by some of the Viennese aristocracy who found her attitude divisive if not downright treacherous. In February 1868, she moved to the palace in Buda, awaiting the birth of what she hoped might be a son whom they could name Stephen, after the patron saint of Hungary. The arrival of a daughter on 22 April, whom they named Valerie, did nothing to dampen their spirits.

Malicious rumours throughout her childhood would insinuate that Valerie was actually the daughter of Elizabeth's close friend Julius

Andrassy, the Hungarian prime minister. As she physically resembled her father more than her siblings did, even more so as she grew older, they gradually died away. However, Valerie was all too aware of the gossip. This, and her mother's insistence on speaking to her only in Magyar, all helped to plant in her a lifelong antipathy toward anything to do with Hungary.

Elizabeth had decided before the confinement that this child would be hers and hers alone. She had almost lost Gisela to her mother-in-law, while at the age of six, Rudolf had been taken from his kindly governess and handed over to a cruel military tutor who turned him into a nervous, highly strung child. Archduchess Sophie chose the best tutors and professors available to teach him, but the military tutor, Count Leopold Gondrecourt, was selected by the emperor. A savage bully with no understanding of children, he resolved to toughen up the small nervous crown prince by firing pistols in his bedroom to wake him up, or shutting him up behind the gates of a wild game reserve and shout that a wild boar was coming at him. It was no wonder that, unlike his parents, he grew up a physical coward. Early one winter morning, the empress woke up to the sound of shouting outside. She looked through the window to see Gondrecourt drilling her son and barking out orders in the snow and rain, under the light of a lantern. Realising the true state of affairs, she accordingly wrote to the emperor, insisting that such treatment of their son was inhumane and unacceptable: 'I cannot stand by and see such things going on,' she told him. 'It must be either Gondrecourt or myself.'[10] The man was dismissed and the more liberal Colonel Joseph Latour von Thurnberg appointed in his place.

The incident had resulted from a rare moment of insight into her son's needs. Rudolf had not been fortunate in his parents. In personality and interests, he more resembled his mother, but with her mania for leaving Austria and travelling outside the empire, she was a thoroughly inconsistent, even erratic presence where he was concerned. When they were at home, if Archduchess Sophie entered a room, the empress would leave, and it had a disquieting effect on him. Much as he loved, even worshipped, her as a small boy, she rarely returned his affection, treating him less like a child and more as a pet to be fussed over at odd moments.

When he was small, he was seriously ill with typhoid, but she refused to cut short her holiday in Bavaria to come and nurse him, leaving the task to her mother-in-law. That same year, he had an accident at Laxenburg, when he fell off a ladder while climbing a tree and hit his head against a stone. The emperor and Archduchess Sophie immediately came hurrying back to his side, but the empress, taking her annual cure at Kissingen, was not told until he was out of danger. Her husband and mother-in-law were keen to shield her from bad news and unpleasantness, a well-meant gesture that increasingly detached her from family life. She returned to Vienna when he was recovering, bringing him a collection of expensive toys. When they were reunited, she held him spellbound for a short time with her stories of what she had been doing while she was away. As ever, on such occasions, once the archduchess entered the room, his eyes lit up with delight with her appearance and his mother immediately disappeared.

Francis Joseph was little more than a distant father figure, rarely showing him any affection or trying to establish a family bond, treating him like a military cadet to be shaped and trained by from discipline so that he might grow up to be manly and industrious. Valerie, who was almost ten years younger than her brother, thought the relationship between father and son was very 'self-conscious'. It was no wonder that he grew up to be highly strung, charming and agreeable one moment, withdrawn and morose the next. As a child, he suffered from nightmares, and at the age of seven, he had some kind of a nervous breakdown. When he was ten, he met Albert Edward, Prince of Wales, who was visiting Vienna. The future king called his much younger fellow heir 'a very nice young man, but not at all good-looking', and thought he was 'treated almost like a boy by his parents'.[11] Bearing in mind the crown prince's tender years, it was a rather strange comment.

In 1869, Beust persuaded the emperor to accept an invitation from the Khedive of Egypt and attend the opening of the Suez Canal. It was important to emphasise Austria's interest in the Near East, by going to the country and also paying a courtesy call on the Sultan in Constantinople, a gesture no Christian monarch had yet made. An itinerary for this imperial tour of the east was gradually extended into a river trip on the lower Danube and visits to Athens and Jerusalem. Elizabeth had decided that she would not accompany her husband for various reasons, and shortly before he left, she tried to change her mind, but by then it was too late to alter the arrangements and include her as well.

This expedition was the longest journey that the emperor had ever made, and never again during his long life would he travel so far from his empire. He returned home refreshed and enriched by the experience. At the same time, it had been a display of friendship towards and support for France, and a useful gift to those in the French war ministry who still hoped for a war of revenge against Bismarck's Prussia.

At around this time, there were unofficial meetings between French staff officers and Austrian representatives, and in February 1870, Baron Franz Kuhn, the Austro-Hungarian war minister, informed the French military *attaché* in Vienna that, should France and the dual monarchy ever declare war on Prussia, he could guarantee full mobilisation of an army of 600,000 men within six weeks. Plans were made for a proposal for France to keep the Prussian force engaged for weeks and to mount an offensive in the direction of Nuremberg, whereupon the Austrians and perhaps an Italian force would cross into Saxony, raise the south German states and join the French in a march on Berlin to destroy Prussia. France was more ready to take the field than either of her allies and claimed she could mobilise in a fortnight as opposed to the six weeks required by Austria and Italy. Archduke Albrecht, commander-in-chief of the army since 1866 until the emperor assumed the title himself three years later and was subsequently appointed inspector-general for life, then proposed that the three powers should begin mobilisation simultaneously, but that Austria should feign neutrality while concentrating two army corps at Pilsen and Olmütz instead of declaring war before she was ready.

A formal agreement between France and Austria was concluded on 13 June 1870, and that same day, Albrecht drafted a plan of campaign, a general scheme of joint action between the two powers and a detailed brief for the distribution and employment of the French army. The French were not convinced of its success, particularly because of the six-week delay, and they suspected the Austrians would wait and see which side looked more assured of victory. Moreover, they thought Emperor Francis Joseph was disinclined to risk another war. On two previous occasions, he had allowed his ministers and generals to persuade him to mobilise and join battle, resulting in disastrous defeats. Nevertheless, discussions with Albrecht and the ministers still took place. While they felt that Austria-Hungary could not stand aside from the inevitable forthcoming conflict, it was evident that the army was unprepared and inadequately equipped for war.

Before matters were resolved, hostilities had broken out between France and Prussia. Despite the archduke's recommendations that they should mobilise as soon as possible on the French side, he was overruled by those who advocated neutrality. Beust believed they should consider entering on the side of France once she had won the decisive battle over Prussia everyone expected, and thus exploit any peace settlement to restore the Habsburg protectorate over southern Germany as a bulwark against France and Prussia at the same time. Prussia's decisive victory over France at Sedan, and the subsequent abdication of Napoleon, forestalled such a move. In January 1871, the proclamation of a German Empire under Prussian leadership, with the title of German Emperor being conferred on King William, finally put an end to the Habsburg voice in German affairs.

In April 1872, Gisela was betrothed to Prince Leopold of Bavaria, her second cousin twice over. Not quite sixteen and still considered a little childish for her years, she was a plain but cheerful, even-tempered girl.

Unimaginative yet sensible, she was quite different in character to the mother who had never seemed to care about her.

Family joy at this news was soon overshadowed by the death of the grand family matriarch. Archduchess Sophie had never really been the same since the tragic fate of her second son, and from then, she aged rapidly. Loss of Austrian prestige and the supremacy of Prussia also deeply grieved her, putting an end to her hopes of a greater Austria that would dominate the German-speaking peoples from the North Sea to the Adriatic. Yet she still presided over high society at Vienna and held a dinner party every Friday evening at the Hofburg until her final illness. In May 1872, she caught a chill that developed into bronchitis, and took to her bed. When she fell into a coma, the emperor placed Maria Theresa's cross and rosary in her hands, and Elizabeth barely left her bedside for several days.

Although both women had remained distant, Elizabeth had also been fond of Maximilian, and her sympathy for the mother of a son who should have met such an ignominious end was genuine. After the archduchess passed away on 28 May, aged sixty-seven, the emperor broke down and sobbed like a child, while the exhausted empress had to be carried from the room. She admitted later that although the archduchess had created problems for husband and wife, she had always meant well. The citizens of Vienna mourned the dead woman deeply, remarking that they had just lost their real empress.

In September 1872, another effort at diplomacy between the three emperors was made when they all visited Berlin. It was the first time Francis Joseph, Alexander II, and William I had met since the inconclusive Warsaw Conference twelve years earlier. The meeting was presented as a demonstration against 'the revolution', as if to try and demonstrate some solidarity between them, as well as to conceal the fact that they had not actually agreed on anything. Yet there was still a degree of mutual antipathy between the men whose ambitions and characters were so different. At forty-two and much the youngest of the triumvirate despite having reigned the longest, Francis Joseph neither liked nor trusted the tsar. As for the elderly, newly elevated emperor who had until recently been the King of Prussia, the state that gained enormously in prestige at Austrian expense, he resented the Hohenzollern's arrogance and vanity.

On 20 April 1873, Gisela and Leopold were married at the Augustinerkirche, the parish church of the Hofburg. The bride was all but outshone by her radiantly youthful-looking mother, but the uncomplicated, easy-going Gisela was not bothered by the lack of attention paid to her. At the ceremony, her mother and brother broke down and wept, while even Francis Joseph had tears in his eyes. Neither did the empress look forward to the festivities that followed the wedding, although at least there was a gala performance of *A Midsummer Night's Dream*, her favourite Shakespeare play—one that her husband had once sat through under duress and found 'indescribably stupid'. She did, however, wonder why a drama in which a princess fell in love with an ass had been chosen to celebrate a royal wedding. The groom saw the funny side of it, jestingly asking his bride whether it was intended as an allusion to him.[12]

4

'The smile of
an angelic sphinx'

For Austria and for Emperor Francis Joseph, 1873 was the year of the great Universal Exhibition in Vienna. Echoing similar recent ventures in London and Paris, it was staged as an international shop window of industry and commerce. A huge building, the Rotunde, was specially constructed for the purpose, 312 feet in diameter with twenty-eight temporary pavilions and a long central arcade.

The opening day, 1 May, was cold and wet. According to Sigmund Freud, a student of almost seventeen at the time, nobody apart from a few street urchins sitting into trees 'broke into shouts of joy at the sight of their Apostolic Highnesses, while His Majesty's humble and obedient subjects took cover under their umbrellas and hardly raised their hats'.[1] Inside the rotunda, the pageantry went on undisturbed by the elements as Archduke Charles Ludwig, imperial patron of the exhibition, delivered a formal speech of welcome to the guests before the emperor declared it open. Beside him on a dais sat the empress, the crown prince, the Prince of Wales, Crown Prince and Princess Frederick William from Germany, and Crown Prince Frederick from Denmark.

During the next few months, there was a carefully organised schedule of visits from several sovereigns and ruling princes of other European territories, including King Leopold II of the Belgians, German Emperor William I, King Victor Emmanuel of Italy, King George of the Hellenes, and Tsar Alexander II, who remained aloof and unsmiling throughout. It was the greatest gathering of royalty hosted by Vienna since the congress of 1815, although they did not all arrive simultaneously. It might have been preferable if they had, as the empress complained privately: '... if only they would all come together for one nightmare week'.[2] Several of these guests were welcomed but reluctantly in the interests of diplomacy. Francis Joseph grumbled that he 'felt like an enemy' to himself when required to don the uniform of the Prussian Guard Grenadier Regiment for his Hohenzollern neighbour, while having to offer the hand of friendship to the King of Italy, the victor on the battlefield at Solferino, was an even more bitter pill to swallow.

The exhibition was dogged by misfortune. A few days after the opening ceremony, Vienna was stricken with an epidemic of cholera that claimed over 2,000 victims. Many of those who had remained healthy panicked and fled the city to avoid any risk of infection, taxi drivers went on strike, and the city stock exchange collapsed, precipitating a rush to sell stocks and shares. The weather did not improve over an unusually wet summer and autumn. Takings were lower than expected, and soon after it closed on 2 November, having counted 7 million visitors through its doors instead of the 20 million anticipated, it was found to have made a loss of around 15 million gulden.

The emperor and empress had a rare short holiday together at Ischl in August. Soon afterwards, Elizabeth fell ill with gastric fever, and suspicions she might have been malingering were disproved when she was too unwell to attend a major horse show. She was still convalescent when the family had another short holiday at Gödöllö, but she had fully recovered by the time of her husband's silver jubilee celebrations in December. These included a procession and a drive around the Ringstrasse in Vienna, the emperor and crown prince driving in an open carriage and the empress following in a closed one, with a ceremony in the Hofburg next day at which the emperor and his generals exchanged compliments and congratulations. In the evening, the emperor and empress attended a gala performance of *The Taming of the Shrew* at the Stadtheater. The actress playing Kate was Katherine Schratt, a grocer's daughter from Baden, destined to become the emperor's closest companion.

Early in 1874, the emperor and empress became grandparents for the first time. The empress went to stay with her daughter and son-in-law at Munich so she could assist at the confinement, and the child, born on 8 January, was named Elizabeth. She had mixed feelings about attaining the status of grandmother so soon after her thirty-sixth birthday, and the baby, she wrote bluntly, was 'extraordinarily ugly but very lovely—in fact, just like Gisela'.[3] The emperor likewise regarded this family milestone as a sign of ageing, as he sighed less than accurately, 'Only forty-four and already a grandfather!'[4]

Despite the unproductive meeting of three emperors just over a year earlier, their ministers persevered, and all efforts bore fruit when Tsar Alexander II and Gorchakov visited Francis Joseph at Vienna in June 1873 for the signing of the Schönbrunn Convention. Bismarck's enthusiasm for resurrecting the old alliance of 1815 as a bulwark against radical movements in Europe culminated in an alliance between all three emperors, agreed in October 1873. Four months later, Francis Joseph visited St Petersburg, partly as a gesture of reassurance to Tsar Alexander II, who was still suspicious of Austria-Hungary's policies in the Balkans. One of the Austrian emperor's first acts was to lay a wreath on the tomb of Tsar Nicholas I and stand at the vault in silent prayer. Next, Alexander took him into his father's apartments, still maintained as they had been at the time of his death. At last, the bitterness of almost twenty years could be laid to rest. Imperial solidarity was sealed, as both rulers knew that mutual support would be invaluable over the years ahead. During his visit, the emperor had discussions with Gorchakov, as well as invitations to lavish entertainments and banquets at St Petersburg, where he met some of the tsar's English and Danish relatives by marriage.

Unusually, Elizabeth stayed at the Hofburg while he was away. She had taken to exploring Vienna incognito, and while he was away, she embarked on one of her oddest escapades. In disguise at a masked ball during the carnival season, she struck up a friendship with a civil servant, Fritz Pascher. She questioned him closely on how people in Vienna felt about the court, the emperor, and the empress, receiving very guarded answers. He realised who he was speaking to, but the empress naïvely assumed he would not recognise her. For some weeks after the ball, she sent him letters signed 'Gabrielle' via her sister, Marie, former Queen of the Two Sicilies, who was staying at a house in London she had leased, and forwarded them to him in Vienna. This, she believed, would protect her anonymity and keep any knowledge of her activity from her ladies-in-waiting. One of his replies made it evident that he had guessed her identity, and the correspondence abruptly ceased. Fortunately, he was discreet enough to keep the letters secret until shortly before his death almost sixty years later, and the emperor remained unaware of everything.

In April 1874, soon after Valerie's sixth birthday, the empress decided the little girl needed a holiday with plenty of sea air and fine weather without excessive heat. England, she decided, would be ideal for a visit that summer. Travelling under the incognito of Countess von Hohenembs, in August, she and her daughter came for a few days at Steephill Castle, Ventnor, on the Isle of Wight. Almost at once, Queen Victoria called on them. The empress did not want to dine with the queen at Windsor, and twice she refused, saying she was indisposed. It was perhaps tactless of her to accept the duke and duchess of Teck's invitation to visit them at Richmond, a move that did not escape the queen's notice. From England, she wrote to the emperor how delighted she was to be there and begged him to join her for a while, visit London, and enjoy some hunting in the countryside himself, but in vain.

One year later, in June 1875, Emperor Ferdinand passed away at the age of eighty-two. He left his nephew a considerable fortune, as his financial advisers had wisely avoided the stock market and left him unaffected by the crash two years earlier. He was followed to the grave three years later by Archduke Francis Charles, the man who would have been his successor and the emperor's father, who died in March 1878 at the age of seventy-five. Although the court was in mourning, Francis Joseph welcomed General Nikolai Ignatiev, Russian Ambassador in Constantinople, whom the tsar had just sent to Vienna to try and reconcile the Austrians to a military presence in Bulgaria, and assure them that St Petersburg would raise no objection to action taken by the Viennese government to secure the provinces. Talks took place between Ignatiev and Andrassy, but the former was not trusted, and after returning to St Petersburg, he tried to intrigue against Andrassy, hoping a more pro-Russian minister might be installed instead. Angered by his behaviour, Francis Joseph called him a 'notorious father of lies'.

The Congress of Berlin, bringing together Europe's greatest statesmen, met in June and July 1878. A revised treaty was drawn up at the end, by which time it was agreed that the new principality of Bulgaria, created as a result of the Russo-Turkish peace treaty signed at San Stefano in March that had brought the war between both nations to an end, would be reduced to one-third of the size proposed, while Austro-Hungary was given its long-coveted mandate to occupy and administer Bosnia and Herzegovina, in order to bring to an end the state of civil war between Christians and Muslims of both territories. Many in Austria saw the gain of these lands as some compensation for the loss of Lombardy and Venetia earlier in the emperor's reign.

In 1879, Crown Prince Rudolf came of age. A slim young man, according to his future sister-in-law, Princess Louise of Belgium, he was 'more than handsome, he was fascinating', in some ways very like his mother, having inherited her manner of speaking, and 'the smile of an angelic sphinx, a smile peculiar to the Empress'.[5] After the ill-chosen Gondrecourt, he had been fortunate in General Latour as his tutor, as he appreciated the importance of providing mental stimulation for the young man. Rudolf was fascinated by scientific subjects, such as ornithology (although like many contemporaries, he was obsessed with killing anything with feathers and wings), and at the age of twenty, he went on an expedition to observe animal and bird life in the Danube forests in southern Hungary, later publishing a book on the subject. The emperor seemed proud of his son and supported him against criticism at court from those, such as the arch-conservative Archduke Albrecht, who thought him a dangerous subversive.

It is uncertain how much the emperor actually knew about his son's political thoughts. As a youth of fifteen, he recorded in his notebook that the fate of King Louis XVI, the nobility, and the clergy during the French revolution was 'a necessary and salutary catastrophe'. Monarchy, he believed, had lost its old power and now clung to the trust and love of the people; it had become 'a mighty ruin, which may remain from today till tomorrow but which will finally disappear altogether'.[6]

At nineteen, he wrote to King Ludwig II of Bavaria that the Christian faith, 'in the narrow forms demanded by our Church, [was] quite unacceptable for any educated man who has reached a stage of mental development that allows him to rise above common life and logically think and ask questions'.[7] Three years later, he wrote to Thurnberg that he had no sympathy at all for the influence of the Church on the State, how he would rather send his children to a school where the master was Jewish than to one where the headmaster was a clergyman, and that a strong Catholic Church always resulted in 'evil consequences'.[8] Those in power, not least his father, would have been disturbed to know that the heir harboured such radical ideas.

On 24 April 1879, the emperor and empress celebrated their silver wedding anniversary, and the family gathered in Vienna for several days of festivities. During their life together, the emperor and empress had come to terms with a largely one-sided marriage. It was apparent that he was still devoted to her and resigned to the fact that he could never totally possess this temperamental wife with her antipathy to court life and obsession with travel, while he toiled at home. When they were apart, he wrote fondly to her from his study where he sat below a full-length portrait of her, telling her of mundane details such as the weather, what he had shot when he last went out with his guns (almost his sole form of relaxation), whom he sat next to at dinner, and the health of their relations. The last few years had showed them and the outside world that they had little in common while he put up with her foibles, her obsession with slimming and dieting, and her passion for riding and for acquiring large dogs. Nevertheless, he was pleased by the public response to their wedding anniversary, although, yet again, she found the various functions exhausting.

Now that the crown prince was of age, it was necessary to find him a suitable consort to allow him to marry and settle down. He had become very promiscuous, and when visiting London in 1878, the Prince of Wales, hardly a paragon of virtue himself, took him for a tour around London and commented afterwards to one of his aides—with, one suspects, some admiration—that for a young man of his age, it was surprising how much the Austrian crown prince knew about sexual matters: 'There is nothing I could teach him'.[9] Rudolf's private comments had an unpleasantly misogynistic ring. To him, women were willing to abandon any principles in pursuit of romance, bored him, and were only good for one thing. He had numerous brief affairs with married and unmarried women, wives of his closest friends not excepted, and it was rumoured that he fathered more than thirty children on the wrong side of the blanket.

It was one of these lovers, Princess Louise of Belgium, unhappily married to his hunting companion Prince Philip of Coburg, who helped to find a crown princess for Austria. Her younger sister, Princess Stephanie of Belgium, had shared her miserable childhood at the hands of their father, King Leopold II, who as parent and sovereign had few if any redeeming features. Even the emperor, who was generally prepared to see the good in anyone, called him 'a thoroughly bad man'.

In 1880, Count Bohuslav Chotek, Austrian Minister in Brussels, was asked to approach King Leopold and arrange a meeting between Princess Stephanie and the crown prince. Rudolf travelled dutifully to the Belgian capital to meet her in March. A tall, plump, and plain girl of fifteen, she was nevertheless eager to please and escape from her miserable childhood home. One of the emperor's aides, Baron Albert von Margutti, later observed pointedly that, in contrast to his feelings for her husband, he was carried away by his admiration for 'that beautiful woman who carried herself with such charm and ease and always had a friendly smile or a few kind words for everyone'.[10] Not everyone would have agreed that Princess Stephanie of Belgium was beautiful with her plain face and red arms. His judgment was probably influenced by his sympathy for her in the light of her fate, but she was clearly a kind-hearted young girl trying to make the best of herself.

While Rudolf was staying in Brussels, the king called his daughter into his study to tell her how much he and Queen Marie-Henriette were in favour of the marriage. Apparently taken aback by the news, she was led into an adjoining room to meet him. It was not to be love at first sight. She later noted with scant enthusiasm that he could not be called handsome: '... but I found his appearance by no means unpleasing'. In spite of this, she thought there was something hard and less than frank about his gaze. He could not bear to be looked at directly in the face, and around his mouth 'was a queer expression which was difficult to read'.[11]

Rudolf came close to losing his future bride when the queen caught him in the arms of his current mistress, Anna Pick, whom he had brought to Brussels for companionship on his journey to woo Stephanie, but despite this, the engagement was duly announced. He entered into the spirit of his engagement with uncharacteristic enthusiasm, telling Thurnberg that Stephanie would undoubtedly become a faithful daughter of the emperor and a good Austrian. She was 'a real angel, a good and faithful being who loves me, a very intelligent and tactful companion for life who will stand successfully and sympathetically by my side in all my difficult undertakings.'[12]

The emperor was pleased that the Habsburgs were to be joined by a king's daughter who was related to nearly all the other royal families of the day. The empress could not disagree more. When she opened and read the telegram bringing her the news, she turned very pale. As she read it out to her lady-in-waiting, the latter replied that she was glad it was not news of some disaster. 'Heaven send that it be not one' was the apprehensive empress's comment.[13] She hated the King and Queen of the Belgians, thought Stephanie's education too shallow and her nature too frivolous, and foresaw that she would not make a suitable wife for her son. Above all, she believed nothing good could come out of Belgium, particularly after the precedent of the ill-fated Maximilian's bride 'Hasn't Charlotte been experience enough for us?' she retorted.[14] Unlike her husband, she believed that Charlotte's thirst for status if not power as empress consort had been partly responsible for Maximilian's tragedy.

A wedding was planned for the summer, until it was revealed that fifteen-year-old Stephanie had not begun to menstruate and was still 'an unformed child'. Further difficulties were caused by the king, who refused to provide her with a dowry larger than the 100,000 gulden given to Charlotte more than twenty years earlier. The emperor then agreed to provide her with an additional sum, as well as an annual allowance from his own funds, while complaining of the king's penny-pinching ways.

The ceremony was accordingly postponed until 10 May 1881. She arrived in Vienna four days before the wedding, which took place at the Augustinerkirche at the Hofburg. Among the guests was Prince William of Prussia, the emperor's grandson, who wrote afterwards to his grandmother, Empress Augusta, that the bride looked 'delightful and sweet', while the groom made 'the least favourable impression' and did not seem 'to grasp the solemnity of the occasion'.[15] They spent their honeymoon at a chilly and unwelcoming Laxenburg. To start with, as they went there, Rudolf was silent and Stephanie nervous, alone with a man she hardly knew. Although it was almost summer, snow was falling when they arrived, they were greeted by the smell of mould, with no fresh flowers in vases or any other homely touches, and no dressing table or bathroom, but only a sink on a three-legged framework in which to wash. The wedding night was a shock to the bride, who 'had not the ghost of an idea what lay before [her], but had been led to the altar as an innocent child'.[16]

In spite of this unpromising overture, both partners initially tried to make a success of their marriage. Stephanie admitted that while there had been 'a lack of affectionate spiritual companionship', and 'nothing more than a sort of enforced association without cordiality', she did her best to try and understand her husband's nature and character.[17] Her sister-in-law, Valerie, thought that her love for him was 'close to adoration'. Rudolf was at first devoted to his young bride, whom he addressed in his letters as his 'Dearest Angel', signing himself 'Coco', while she accompanied him on his official visits and sometimes on hunting expeditions and shoots. Having been so unhappy at home, she looked forward to a happier time as a wife than as an unwanted daughter. He appreciated her readiness to learn and was encouraged by the interest she showed in politics as they discussed contemporary issues and current affairs together.

In June 1881, there was a renewal of the League of the Three Emperors. The imperial foreign minister, Heinrich von Haymerle, secured from Germany and Russia virtual recognition of Austro-Hungarian supremacy over the western Balkans, including the eventual annexation of Bosnia and Herzegovina. In return, Francis Joseph pledged the monarchy's benevolent neutrality if either of his partners should be at war with a fourth power, other than Turkey. The minister died suddenly in October 1881 and was succeeded by Count Gustav Kàlnoky, Ambassador to St Petersburg. Rudolf had admired Haymerle but did not extend this admiration to his successor.

Soon afterwards, Rudolf was introduced to the journalist Moritz Szeps, editor of the radical *Neue Wiener Tagblatt*. He maintained regular correspondence with Szeps, who replaced Latour as the main recipient of his political observations, and regularly contributed anonymous articles himself. He had to try hand to keep such contacts secret, as he knew that the authorities were keeping him under surveillance, on the pretext of protecting him from would-be assassins. Thanks to the private intelligence connections of Archduke Albrecht, the emperor was aware of, and strongly disapproved of, the company he kept. As a profession, he thought journalism the lowest of the low, a calling only fit for troublemakers and subversives. Most German journals were openly critical of the government, and he asked his chancellor, Count Taaffe, to invoke a press law empowering the confiscation of publications containing any potentially offensive articles. However, he was still prepared to treat his son indulgently. As long as Rudolf was a good and faithful husband, and showed promise as a regimental officer, he was prepared to accept a little waywardness in his stride, assuming the young man would grow out of his radical inclinations with increased maturity and wisdom.

For the first two years of their marriage, Rudolf and Stephanie appeared to be settling down well together at Hradcany Palace, Prague. Despite their differences in temperament and background, they had reached a mutual understanding. She was more willing to take part in court functions than he was, which won the emperor's approval. In the spring of 1883, she became pregnant, and a delighted Rudolf went to Vienna to tell his father in person. When military duties took him away from home, his letters to her referred to their unborn child as Vaclav, the patron saint of Bohemia. This may have been a subconscious wish of his to name the infant thus if it was a boy.

On 2 September 1883, at Laxenburg, Stephanie gave birth to a daughter. When told after a long and painful labour that she had not produced the eagerly awaited son, she sobbed bitterly, but Rudolf reassured her that little girls were 'nice and affectionate'. Two days later, he told Latour that the young mother 'looks as blooming as ever, as though nothing had happened, and the little one is a strapping girl weighing seven pounds, completely healthy and strongly developed'.[18] Named Elizabeth after her grandmother, she was known in the family as 'Erszi'. Stephanie thought he 'was absolutely stricken, as he had set his heart upon an heir to the throne'.[19] Yet he was a doting father, though he naturally hoped a son would follow.

By this time, the empress was about to have a residence of her own in Vienna. In the autumn of 1881, the emperor had agreed to the building of a modest-sized villa for her personal use, a family lodge free of all court ceremonial in a secluded part of the Lainzer Tiergarten park. He planned to meet the costs from his personal funds, it would be completed within about five years, and he saw it as a way of encouraging her to stay in the capital more.

At the age of forty-four, Elizabeth was losing interest in riding and suffered from sciatica. She sold her stud and never returned to England or Ireland, where she had enjoyed her hunting so much. Now she had an all-consuming urge to exercise, with gymnastic routines every morning, later supplemented with fencing lessons. Next she began to take long walks, sometimes of 20 miles or more, spending up to eight or nine hours a day on foot. Obsessed with her appearance and figure, saying that life would no longer be worth anything to her once she was no longer desirable, she took very little nourishment each day, drinking a glass of milk or orange juice instead of a proper meal. To the emperor's alarm, she became increasingly thin and pale. Ironically, something of her beauty remained into middle age, and neither of her daughters were really attractive as adults. Motherhood made Gisela look older than her mother, while Valerie was a pale, plain-faced young woman, admittedly with attractive hair and a graceful figure. The empress's parents, now in their mid-seventies, were deeply concerned about the change in her attitude to people and her various obsessions. In particular, she had developed an attachment to her cousin, King Ludwig, whose behaviour was becoming ever more erratic and his personal extravagance increasingly untenable. Although homosexual, he had once been briefly betrothed to her sister, Sophie, before jilting her, and Elizabeth was the only member of the family ready to forgive him.

In May 1886, Elizabeth excitedly took her husband and youngest daughter to visit her new hideaway, now almost complete. It was originally to be called the Villa Waldruh, until she changed her mind and decided it would be the Hermes Villa. The emperor tactfully admired its decoration, although he admitted he did not like the idea of going to visit as he was afraid of spoiling things inside. Valerie took an instant dislike to it, noting in her journal how she disliked 'these marble reliefs, these luxurious carpets, these fireplaces of chased bronze, these innumerable angels and Cupids, the carvings in every hole and corner, this mannered rococo style', and heartily longed to be back home again.[20]

When it was ready, Elizabeth was delighted to be there, and for the rest of her life, she enjoyed the luxury of having her own secluded *pied à terre*. She and the emperor spent a few days together there annually in late spring. Yet it did not stop her desire for yet another hideaway. A couple of years later, she told the emperor that now she wanted a small palace on Corfu, dedicated to Achilles. In the *Reichsrat*, opposition deputies were beginning to ask questions about the vast sums being spent on these buildings. Francis Joseph admitted sadly that it would do him 'no good with the Viennese', but he could refuse her nothing, and before long she also had her Achilleion.[21]

The emperor would also soon have additional (and less complicated) female company. In 1883, his mistress, Anna Nahowski, gave birth to a daughter, named Helène, and he was believed to have been the father. However, with the twenty-nine years that separated them, they had little in common. Although their relationship lasted a few more years, he soon found a more congenial companion, the actress Katherine Schratt, to whom he had been presented on a visit to the Burgtheater in 1884. Five years earlier, she had married Nicholas Kiss von Itebbe, retired from the stage, and given birth to a son. In 1882, her improvident husband fled from their creditors, leaving her and their child at the mercy of bailiffs. As a single parent, she had no choice but to resume her theatrical career. Shortly afterwards, she was introduced to the emperor. In the summer of 1885, she accepted a seasonal engagement at Ischl, where he generally celebrated his birthday. On 17 August that year, he, the crown prince, and the crown princess, Prince Leopold of Bavaria and Archduchess Valerie, all went to see Katherine at the Kurhaustheater in *Der Verschwender* (*The Spendthrift*).

Nine days later, she appeared before the emperor and Tsar Alexander III in a one-act comedy at a command performance in Kremsier, during an Austro-Russian summit conference in the Moravian archbishop's summer palace. At the tsar's suggestion, all the leading actresses joined the crowned heads for supper that evening. The slightly tipsy monarch had been ogling Katherine ever since they had been introduced, paying her unsubtle compliments, and after they had eaten that evening, he insisted on taking her for a stroll through the illuminated gardens. Next morning, Francis Joseph told Elizabeth that their Romanov guest's behaviour had been unpardonable, but she was rather amused. Unlike his late father, the tsar was normally the most faithful of husbands, and she wondered if her husband had taken offence.

Elizabeth was unfailingly supportive of his liaison with the actress. Although often increasingly self-absorbed, she undoubtedly felt some guilt at leaving her husband alone so much, and she felt that encouraging him in this relationship was the least she could do to make amends. Among other things, she commissioned a portrait of Katherine from the court painter Heinrich von Angeli as a gift for him.

A close, untroubled personal relationship for the emperor was some consolation in an often-troubled life. Not for the first time, his empire faced the threat of yet another war in which they would have to act with firmness to avoid being embroiled. Emperor and tsar were keen to preserve good relations and reaffirm their belief in the League of the Three Emperors, but neither Elizabeth nor Rudolf trusted the tsar's offers of friendship. Shortly before the Kremsier meeting, Francis Joseph had received Prince Alexander of Battenberg, now sovereign Prince of Bulgaria, who proclaimed the union of the two Bulgarias, linking the predominantly Bulgarian Ottoman province of Eastern Rumelia with his principality. Neighbouring Serbia, alarmed by the shift of power in the Balkans, invaded Bulgaria, only to be defeated by Alexander at the Battle of Slivnitsa. Francis Joseph and Kàlnoky both strove to keep the peace, holding Austria-Hungary to a common policy of mediation agreed by its partners in the League of the Three Emperors, as they were not prepared to risk a war in which they could not count on unqualified German support.

Meanwhile, tragedy was about to strike the Wittelsbachs. In June 1886, King Ludwig of Bavaria was compelled to abdicate his throne on the grounds of his increasingly abnormal behaviour and paranoia and placed under house arrest. On the evening of 13 June, his body and that of Dr Bernhard von Gudden, his physician who had tried to restrain him, were found by Starnbergersee, a large lake in Bavaria. Both men had drowned, but the exact circumstances as to how and why were never established, although the courts ruled that the king had killed his doctor and then himself. The empress was breakfasting with Valerie when the normally cheerful Gisela came in tears, asking to see her alone. At once the empress guessed what had happened. Too shocked to weep at first, she muttered to herself that 'they might have treated him more gently and so spared him such a terrible end'.[22] For several days, she locked herself in her room weeping, convinced the Bavarian authorities had conspired to murder him.

Her hysterical reaction to her cousin's presumed suicide seemed so exaggerated that her children thought her sanity needed to be called into question. At first, Rudolf, who had also been close to Ludwig, had only to enter the same room as his mother for her to start weeping. Gisela longed to help comfort her, but ironically it was her father-in-law, Leopold, Regent of Bavaria, who had signed Ludwig's arrest warrant. Elizabeth accused him of being 'an assassin and a traitor' and held it against the completely blameless Gisela. Elizabeth had had an irrational antipathy to her daughter ever since the latter's childhood, blaming her for passing on the infection that had killed her elder sister, Sophie. This latest unfortunate connection did nothing to reconcile them. As Elizabeth was in no fit state to attend the funeral, Rudolf went to represent her. After he returned, he and Gisela, deeply concerned about the mental state of the empress, questioned Valerie searchingly about their mother's behaviour and conversations. Shocked and deeply distressed at having to discuss such a sensitive matter, she was unable to say much without leaving their presence in tears.

Francis Joseph was still heavily preoccupied with affairs in the Balkans. In August 1886, the Russians kidnapped Prince Alexander of Bulgaria, who was too independently minded for their liking. It was thought that Tsar Alexander III intended to nominate a more subservient ruler himself, so as to ensure Pan-Slav control throughout the Balkans. Francis Joseph agreed with Kàlnoky that this was unacceptable for Austria-Hungary, and for a time, war seemed possible. Bismarck, who had been elevated to the post of German chancellor in 1871, made it clear that Germany would provide no military assistance, and only the recall of General Alexander von Kaulbars, the tsar's *aide-de-camp*, from Sofia to St Petersburg averted such a crisis.

Although father and son were very different, Francis Joseph was proud of Rudolf, his range of interests, and the way in which he discharged his duties. The crown prince, a good public speaker, had made an excellent speech at the opening of Vienna's electrical exhibitions in August 1883. At the same time, he published a book on one of his hunting expeditions, *Fifteen Days on the Danube*, for which he was awarded an honorary doctorate from Vienna University, and followed it with another on a journey he had made to the Middle East. Next, he assisted in the preparation of a multi-volume encyclopaedic survey of the Habsburg Empire, to which he contributed substantially. The emperor was so impressed by his son's introduction that he asked, a little tactlessly, whether it had really been his own work.

Despite these literary activities, Rudolf still regarded himself as a professional soldier, and recognised the army's role in binding the different provinces of the monarchy together. However, father and son differed in their aims. Francis Joseph placed increasing importance on the traditional role of his officers in bringing a splendour to distant towns scattered across the empire, while Rudolf was ever searching for new ideas in the old regiments, looking for greater efficiency, and planning ideas such as backing a preventative war during the Bulgarian crises. The emperor thought he was too immature to be entrusted with major military responsibility. So did Archduke Albrecht, who regarded the heir as a dangerous liberal. He and Prime Minister Eduard Taaffe were alarmed by his links with radical journalists in Vienna. Archduke Albrecht warned the emperor that all journalists were Jews and subversives, intent on destroying the empire, and that Szeps was responsible for filling the crown prince's head with dangerous ideas.

In the spring of 1888, Rudolf expected to receive the command of the Second Army Corps, with headquarters in Vienna. Instead, he was made inspector-general of the armed forces, a somewhat inferior post created for him, with ill-defined duties carefully monitored by Archduke Albrecht. He suspected, and complained to friends, that he was under surveillance from the emperor's inner circle of military advisers.

By this time, Rudolf's health was deteriorating. Early in 1886, he fell seriously ill, with what the public were told was severe rheumatism and a bladder infection, but was in fact syphilis, and he was confined to bed for several weeks. He passed the infection to Stephanie, who thought at first she had a severe case of peritonitis until two gynaecologists examined her, confirmed it was venereal, and told her she would never again be able to conceive.

Towards the end of the year, persistent bronchitis and rheumatic pains left him increasingly weak, and the emperor suggested he should go and convalesce on the island of Lacroma, off Dubrovnik, which he declined. But from that time onwards, he was a very sick man, heavily dependent on morphia, and drinking too much. Since falling out of a tree in childhood, he had been prone to severe blinding headaches, which were now becoming more frequent. Ill-health and self-indulgence were slowly destroying him, and a severe eye complaint made it difficult for him to enjoy his old passion of shooting.

He was still capable of displaying great charm. In the spring of 1887, he was chosen to represent his father at Queen Victoria's golden jubilee celebrations in London that June, and while there, he made a favourable impression on both the queen and the Prince of Wales, who had become a close friend. Ironically, Stephanie did herself little good by refusing to accompany him. She had heard from her sister, Louise, that Mary Vetsera, a notoriously fast member of Viennese society aged only sixteen with a shocking reputation, was going to be in London at the same time. At a court ball, she had been flirting shamelessly with Rudolf to the extent where gossips were talking about her intentions, and Stephanie was sure they intended to meet in England. Rather than face any humiliating scenes, she decided to stay at home, much to the anger of her husband, his father, and of Queen Victoria.

The marriage had not been a success. Although he only had himself to blame, Rudolf was angry that they would never be able to produce a son and heir, as she was herself. She was also thoroughly dismayed to find that his outward piety was only surface deep: '... he lacked a sense of duty and responsibility, so that later when life came to make its claim on him he lacked the power of religious faith and moral restraint'.[23] Among the rest of his immediate family, only the emperor was always gracious to her, if not particularly supportive. The empress continued to treat her with disdain, deriding her to others as a narrow-minded bigot and making no effort to help. Valerie also disliked her, noting in her diary that one could never warm to her, and wondering how her brother could love such a 'cold and arrogant woman'.

By the spring of 1887, Stephanie had noticed a severe change for the worse in her husband as his physical health deteriorated, he became increasingly restless and could not settle down to anything. Though she was certainly the more faithful partner of the two, on one visit outside the empire, she reportedly had a brief liaison with a Polish count. Rudolf was in no position to criticise. He still had his bachelor quarters in the Hofburg where he entertained his mistresses, and where she was never allowed to enter, and he never made any effort to conceal his infidelities from her, often insisting on sharing with her the most unnecessary details of these liaisons.

At the same time, he was increasingly embittered at not being allowed to take any part in the business of government. Some thought this the fault of the emperor, who kept him at a distance and regarded him as too immature, too eager for change, and, above all, distrusted by those closest to him, namely Archduke Albrecht and Taaffe. He never appreciated that it might have been worth taking the risk and entrusting him with some responsibility, hoping he would mature and that his ill-thought out radical ideas would be tempered by age and experience. A measure of productive work would have certainly made the crown prince feel more of use. Whether he was mature enough to take on any such responsibilities was another matter. If not trusted by his father and the elder generation because of his association with the 'wrong' people, he had to take a share of the blame. Unlike his friend and contemporary, Albert Edward, Prince of Wales—who had compensated to some extent for being heir to an apparently immortal sovereign and parent through his connections and activities as a royal ambassador to the other courts of Europe in all but name—he lacked the temperament to be able to make the best of a frustrating situation.

On 9 March 1888, German Emperor William died in Berlin at the age of ninety. Emperor Francis Joseph never mourned the man who had been a mere mouthpiece for his chancellor, Bismarck, and was more interested in what changes there might be under his son and successor Frederick III, the Prince of Wales's brother-in-law. Yet Frederick was in the advanced stages of cancer of the larynx and was unable to speak above a hollow whisper. He died after a reign of three months to be succeeded by his young, unstable, and headstrong son, Emperor William II. William and Rudolf, between whom there was only five months' age difference, had met each other on occasion and formed a pronounced mutual dislike. Francis Joseph hoped that William would maintain the traditional Austro-German friendship. Rudolf had been on excellent terms with the liberal Frederick and his consort Victoria, eldest child of Queen Victoria. When they were eclipsed by their son, William, he was deeply dismayed.

The emperor may have been too busy or perhaps too insensitive to notice the change in his son, particularly as they had little contact by now, apart from their joint hunting and sporting activities. They differed so much in outlook and personality, and Francis Joseph may have found it difficult to understand his heir.

It took one potentially serious incident to warn the elder man of impending trouble. In January 1888, father and son were shooting together when Rudolf suddenly saw another herd of deer. Though he was standing close to his father, he fired suddenly, and a beater raised his arm to protect the emperor. The man's forearm was shattered, but he had saved his sovereign from serious injury, if not death. A probably thoughtless but very dangerous action on Rudolf's part could have been construed as an attempt to assassinate his father.

Some said that Rudolf was banned from subsequent shooting parties, others that he was merely ordered not to take part the next day after his father had spoken to him severely and exacted an undertaking that nothing of the sort must ever happen again. What had probably angered him even more than his son's wilful disregard of basic safety precautions was the fact that Viennese gossips would surely say that his son had tried to kill him. Stephanie was sure Rudolf had meant to do so and disguise it as an accident.[24] It was well known that he resented his exclusion from any position of responsibility in the empire. Many people would have suspected that it was deliberate. After that, the emperor refused to see his son alone and ensured that he was kept under surveillance as much as possible.

Rudolf's mother and sisters were painfully aware of the changes in him. In April, Valerie wrote sadly of his recent behaviour, when he stared at them, she noticed, 'with glances of such deep and bitter hate that one is overcome with a feeling of anxiety'. Even Gisela, a tougher character less prone to worry than her mother and younger sister, 'whose love for Rudolf tends always to embellish his behaviour', was deeply perturbed to notice on one of her visits to Vienna that all the family regarded him as somebody to be treated with the utmost caution because his behaviour and temper were so unpredictable. She admitted that his stare thoroughly frightened her as well, and it eventually reduced all three of them to tears. His behaviour made them fear deeply for the future.[25] Several people outside the family also shared their sense of alarm.

5

Death at Mayerling

Rudolf and Stephanie had been living increasingly separate lives for some time, but when they paid a joint visit to Sarajevo in the summer of 1888, she saw a deeply disturbing change in his character. He was more restless and distraught than ever before, and prone to outbursts of fierce anger on the most trifling occasions. She had long become used to the fact that the 'conventionalities of our life together as husband and wife' contrasted glaringly with his everyday behaviour. However, he now seemed quite unrecognisable to her, as if he had 'lost any sense of good form'. He did not hesitate to talk to her openly 'about his distasteful amours', and his health was visibly declining, a venereal infection exacerbated by excessive reliance on alcohol and drugs.[1] After imbibing generous quantities of champagne and Cognac, he could not function coherently, and quick-witted members of his suite sometimes had to remove him discreetly from public functions to spare everyone else embarrassment and avoid scandal. He rarely slept more than four or five hours a night, and he suffered from headaches, painful joints, and eye infections. To ease the pain, he injected himself with morphine several times a day, and when the court physician Dr Herman Widerhofer suggested he should reduce the amount, he not only disregarded the instruction but increased the dosage.

As his strength ebbed, he neglected his intellectual interests and plunged into more military routine work. It was rumoured that he wanted an annulment of his marriage, and that he had talked to family members and friends about killing himself or suggesting suicide pacts, among them his wife, Lieutenant Victor von Fritsche, his personal secretary, and one of his mistresses, Mitzi Caspar, a former Viennese dancer. When he first mentioned it to the latter, she assumed that he was completely under the influence of alcohol or narcotics, and tried to pass it off as a joke. When he repeated the idea a few weeks later, she realised he was serious, and it worried her so much that she reported it to Baron Francis von Krauss, the Viennese chief of police. Probably taking the view that his crown prince was a tiresome neurotic accustomed to making foolish threats, he made her sign a declaration for his office records, and then warned her that if she told anyone else, she would be prosecuted. He had probably already been warned about Rudolf's suicide talk and discussed it with Taaffe, a man who disliked the crown prince so much, thought he would be a complete liability as emperor, and would have been relieved if the heir was to meet an untimely end. Rudolf himself sensed he would never reign or rule; during a shoot, he once pointed to Archduke Francis Ferdinand and told others that they were looking at the next emperor of Austria.

The crown princess's concern about the state of her husband was not shared by his parents. Although Elizabeth knew something was wrong, even if not to quite the extent that her ever-loyal younger daughter had suggested, there was a conspiracy of silence among Elizabeth's entourage, to shield her from hearing about her son's infidelities and over-reliance on drink and drugs. Self-absorbed she might have been, but had she spent more time in Vienna, or at least seen more of him, she would surely not have been totally oblivious to his physical deterioration. As for Francis Joseph, he was presumably too unobservant or too proud to admit anything could be seriously wrong with his son. In the same way that he refused to face the possibility that his wife was mentally unbalanced, he also turned a blind eye to Rudolf's condition. Ill-health, whether physical or mental, was beyond his limited experience. Having passed almost sixty years without illness or psychological problems, he must have found it impossible to recognise such frailties in others, least of all his closest relations.

Francis Joseph's youngest child, Valerie, was now almost an adult. For a couple of years, Elizabeth had spent more time in Vienna than usual, as several balls were held in the Hofburg to which the young archduchess's closest friends and young men attached to the court were invited. While her mother made an effort to put herself out for their guests, her remote manner tended to intimidate them. On the other hand, Francis Joseph, who genuinely liked the company of younger people, was at his most charming on such occasions.

By the time of her twentieth birthday in April 1888, Valerie had become attached to Archduke Francis Salvator, her second cousin from the Tuscan branch of the Habsburgs. They had been friends since childhood, an affinity that deepened while attending a ball together a couple of years earlier. Although dreading the prospect of her favourite child leaving home, Elizabeth saw the advantages of a marriage that would keep her in Austria and still hopefully under her mother's control to some extent. Rudolf initially thought Francis Salvator not good enough for his sister, while the emperor thought his daughter should seek a husband from another foreign house instead of marrying a kinsman of limited means. That winter, Crown Prince Frederick Augustus of Saxony and Crown Prince Carlos of Portugal planned to visit Vienna, mainly in order to ask the emperor for the hand of Valerie. If either the emperor or Rudolf dared to suggest the virtues of a marriage to the right man, Elizabeth would burst into tears and complain about their cruelty to Valerie, or about how lonely and unhappy she would be once her daughter had gone. It was hardly tactful of her to suggest that her life would be worthless after a perfectly normal family event such as a child's wedding.

The Austro-German affinity was to have unfortunate repercussions that autumn in what became known as the 'Vienna incident'. During the summer, Francis Joseph had invited the Prince of Wales, as honorary colonel of the 12th Austrian Hussars, to attend the autumn army manoeuvres. The prince knew Emperor William II was about to pay an official visit to Vienna at the same time, and wrote to express his pleasure at the likelihood of a meeting between them. Although the letter was not acknowledged, he went to Vienna as planned, arriving on 10 September. When he met the emperor and crown prince, they drew up a programme involving his absence on 3 October, the date Emperor William was expected to arrive. On the next day, he was told the emperor had insisted there should be no other royal guests in Vienna during his visit. Genuinely astonished and hurt, the prince told Sir Augustus Paget, the British ambassador, that he would avoid provoking ill-natured gossip by staying away from the capital while his nephew was there. Yet next day it was common knowledge that Emperor William had threatened to cancel his visit unless the British heir was asked to leave. The Austro-Hungarian Empire could not afford to offend her most powerful European ally, and the prince had to withdraw. Emperor Francis Joseph accordingly paid host to the young German sovereign, but found his presence as tiresome as his effrontery after an Austrian military review, when he criticised the efficiency and turnout of the Austrian infantry.

Differences between the young German emperor and the Austrian heir had already led to undignified exchanges behind the scenes. During a routine military inspection on his visit to Vienna, William belittled Rudolf's infantry and the rifles they used, saying they would be inadequate in any armed conflict. More was to come, for after he returned to Berlin, he sent Francis Joseph a letter drafted by Bismarck, suggesting in his capacity as head of Austria-Hungary's major military ally, the crown prince should be relieved of his post as inspector-general. Afraid of offending the German emperor, Francis Joseph cravenly asked his son to resign, a request he angrily refused. This was followed by a series of fiercely critical articles about Rudolf in the German press, referring to an eminent person in the Austrian Empire who hated Germany and was leading an extremely dissolute life. It was obvious to whom they referred. The eminent target himself responded by writing several fiercely anti-Prussian articles for a couple of Austrian journals. At the same time, he advised Moritz Szeps that the German emperor was having an affair with an Austrian woman of doubtful reputation, and who had stolen the All-Highest's monogrammed cufflinks. If the attacks in the German press did not stop, he said, this information about Emperor William—whose public image had long been that of an unimpeachably faithful husband to the very straitlaced Empress Augusta Victoria—should be published.

After the Prince of Wales was able to return to Vienna, he made a much more welcome guest than his nephew. When he attended the gala opening of the new Burgtheater on 14 October, he saw the seventeen-year-old Mary Vetsera in the audience and pointed her out to Rudolf, who had never met her though he had previously been pursued by her flighty mother Helene. A meeting was accordingly arranged by Countess Marie Larisch, the daughter of Elizabeth's eldest brother who had married the actress Henriette Mendel, now Baroness von Wallersee. In her younger days, Marie Wallersee had thrown herself shamelessly at Rudolf, and to try and keep her in order, Elizabeth had helped to arrange a marriage between her and the uninspiring Lieutenant George von Larisch von Moennich. Marie had sought revenge by indulging in spiteful gossip about the imperial family, and she became the confidante of Countess Vetsera and her family. On 5 November, Marie Larisch led Mary Vetsera to Rudolf's apartments at the Hofburg and formally introduced them.

Francis Joseph was more concerned at this time with his youngest daughter's future. Valerie was about to become betrothed, and he knew how it would sadden Elizabeth to be deprived of the constant companionship of her favourite child. The previous December, she had told Valerie that she was the only person she really loved, and that if she left her, her life would be at an end. She had never forgotten how Archduchess Sophie had taken the place of a mother towards the other children, and from the moment of her birth, she had determined it would be very different with this new daughter.

Elizabeth also had other family concerns. Her father, Max, had been ailing since a mild stroke in the summer and a more serious one on 10 November. When told he was gravely ill, she was at Corfu, and she desperately wanted to leave for Bavaria and see him again before it was too late. Knowing she was in low spirits at the time, the emperor advised her not to do so, as he feared the effect a deathbed meeting might have on her. The duke died on 15 November, and when told that he was gone, her sadness at his death was exacerbated by guilt at what she confessed was her 'unpardonable neglect of the most charming and original of fathers'.[2] The court at Vienna went into mourning, but Elizabeth did not attend the funeral, leaving her husband and son to represent her. On her return to the capital, much to the emperor's horror, she revealed that she had had an anchor tattooed on her shoulder, to show her love for the sea.

By now, Crown Princess Stephanie was increasingly desperate at the change in her husband. Breaking with the stiff Habsburg court etiquette that required her to seek an audience with the emperor first, she insisted on seeing him privately as her father-in-law to draw his attention to Rudolf's erratic behaviour and worsening health. She implored him to give his son a complete change, such as sending him on a goodwill voyage around the world, or something similar to remove him from a hollow life of idleness and dissipation that was slowly destroying him. The emperor still seemed unaware that anything was seriously wrong with his son, and he told her patronisingly that she should not be so anxious or give way to fancies. There was nothing wrong with Rudolf, he opined, except that he was rather pale, expected too much of himself, and ought to stay at home with her more than he did. With that he rose, embraced her, and then dismissed her. It said much for the emperor's lack of understanding, and it demonstrated how remote father and son had become with each other.

Although she was absent much of the time, the empress also had concerns about her son. Yet unlike the daughter-in-law whom she had never liked, she did nothing to try and help him. It was not in her power to do much, but had she been sufficiently worried, she could also have tried to intercede with her husband, or at least spoken to her son and offered him some moral support, but such gestures were now evidently beyond her. When Valerie became betrothed, she was so afraid of Rudolf's 'unstable, often bitter, sarcastic expression', and of even being alone with him, that at first she shrank from breaking the news to him.[3]

Nevertheless, she invited him and Stephanie to a family dinner on 16 December, adding that she had a secret to reveal. Although they were all anxious as to how he would take the news, to their surprise, he seemed unusually friendly that evening. For the first time in her life, Valerie noted afterwards, when she had given him the news, they embraced each other fondly as he wished them well for their future together. He was clearly touched, and when the empress asked him to be good to Valerie and her husband, he gave her his word that he would be the best of brothers. For the rest of that evening, he was very affectionate towards them, and it ended with Valerie embracing them both as she told them all that 'this is how we ought always to be'.[4]

This brief display of family togetherness could not prevent Christmas at the Hofburg that year from being a cheerless one. Gifts were exchanged on the afternoon of Christmas Eve, Elizabeth's fifty-first birthday, and Rudolf presented his mother with eleven autograph letters by her favourite poet, Heinrich Heine. Stephanie presented the emperor and empress with a set of drawings she had done of the Adriatic coast, while they produced for little Elizabeth a set of miniature garden furniture that had been made in Corfu.

That evening, they formally celebrated Valerie's betrothal. Elizabeth was now resigned to her forthcoming marriage but still depressed at the prospect of losing her, saying bluntly that Francis Salvator was a robber and by taking her away he was depriving her of the only real joy of her married life. She had arranged to go to Munich on 26 December and join her widowed mother, taking Valerie for a last family visit before the wedding. Francis Joseph was denied the pleasure of Katherine Schratt's company, for she was in quarantine as her son was ill with measles. She was not even allowed to write to the emperor, only to send him telegrams. In his loneliness, he paid what was to be his final purely social visit to Anna Nahowski.

Because of court mourning for the empress's father, there were no court balls during the new year season, only official dinners. Rudolf had been for a short holiday with Stephanie at Abbazia, on the Adriatic coast on 27 December, but he returned suddenly two days later, leaving her to return about a fortnight later.

During the first two weeks or so of January 1889, apparently in rather better spirits than he had been for some time, he continued with his usual routine. He went shooting again with the emperor and had presumably taken to heart the lessons to be learnt from that occasion a year earlier. On other days, there were visits from German and Russian dignitaries, regimental duties and the like, while in the evenings, there were assignations with Mitzi Caspar and Mary Vetsera, and the usual liberal consumption of alcohol and drugs. He and Stephanie were again leading almost separate lives, and when she saw him at Vienna on 11 January, yet again she was struck by his further deterioration, irritability, restlessness, and lack of sobriety as he 'spoke menacingly of horrible things' and toyed about menacingly with a revolver in her presence.[5] Like so many other family members, she was now frightened of being alone with him. It was perhaps fortunate that he made it clear he now wanted her company as little as possible.

On 13 January, Rudolf and Mary Vetsera, who had been having an affair with varying amounts of discretion since April 1888, saw each other again when his coach driver delivered her to the Hofburg for an assignation. Returning home, she told a friend that she had been with the crown prince, they had both 'lost [their] heads', and that 'now we belong to each other with body and soul'.[6] Her mother, Helene, had previously supported and encouraged her daughter in the affair, but now she flew into a panic. When Mary was out of the house, the baroness broke open her daughter's jewellery case and discovered photographs of Rudolf, her will made and dated 18 January, and a silver cigarette case engraved with his name, his regular farewell gift to each of his mistresses. Once Mary was back, mother and daughter argued violently. Mary then fled to a hotel and sought the companionship of Marie Larisch, begging her to get her away from Vienna as she felt she would die if she stayed at home.[7] Marie calmed her down and took her home, after which Mary fainted and was put to bed. Marie asked her what she had done to her daughter, but the baroness was too angry to reply. In order to try and calm her, Marie lied that the case engraved with Rudolf's name had been presented to her and she had given it to Mary.

One week later, Rudolf made plans with his friend Count Joseph Hoyos and his kinsman by marriage Prince Philip of Coburg to go shooting at Mayerling, his hunting lodge. When Stephanie learnt of this, he told her bluntly that her presence was not required. She suspected that Mary Vetsera, who had been flaunting her infatuation with the crown prince brazenly, was to be on his guest list. She gave him a gold cigarette case inscribed with the date 13 January 1889, and the words 'Thanks to a lucky chance'. When she and her mother were in their box at the opera, she wearing a conspicuously low-cut dress that did full justice to her generous figure, her eyes would be focused on the royal box, shrugging off any disapproving glances that came her way. His other mistresses would have almost certainly received a sharp reprimand from him for behaving thus, or else have been cast aside altogether. That she was allowed to get away with it suggested she had some special hold on him that her predecessors had not.

With hindsight, it was apparent that he had found the one person on earth foolish enough to die in a suicide pact with him. She was a voracious reader of romantic fiction, and in her infatuation with the heir to the throne, she probably saw herself as a heroine ready to sacrifice herself for her lover and die with him. Vienna had long had the dubious reputation of being the suicide capital of Europe, and the previous few months had seen a worrying increase in such statistics. Adults of all ages were killing themselves, often in public, sometimes taking colleagues, partners, and members of their family with them for the most absurd reasons. Like his contemporaries from all walks of life, Rudolf, and perhaps Mary, too, had a morbid fascination with those who chose to end their lives thus, and studied reports in the papers with obsessive attention to detail.

On 24 January, Rudolf attended a dinner given by British Ambassador Sir Augustus Paget. Lady Paget thought he seemed in rather better form that night than on previous occasions. She had a long talk with him, and found him 'less sarcastic, less down on people, and for the first time, he looked me in the eyes when speaking'. The only person he spoke of disparagingly was the German emperor, remarking: 'How horrible is this constant fight with the ghost of his father'.[8] Later that evening, he went to the opera, with the emperor arriving soon afterwards. It was noticed that father and son had what looked like a strained conversation, and the emperor left abruptly after the second act of the performance.

On the morning of 26 January, the emperor summoned the crown prince to an urgent audience. Rumour had it that he was shocked by some news he had just received, either from a member of his entourage or through the newspapers. There is no record as to what they discussed, but according to at least one court dignitary, shouting was heard. When Rudolf left the study afterwards, shaking and on the point of collapse, it was evident that something serious had passed between them. Maybe the emperor was ordering Rudolf to sever his connections with journalists and not for the first time, or maybe the crown prince was urging a change of military or governmental policy. A more likely theory is that his private life was questioned. The emperor was in little position to lecture his son on fidelity, but his liaisons were less numerous, more discreet, and at least took place with the approval of his frequently distant wife. Yet another, possibly speculation but not impossible, concerned his affair with Mary Vetsera. He might have confided as much to his father, who would have been angry but surely understanding, in view of his own relationship with Anna Nahowski.

There may have been more to it than a simple order to him to break off his affair with Mary, on the grounds that she was 'undesirable' and scandal would surely follow, and not merely a matter of the crown prince consorting with one of Vienna's most notorious courtesans who might be expecting his child. It concerned the dalliances Helene Vetsera had been enjoying in 1870, when she became pregnant with Mary. The young girl was nicknamed 'Le Picnic' by some, as her mother was not certain that her husband, who had been on diplomatic service at the court of Darmstadt when the baby was conceived, was the father. It might well have been a much more eminent figure in public life altogether. Had Francis Joseph, and subsequently Rudolf, been confronted with the possibility that Mary Vetsera was the emperor's secret love child, and that after investigating the baroness's past, some newspapers were publishing the rumour? Furthermore, if the young girl was pregnant, was she carrying her imperial half-brother's child? If so, details would inevitably emerge, with surely calamitous consequences for the Habsburg monarchy. Whatever the truth of the matter, Rudolf was in absolute despair when he left the Hofburg.

On 27 January, the emperor, crown prince, and crown princess attended a reception and state dinner at the German Embassy in Vienna to celebrate the thirtieth birthday of Emperor William, hosted by German Ambassador Prince Reuss. Like his heir, the emperor found little to admire in the personality of his young fellow monarch, and he confessed privately that it would hardly please him, particularly as courtesy required them to appear in German uniform. Ironically, eleven days earlier, the new issue of a new weekly journal, *Schwarzgeld*, that had Rudolf's backing and which was strongly anti-German in tone, carried a front-page article, 'The Ten Commandments of an Austrian', strongly critical of Prussia. Newspaper articles elsewhere in the press suggested that the crown prince favoured a reversal of alliances, with the dual monarchy abandoning Germany and Italy in favour of France and Russia. Although he hesitated to usurp his father's prerogative and go against his government's policy by approving publicly, with his increasing distaste for Germany, he doubtless approved of the general principle.

Lady Paget noticed that when the emperor arrived, Rudolf bent low over his father's hand, almost touching it with his lips. It was to be the last meeting between father and son. According to the somewhat dubious memoirs of Marie Larisch and others, there were some dramatic scenes at court that evening. The emperor was said to have turned his back on his son, while the crown prince and Mary Vetsera were observed speaking twice to each other during the evening. When the time came for the imperial party to leave with the emperor and his son passing along the rows of guests who bowed and curtseyed, Mary remained standing as the crown princess walked by, looking her defiantly in the face. As soon as she noticed, her furious mother ordered her to remember her manners and drop to her knees, but the girl had made her point, and everybody in the room noticed. How the emperor and crown prince reacted was not recorded—perhaps they wisely kept their reactions to themselves in public, far too conscious of their own dignity to consider causing a scene—but the crown princess blushed and was rightly affronted at such a breach of etiquette.

Later, the emperor made a remark to Lady Paget about the year that had just closed. She replied that she did not regret the passing of 1888 as it had been 'a very bad year', perhaps referring to the deaths of two emperors in Germany, but she feared 1889 would be 'far worse'.[9]

Although Mary Vetsera might have been his mistress of the moment, Rudolf then spent the rest of the night with Mitzi Caspar, entering her house with a bottle of champagne, and drinking for a couple of hours. He had already told his servants that he would be leaving the Hofburg for his hunting lodge at Mayerling before noon on 28 January. Now, he rambled on at length, telling her that honour demanded he take his own life at Mayerling, and that Archduke Francis Ferdinand could take his place as heir. A few hours before dawn, he staggered to his feet, raised his hand, and made the sign of the cross on her forehead, a strange act for a self-proclaimed atheist.

On the evening of 29 January, Francis Joseph and Elizabeth hosted a family dinner at the Hofburg to celebrate the engagement of Valerie and Francis Salvator. Rudolf and Philip were among those expected to attend. When Philip arrived at Mayerling early that afternoon, he found Rudolf looking distraught, saying he had a feverish cold and would not be there. After Philip had left to join the others, Rudolf sent a telegram to Stephanie to apologise for his absence. When she read it, she was deeply disturbed. For him to make his excuses for such a minor indisposition, not join a major family occasion, and only tell them at the last minute was a calculated insult to them all. Unlike her parents-in-law, she was not prepared to shrug it off as mere wilfulness. She had an instinctive feeling that worse was to come. Philip confirmed that the crown prince had not been well enough to go shooting that morning with him and Count Joseph Hoyos, the court chamberlain, but it did nothing to allay her fears.

Rudolf had been increasingly distant from her for the last few years, and almost never confided in her anymore, apart from his infidelities. Yet she believed that the main reason for his decision to end it all was because he was deeply involved in high treason against his father. His secret plans, she wrote in her memoirs, 'led him into a blind alley', he did not have the stamina to face such a situation and was unable to back out of it.[10] There were rumours of an independence movement in Hungary, and of an offer by Count Tisza, to defuse the aims of the radicals by keeping the country within the Habsburg dominions and making Rudolf king. Such a move would have been anathema to the emperor, who intended to maintain his prerogatives and had no wish to be faced with a rival monarch, least of all his own son. He would have been even angrier had he known—according to subsequent historians on admittedly slender evidence—that Rudolf had signed a document promising the Hungarians he would press for a completely independent nation with its own government and army. These theories may have no foundation in fact, but Rudolf had inherited his mother's admiration for Hungary, and any separatist movements supported by radical Magyar politicians knew or assumed they would have a ready supporter in high places. For Rudolf to have offered any encouragement, no matter how slight, would have been seen as treason against his father.

Meanwhile, Countess Vetsera was increasingly anxious that Mary had not returned home. She and her brother, Alexander Baltazzi, went to report to Krauss that her daughter was missing, and that Marie Larisch suspected the crown prince was involved. Krauss warned her that if he launched an official enquiry, her daughter's name was bound to appear in the press. She was sufficiently worried to agree, and when she handed him a photograph of her, he assured her he would keep the matter as secret as possible. Krauss then reported everything to Taaffe, who reminded him of the Vetsera family's dubious reputation and instructed him to take no further action. Shortly afterwards, the countess walked into Taaffe's office and demanded an immediate audience. He said he was in no position to speak directly with the crown prince, as they were not on good terms and he had no wish to enquire about his private life. The heir was expected back in Vienna that evening, and if he did not appear, he would ask detectives to make enquiries. Until and unless the crown prince failed to return, she must keep silent. When she threatened to go directly to the emperor, he asked her what made her think that Mary was with the crown prince. After one or two further remarks about the young girl's notoriety, the countess blushed and hurriedly left.

Taaffe was unaware that Rudolf had already excused himself from dinner at the Hofburg. When he learnt that the young man had been absent from such an important family occasion, he realised the situation was serious and advised Krauss to send an inspector to Mayerling next morning.

Meanwhile, Rudolf was in his rooms at the hunting lodge, where Mary had been carefully concealed with nobody else there initially aware of her presence. In the afternoon, he told Hornsteiner, one of his gamekeepers, that he would not be taking part in the shooting next day after all. Early that evening, he invited Count Hoyos for an informal dinner, at which he ate and drank heartily. Hoyos later revealed that the crown prince seemed more his old self, and added that he was unaware Mary Vetsera was in the bedroom all the time. Rudolf then excused himself early, complaining again about his cold. Once Hoyos had returned to his lodgings in a separate building nearby, Rudolf called Joseph Bratfisch, his cab driver, and asked him to wait with his carriage early next morning as Mary Vetsera was with him and she would be returning to Vienna. Next he instructed Johann Loschek, his valet, not to let anybody in—not even the emperor. It was an odd order, for nobody would expect His Imperial Majesty to visit his son's hunting lodge 15 miles from Vienna in person.

At shortly after 6 a.m. on 30 January, Rudolf was dressed in his hunting clothes. Coming out of the bedroom, he asked Loschek to see to the horses and carriages needed for sport that day. Breakfast was ordered for 8.30 a.m., by which time Philip should have returned from Vienna. That would allow him a little more sleep, and he needed to be woken at 7.30 a.m. He then returned to the bedroom.

According to Loschek's testimony, the crown prince seemed unusually light-hearted, even whistling a tune to himself. Within a few minutes, he heard two gunshots, fired in quick succession, and as he ran back to the anteroom, he thought he smelt gunpowder. He tried the door on Rudolf's bedroom, which was usually unlocked, but this time it was locked on the inside. Without alerting anybody else, he walked across the courtyard to order breakfast and carriages for the hunt. As requested, he went to wake his master at 7.30 a.m., but the door was still locked and there was no response to his knocking. Now quite worried and hoping that despite having been alert only a short time ago, the crown prince had merely passed out from the effects of morphine or alcohol, he left the anteroom and walked round to the corridor towards the bathroom. When he tried to open the door there leading to the bedroom, he found that locked as well, and fetched a piece of firewood to bang on the door, but in vain. Alois Zwerger, the lodge warden, was sent to fetch Hoyos, who was having his breakfast and suggested they should let the crown prince sleep as he was probably tired, but gave in at Zwerger's insistence that something must be wrong. Back at the lodge, Loschek was still banging on the door. Hoyos knocked loudly, calling the crown prince's name. He then insisted that Loschek must break into the room, but the latter refused, admitting that he knew Mary Vetsera was also in there.

Between them, they decided that when Philip returned from Vienna, as he was a member of the family, he would be given responsibility for forcing an entrance. When he returned shortly after 8 a.m., the others explained the situation and he ordered Loschek to break down the door with an axe. As this failed to break the lock, he cut a hole through the upper panel and peered through. Even though it was not yet fully light outside, the curtains were drawn, and the windows were shuttered, he could see two dead bodies.

Reaching through the panel, he found the key, and unlocked the door at last. Rudolf was on one side of the bed, fully dressed, with Mary naked on the other, their heads hanging down. The top of Rudolf's skull was gone, while a single bullet wound to Mary's head had shattered one side of her skull. A revolver lay beside them. Loschek realised at once that he had killed her and then himself. Her dead hand was clutching a handkerchief, as if she had been crying during her final moments. She had been shot in the left temple, presumably several hours before her imperial lover.

Still suffering from shock, Philip and Hoyos realised the most important thing to do was to try and keep everything secret until the emperor had been informed. Hoyos persuaded the stationmaster to stop the next train and allow him to board, but only after having to reveal that the crown prince had shot himself. Once Hoyos was on board, the stationmaster telegraphed Baron Rothschild, who owned the Southern Railway on which the Trieste express was travelling. The news was immediately passed to the Austrian, German, and British embassies in Vienna, and the diplomatic world therefore knew before the dead man's family. Meanwhile, Loschek was asked to telegraph Dr Herman Widerhofer, summoning him to the lodge immediately. At mid-morning, a thoroughly distressed Hoyos arrived in a cab at the Hofburg, sought out Charles von Bombelles, the emperor's adjutant, and told him of their discovery.

The emperor was working on papers at his desk as usual, while the empress was having one of her Greek lessons. Neither of them wanted to break such dreadful news to His Majesty. Philip was so devastated that he was temporarily incapable of doing almost anything, and Hoyos was left to undertake the task. At this stage, he hesitated to tell anyone the full facts at once. He informed Bombelles that the crown prince had apparently been poisoned by one of his mistresses, who had then killed herself the same way.

Ironically, in view of the fact that the emperor and his entourage had always insisted that his wife should be spared emotional shocks as far as possible, it was to the empress that they gave the news and asked her to tell her husband. Totally self-absorbed, frequently absent from Vienna, and largely preoccupied with Valerie's romance during the past few months, and shielded by her family from much bad news, she had appeared unaware at times of Rudolf's deterioration, and perhaps even of the existence of Mary Vetsera. Nevertheless, she rose to the occasion and steeled herself to let her husband know that their son was dead—by the hand of his mistress.

By coincidence, Katherine Schratt had arrived that morning to see the emperor. She was unaware of the news until the empress told her, urging her to go and help him as she, his wife, could do nothing more. Next to learn was Valerie, who found her mother weeping in her bedroom. She told Valerie that Rudolf was very ill, and there was no hope. Instinctively, Valerie immediately asked if he had killed himself. The empress asked her why she should think that, but said 'the girl' had poisoned him. It was left to a lady-in-waiting to inform Stephanie, who was interrupted during her singing lesson, and now learnt that her worst fears had been realised. Later that morning, the emperor and empress summoned her to a formal audience. Instead of showing any sympathy, she later related in her memoirs, they seemed to look on her as a criminal, assailing her with a crossfire of questions, some of which she could not, and others would not, answer. Sensing that they held her responsible for the tragedy, she mentioned Rudolf's erratic behaviour over the years and how the emperor had dismissed her warnings and anxieties. The empress refused to listen to her.[11] Before they dismissed her, they told her that he had died of heart failure. At this stage, she was probably unaware of the full details. On returning to her apartments, she collapsed, her doctor gave her a sedative and put her to bed.

Soon afterwards, a worried Countess Helene Vetsera called on Taaffe again. He told her that if she considered the matter urgent, she should seek an audience with the empress and ask her to intervene. When she came to the Hofburg, seeking news of her missing daughter, Ida Ferenczy tried to order her away, but she persisted. Coldly, Elizabeth told her that her daughter was dead, adding that her own son was as well. As she swept away, still believing that Mary Vetsera was a murderess as well as a suicide and that her son was the scheming girl's victim, she warned the countess coldly to remember that Rudolf had died from a heart attack. One day later, Count Taaffe came to see the baroness briefly and advise her that it would be in her best interests to leave Austria for a while.

Next, the people had to know that the imperial heir was dead. Shortly after midday, in accordance with regular ritual, the changing of the guard outside the Hofburg was followed by a rousing piece of music from the regimental guard. Almost at once, it stopped without explanation. Theatres, music halls, and other places of public entertainment were ordered to stop playing and close their doors, as there was grave news concerning the crown prince. Telegrams were despatched that same day to other European sovereigns, including German Emperor William, Queen Victoria of England, and Dowager Queen Maria Cristina of Spain, saying he had died suddenly, 'probably from heart failure'. At about 3 p.m., Taaffe released a short bulletin to the press saying that the crown prince had died that morning at his hunting lodge, giving the same reason. One hour earlier, he had informed Krauss that the heir was found dead in bed 'with the Vetsera woman', after they had poisoned themselves. A commission had left for Mayerling, and it was imperative that her body was taken away and secretly buried. Nevertheless, news of the baroness's visit to the palace had spread and gossips, who knew about the affair, instantly realised there must be some connection. In a special edition of the official *Wiener Zeitung*, it was noted that he had succumbed to a stroke.

At that time, the court still believed Rudolf had been poisoned, and as a good Roman Catholic, Francis Joseph hesitated to lie to the Holy Father, so he decided to tell him as little as possible. The telegram informing Pope Leo XIII, despatched on 31 January, merely informed him 'with most profound grief' of the sudden death of his son, but no mention was made of the cause. A reply from the Pope assured the emperor of his sympathy and informed him that he had said a Requiem Mass for the late crown prince that morning.

Few people could believe that their crown prince could have died at such a young age from natural causes. Even when the truth became impossible to suppress and it was admitted two days later that he had taken his own life, it did nothing to quell any of the rumours. Some said he had been the victim of a political murder—a group of Hungarian separatists having killed him for going back on his word and betraying them; others believed he had taken his life after attempting a coup in Hungary. Others whispered that a cuckolded husband had sought revenge, or that he had been so deeply involved in treason that Count Taaffe, aware that he and his mistress had gone to Mayerling, had arranged for agents to stage an assassination that would look like suicide. Other stories were that after learning that Mary Vetsera was believed to be the emperor's illegitimate daughter, the shame of their incestuous affair left them with no alternative but to take their own lives; that he had been killed in a drunken orgy after being hit over the head with a bottle; or in a hunting accident. Within less than a week, a Munich newspaper printed the full story of Mary Vetsera having died with the heir to the throne, and before the authorities could act, copies were on sale in Vienna.

The emperor had been misinformed. Only when he received a report of the autopsy from Widerhofer, on 2 February, with a verdict that the crown prince had died as a result of the shattering of his skull and the anterior parts of his brain, produced by a shot fired against the right temple at close range, did he realise his son had murdered his mistress and then turned the weapon on himself. Having previously been given to understand that he had been killed by her, the even greater shame that he was not a victim, but a murderer and a suicide appalled him even more, and it was a while before he regained his composure. The doctor valued his professional integrity more than his position at court and insisted on telling the truth in his *post-mortem*. He did concede, perhaps in all good faith, that an examination of the brain revealed 'pathological disturbances', signifying that the heir to the throne had shot himself in a moment of mental derangement. Queen Victoria wrote bluntly in a letter to her prime minister, Lord Salisbury, that there could be no doubt 'the poor Crown Prince was quite *off his head*'.[12] Her suspicions were confirmed in a letter from her grandson, Emperor William II, who had been told by Philip of Coburg 'that lunacy was looming in the background & that the monomania of suicide had done its silent but sure work on the overexcitable brain'.[13] Widerhofer also reported symptoms of advanced paralysis that would have probably resulted in the heir's death within the year. To his surprise, the emperor found some consolation in this, remarking that God's ways were inscrutable: '... perhaps he has sent me this trial to spare me a yet harder one!'[14]

It was agreed by all concerned that papal permission should be sought for a full Christian burial, despite the stigma of suicide. Evidence of abnormal mental conditions was enough to obtain permission from the Pope to approve the full rites of Christian burial. If he was denied one, it would have caused yet another astonishing scandal from which none of the parties involved would emerge with credit.

A further loss for the emperor to bear was that Rudolf had left several farewell notes, including to his mother, wife, youngest sister, Loschek, Hoyos, and to an abbot to come and pray over their bodies—but none to his father.

The whole episode added to Elizabeth's fears that she had brought into the family the strain of insanity that had long haunted the Wittelsbachs. She told one of the court physicians sadly that the emperor should never have married her, as she had inherited the taint of madness. Rudolf had as well, 'or else he would never have treated me thus!'[15]

Meanwhile, the presence of Mary Vetsera had to be concealed from press and public. On the day after his death, his body was laid out on a bed in the Hofburg for burial. Stephanie brought little five-year-old Erszi in to say goodbye to him and to lay her own wreath of white roses. The tearful girl clung to the skirts of her attendant, screaming when she saw the bandaged head, saying over and over again that the lifeless form was 'not my father', and begging to be taken away. Valerie had been dreading the ordeal of coming to see him, but found some comfort in looking at the brother whose 'erratic, bitter expression that he had so often had in life had given way to a peaceful smile'.[16] The usually placid Gisela came from Bavaria, in an uncharacteristically nervous state, insisting that it was impossible her brother was dead. She was kept from viewing the corpse with some difficulty.

There was no possibility of a state funeral, and the emperor requested that no crowned heads should attend the ceremony. Emperor William said he wished to come, presumably more out of solidarity with the emperor and as a demonstration of his adherence to the Austro-German alliance rather than out of any feelings for a late prince for whom he had had little but contempt. Francis Joseph telegraphed him asking him to stay away. He also tried, but in vain, to dissuade his son's parents-in-law, King Leopold and Queen Marie-Henriette of the Belgians, from coming. Having never cared much for his daughters, while in Vienna, King Leopold appeared quite unaffected by the tragedy.

Neither Elizabeth, Stephanie, nor Valerie attended the funeral on 5 February. Out of consideration for her feelings, knowing her increasing dislike of public appearances, the emperor begged his wife not to attend, so she and their youngest spent the afternoon praying together in a nearby chapel. It fell to the sorrowing but composed father and his elder daughter to say farewell to their son and brother at a mournful ceremony at the Hofburg chapel. Gisela was the only one who had really been close to her brother, and it sometimes occurred to her that if only she had stayed in Vienna, her companionship and common sense might have persuaded him to live. At the end of the ceremony, the emperor stepped out from his seat, walked up to the coffin, and knelt beside it in silent prayer. Afterwards, he rose and walked back calmly to his place. He told the empress and Valerie that he thought he bore up well, and only in the privacy of the crypt could he endure it no longer: '… never did a funeral take place in such circumstances as today'.[17]

Several other male members of the family, including his two surviving uncles; his cousin, Archduke Francis Ferdinand; his brother-in-law, Prince Leopold of Bavaria; his future brother-in-law, Archduke Francis Salvator; and Prince Philip of Coburg, were also there. They accompanied the emperor to the vault where his son was laid to rest among his ancestors, and where his composure gave way as he broke down weeping bitterly as he fell to his knees, embracing the coffin and repeatedly kissing the lid.

Mary Vetsera was denied any such dignity in her burial. Her body had been thrown into a storeroom until her uncle was summoned by the police to come and identify her. She would probably have been thrown in an unmarked grave but for the intervention of Katherine Schratt. Furious at the way the police and Count Taaffe were treating the Vetsera family, she suggested tactfully to the court officials that if the family was denied a Christian ceremony for the girl, the court would suffer even more once the news became public, as it surely would. She was eventually given a funeral, a squalid late-night affair. It came at the end of a macabre journey in which her uncle and her brother-in-law escorted the body from Mayerling in a closed carriage, with a stick placed along her spine and her head held up by scarves knotted over her forehead and chest to stop her head from lolling forward.

Within a fortnight, the emperor was trying to put the tragedy behind him, yet some of those around him thought that he had become a completely different person. When he was not talking to others, he acted as if he had been knocked on the head. He told his adjutant, Count Eduard Paar, how grateful he was for the empress's support, and that if it had not been for her who helped to keep him going, although she was stricken with grief herself, he would 'have gone under altogether'.[18] Although they had been so distant from each other for the greater part of their married life, it seemed as if their son and heir's tragic end had brought them closer together than they had been for many a year, albeit briefly. He reputedly told associates that his son had died like a coward, although when writing to other sovereigns, and to Katherine Schratt, he paid lip service to family solidarity, calling him 'the best of sons and the loyallest of subjects'.[19]

Countess Larisch's responsibility for the tragedy in having acted as a go-between between Rudolf and Marie was soon revealed. She was banished from appearing at court ever again and sought revenge in two subsequent books, a volume of highly inaccurate recollections and a spiteful memoir of the empress, despite being paid by the authorities to keep her silence. One of her five children, aged only two at the time of the tragedy, was so horrified when he learnt of his mother's role that he took his own life. Thrice married, she lived to her eighties, dying in poverty in a nursing home.

As Rudolf had left no sons, a direct male heir had to be nominated. Next in succession was the emperor's eldest surviving brother, Archduke Charles Ludwig. Now in his mid-fifties, he was a pleasant, if ineffectual, unambitious character, who had survived all three of his wives. Somewhat unworldly, he was given to quoting the Bible at length and making the sign of the cross whenever he greeted anyone. He took a keen interest in arts, crafts, and industries in the empire, regularly attended exhibitions and conferences in an honorary capacity, and presented annual prizes for pictures and sculptures at the academy. Otherwise, he took little part in public life, had never expected to succeed to the throne, and never attempted to exert any political influence. It was widely believed that he would renounce his place in the succession, and that he asked his brother to allow him to do so. The emperor reportedly refused, as he had grave doubts about the suitability of the next in line, Charles Ludwig's eldest son.

Archduke Francis Ferdinand was aged twenty-five at the time. A strong supporter of closer ties with Berlin, he was firmly opposed to the idea of war with Russia, hated the Magyars, regarding their separatist ambitions as a threat to the stability of the dual monarchy, and had a profound loathing of the kingdom of Italy. Moreover, he had inherited the tubercular condition of his mother, Princess Marie Annunziata of Naples, was often sent abroad during the winter months for the good of his health, and the doctors feared that he would be unlikely to reach middle age. For all his faults, among them hypersensitivity, paranoia, a reluctance to trust people, and an explosive temper, he was a dedicated and conscientious soldier, and although still unmarried, he had none of the debauched tendencies of his younger brother, Otto. Some of those closest to him saw a strength of character that suggested he would make a perfectly capable, if not necessarily popular successor as emperor to his uncle and father.

Death at Geneva

For the emperor and empress, the next few years were bleak indeed. Now aged almost sixty, Francis Joseph's life had become one of ritual and dedication to his empire, with only the company of Katherine Schratt for consolation. Any hopes that the tragedy of their son's death might have brought husband and wife together for more than a short interval were unrealised. During their rare times together in Vienna and occasionally Budapest, Elizabeth alternated between listless apathy, acute melancholia, and tears. Those who knew them well thought that he was still very much in love with her, while it was as if she had been wounded too often, and tried to keep her distance from him and the official world with her aimless travels abroad. He found her persistent negativity and self-pity irritating, and her repeated references in conversation to weariness and looking forward to death thoroughly depressing.

Lady Paget considered that after the Mayerling tragedy, the emperor was managing as well as possible. He continued to work hard at his desk, seeing people, giving dinners, appearing interested in and pleased with everything. It was a painful contrast to the empress, who had 'become a ghost during her own life'. She had borne up well at first, but the effort was evidently too much and she then slid back into her old ways: 'Having lived a life of unalloyed selfishness, worshipping her own health and beauty as the sole objects in life, she has nothing but herself to fall back on'.[1]

On the first anniversary of the tragedy at Mayerling, emperor and empress jointly visited the site of the hunting lodge, which had been demolished and replaced by a Carmelite convent, with a chapel on the spot where Rudolf's bedroom had been. Mass was read by the court chaplain, and as she watched her parents, Valerie felt deeply conscious of everything that divided them. In particular, she was struck by her father who seemed so humble, devout, and resigned to his son's fate, while her mother remained dry-eyed, her face a mask, confessing afterwards that she felt as if her son's bullet had also killed her faith.[2]

Although about to be married, Valerie felt obliged to spend what time she could with one parent or the other in the months following her brother's death. While she did not approve of what she called bluntly 'his unfortunate relationship with the Schratt woman', her sympathies were overwhelmingly with her father, who had sacrificed so much in the name of imperial duty and received so little thanks from his ungrateful wife, and she was sad to see how much they got on each other's nerves.[3] He was increasingly deaf, which, given his wife's persistent talking about her obsession with mortality, was possibly an advantage, and in what might have been a subconscious way to irritate him, she now spoke more softly than ever. Valerie urged her mother to raise her voice when speaking to her father, only to be told that she could not shout. Yet even Valerie found him becoming increasingly ponderous, narrow-minded, and easily worked up over trivial matters, one of the few things he had in common with his wife.

The mere mention of Valerie's marriage made the empress bewail tearfully her loneliness once her youngest child had gone. Further sadness came when she was called back to Bavaria to the deathbed of her sister, Helene, whom she saw for the last time before stomach cancer killed her in May 1890. The wedding took place on 30 July at Ischl, with over 100 family guests present. Francis Joseph was glad to see their daughter so radiantly happy in what was the first cheerful occasion the family had seen for a long time. Elizabeth, who had sometimes said that she had lost all her religious faith, admitted to having prayed a great deal in the days prior to the wedding. She made an effort to be calm and supportive throughout the ceremony, but afterwards she broke down and asked what was to become of her now.

The young couple enjoyed a honeymoon in Italy, Switzerland, and Bavaria, and then made their home at Lichtenegg Palace. Ironically, the first of her ten children, a girl named Elizabeth after her grandmother, was born on 27 January 1892, the day news reached them of the death two days earlier of the empress's mother, Duchess Ludovica in Bavaria, aged eighty-three. In 1895, they purchased Wallsee Palace on the river Danube, renovated it, and made it their home for the rest of their married life. Though relieved to be escaping from a home that had become one of sadness, and very much in love with her husband, throughout her first weeks of marriage, Valerie remained anxious about her mother's state of mind. The empress had been so preoccupied in helping her daughter through the confinement that the shock of her mother's death only sank in afterwards. Again, she absented herself from the funeral, again leaving her husband to represent her while she sought solace on her own in Corfu.

The emperor's friendship with Katherine remained the only consolation in his private life. For much of the time he lived more or less alone, surrounded by obsequious courtiers and servants. He had regular visits from his daughters and their families, loved youngsters, and was always thrilled to see his grandchildren. Erszi, who lived with her mother at Laxenburg, had become a particular favourite of his. It was a matter of some concern that the little girl should not have to suffer any more than possible just because of her father's fate.

Stephanie had found it in her heart to treat her impossible husband, or rather the memory of him, as someone to be pitied and helped more than condemned for his behaviour in the last few weeks of his life. Unlike his father, he had not tried very hard to be a good husband, and she had suffered too much from his infidelities and boorish behaviour to mourn his death too deeply. Yet it was humiliating for her to lose her position as crown princess, especially as her father, King Leopold, was notorious for his ill-treatment of the family, and there was no question of returning to her old home in Belgium, even if she had wanted to. Now no longer wife to the next emperor, she had to take second place at court to Archduchess Maria Theresa, wife of Archduke Charles Ludwig. Normally, her father-in-law was the most fair-minded of men, but he did nothing to dispel the impression that he held her partly responsible for her husband's suicide, and the mere sight of her reduced the empress to floods of tears. The latter never attempted to conceal her detestation of Stephanie, who was guilty of nothing more than having the misfortune to marry a totally impossible husband, and she was coldly indifferent to the granddaughter who bore her name.

From this time onwards, foreign ambassadors complained increasingly about the dullness of the Viennese court. The long period of mourning and the empress's extended absences made it a lifeless place, especially as she would never let any of the archduchesses deputise for her, and the emperor found balls and other functions an unpleasant ritual. Yet he remained as considerate to those around him as ever. Returning to his room early during a court ball one evening, very hot, tired, and needing a cool drink, he had to make do with tepid tap water. When he told Katherine afterwards, she asked why he had not rung for a valet to bring a bottle of champagne, as the ball was still going when he left. He said that he did not wish to disturb anyone at that time of night.

Occasionally guests from foreign courts, some more welcome than others, came and brought some variety to the often tedious Hofburg state dinners. Among them were Carol and Marie, Crown Prince and Princess of Romania. When she and her husband visited Vienna not along after their wedding in 1893, Marie was seated next to the emperor. He was very impressed with her, and told Lady Paget afterwards with a smile that the British court 'sent something much too beautiful to Roumania'.[4]

While the emperor was very set in his ways, he still understood the need to move gently with the times. He abhorred anti-Semitism, telling Count Taaffe that the Jews who lived in the empire were brave and patriotic men, always ready to risk their lives for emperor and fatherland. While he shared something of his class and his generation's suspicion of Jews, occasionally expressing impatience with them, he was dismayed by increasing support for the reactionary major of Vienna, Karl Lueger, and his anti-Semitic Christian Socialist Party.

Taaffe had held office continuously as minister-president since 1879. For over a decade, he had overseen the running of a parliamentary system that showed no favours to any particular grouping or national faction within the empire. Increasing militancy among the dissatisfied Czechs and then in other provinces persuaded Emil Steinbach, the minister of finance, to consider extending the franchise. He argued that nationalism was a middle-class phenomenon, and if the working classes had the vote, nationalistic antagonism threatening the structure of the monarchy would be contained. Taaffe and the emperor both approved, and Steinbach was asked to prepare a suffrage bill giving the vote to almost every literate male in the empire aged twenty-five or over, and to preserve the electoral system by which the proportion of deputies was weighted towards large landowners and businessmen. The resulting proposals were unpopular with most parliamentary groups except the young Czechs. Taaffe resigned and was replaced by Prince Alfred Windischgrätz, grandson of the general who had been the monarchy's saviour in 1848. The new minister was told that Steinbach's should be referred to a parliamentary committee for scrutiny. After further disagreements in the house, Windischgrätz resigned in July 1895, and Count Erich Kielmansegg held office for only a few weeks before being succeeded in September by the former governor of Galicia, Count Casimir von Badeni. Seen by many as a 'strong man', even a Polish Bismarck, Badeni was thought by the emperor to be the man most able to control the troublesome *Reichsrat*.

The three major issues concerning the emperor and his head of government were suffrage reform, appeasement of the Czechs, and renewal of the *Ausgleich* with Hungary, now due for renegotiation. The bill extending voting rights was passed, and after an election held in March 1897, representatives of twenty-five parties sat in parliament. As the Young Czechs had polled strongly, Badeni felt obliged to seek their support, so in April, two language ordinances were issued, substantially extending concessions granted to the Czechs in the previous decade. Within four years, every civil servant in Bohemia would need to speak and write Czech as well as German. It was resented by the German Austrians, who thought it absurd to force Czech, 'a mere dialect', on Germans, especially without parliamentary debate first. After angry scenes in the chamber, the emperor issued a decree closing the assembly down for a brief period. When it reconvened in the autumn, violence resumed, Badeni's resignation was demanded, and troops and police patrolled the streets to keep agitators in order, while admitting they could do little without resorting to force. Fearing it might lead to a return of the events of 1848, the emperor dismissed Badeni and accepted that the language ordinances were unpopular and impracticable, having them withdrawn.

It was the end of effective parliamentary government in the Austro-Hungarian Empire. Representatives on all sides in the *Reichsrat* knew how easy it was to obstruct measures with which they disagreed, and Francis Joseph saw the impossibility of trying to reign as a constitutional ruler. From now on, he would rule as an absolute monarch within a legal structure of constitutionalism. If parliamentary consensus could not be reached, he would resort to Article 14 of the Constitution of 1861, empowering him to rule by 'imperial emergency decree'. With a parliament that found itself unable to agree, he would need it regularly within the next few years. One parliamentarian, Joseph Redlich, later one of the emperor's first biographers, believed that 'the constitutional principle had been smashed', and from then onwards, 'the Habsburg realm was doomed'.[5]

Meanwhile, the empress's wanderlust continued unabated. After Valerie's wedding, she travelled to Corfu, Switzerland, the French Riviera, the Azores, and North Africa. She repeatedly urged the emperor to put his duties aside for a while and join her sometimes. In March 1893, they spent a fortnight in Switzerland, enjoying walks together to the Castle of Chillon, but he did not find it much of a respite. Within twenty-four hours, the hotel had seen through his incognito and flew the gold and imperial standard from its flagpole, and he had to spend the next morning dealing with official papers a courier had brought him from Vienna. He left alone, with Elizabeth planning to travel for a few more months.

In June 1893, she made a rare appearance at a court reception held to mark the betrothal of Gisela's eldest daughter, Augusta, to her distant cousin, Archduke Augustus. The retiring British ambassador and his wife, Sir Augustus and Lady Paget, were astonished to see how she had aged. Lady Paget wrote sadly that the beautiful woman of less than ten years earlier in a white dress embroidered with gold and silver, and jewels in her hair, now stood in transparent but deepest black, with a crown of black feathers on her auburn hair: 'A ruche of black gauze disguised, as much as possible, the thinness of her throat. The face looked like a mask, the lips and cheeks too red, the hair too dark at the roots, the eyebrows too marked, the skin lined about her eyes and cheeks.' Her figure remained 'matchless ... but at the expense of everything else'.[6] That evening, she told the German ambassador she was preparing herself to become a great-grandmother, and then she would be allowed to retire from the world for good.[7]

In Vienna, the emperor still had the companionship of Katherine Schratt, who was now the main link between husband and wife. When they did not have their grandchildren to talk about, they had very little to say to each other. Elizabeth took only an occasional interest in matters of state, while Francis Joseph could not share her enthusiasm for foreign travel. Moreover, Katherine's common sense and sympathy had helped to steady Elizabeth's nerves after Mayerling, as well as giving Francis Joseph himself much comfort, and the empress remained as supportive of the relationship as ever. After Rudolf's death, the emperor added a codicil to his will, leaving her half a million florins in recognition of all she had done for him.

The shy, straitlaced, and unworldly Valerie resented people continually speculating about her father and 'the uncrowned Empress of Austria', and never understood why her mother readily condoned the relationship, or why she always called Katherine 'the friend' or her adopted sister. While she saw that her father was so emotionally attached to her, it annoyed her that her mother was much to blame for what she called 'Papa's unfortunate entanglement' by being away so much. She knew he had been lonely for years, but it seemed completely at odds with his wedding vows to take pleasure in such a liaison with somebody else's wife. Francis Salvator agreed with Valerie, insisting that the emperor 'should not be talked about'.

Elizabeth spoke of Katherine with great affection, regretting that she herself was coming between her husband and 'the friend', so that she felt ridiculous, envied Rudolf, and wondered what point there was in still living. Lady Paget thought that Viennese society considered *Frau* Schratt rather stupid, but with a naïve way of blurting out the truth, thus suggesting she had a way of telling the emperor things nobody else would. She also heard a rumour that Katherine was Francis Joseph's love child, and whatever the truth or lack of it, believed their relationship was completely platonic.[8]

This most self-effacing of crowned heads knew how tiresome he could be to those around him. In some of his letters to Katherine, he would apologise for being such a bore and tell her how marvellous she was to put up with him. It never stopped him from becoming more and more possessive of her, slightly jealous of her zest for life, and resentful of what he considered her extraordinary craving for publicity.

Elizabeth and Valerie both kept diaries, unlike the emperor, who poured out his feelings in long letters to Elizabeth and Katherine instead. To the former, he generally wrote during her travels on alternate days. Nearly 500 surviving letters from husband to wife written between September 1890 and September 1898 survive, most of them simply descriptive, with news of his activities, their daughters and of 'little Erszi', of whom he was much fonder than Elizabeth, and of visits to plays, especially those in which Katherine appeared. During the same period, he also wrote more than 200 letters to Katherine. These were lighter in character than those to the empress, with a certain amount of self-effacement and occasional self-pity, and sometimes warning her against hazardous ventures such as ballooning, mountaineering, and excursions to the glaciers.

From 1894 onwards, husband and wife made four annual visits to the French Riviera, each lasting between one and three weeks. They brought some liveliness and colour back to the emperor's increasingly lonely and duty-bound existence. The novelty of staying in a hotel appealed to him, although he could not be persuaded to break the habit of a lifetime and go to bed later than his customary early hour. However, when the head of the police at Schönbrunn went to Cap Martin with a squad of detectives, the emperor asked them not to accompany him as guards. It was a private visit, he reminded them, and he had no fear of assassination abroad. The remark would soon have a hollow ring.

On their first visit to the French Riviera, Elizabeth had suggested that *Frau* Schratt should be invited as well, but then changed her mind as she feared that the presence of so many other European royalties, and censorious tongues, would give rise to the innuendo they wanted to avoid. By the time of their second French break, in February 1895, she no longer had any such qualms. An *aide-de-camp* was instructed to reserve rooms for the actress, but she chose to visit nearby Monte Carlo on her own instead.

On the imperial couple's arrival in 1896, the emperor wrote to Katherine, they dined in their suite at 7 p.m., and were soon lulled to sleep by music from the hotel lounge. Once, the emperor visited the gambling rooms at Monte Carlo, maybe on her recommendation, but he was dissuaded from trying his luck at the tables by the number of onlookers present and a fear of what gossips might say about him afterwards. It was indeed unlikely that a man of his extreme caution and personal reserve would indulge in such an activity in public. Even so, for once, he was able to enjoy his food in comfort and try the local restaurants. A little guiltily, he wrote to Katherine about the different establishments they visited, and his apprehension that they were perhaps eating a little too much and too varied a fare. After leading such a Spartan existence for so long, the idea of him enjoying himself like any other holidaymaker for possibly the first time in his life must have been novel indeed.

In March 1896, the emperor met the head of a French republic for the first time, when he visited the president, Felix Fauré, who was on an official tour of the Alpes-Maritimes. He was interested to watch the Alpine infantry carrying out field exercises with live ammunition. This area of the republic and its coastline were host during the winter to several European royals, among them the Prince of Wales and Empress Eugenie. That same month, Queen Victoria was on holiday at Cimiez and received the emperor and empress together for the first and only time. She wrote to Lord Salisbury afterwards that the emperor had been most cordial, that she hoped both countries would always be united, how important it was 'that England and Germany should be on the best terms together, and one thing he felt sure of, *viz.* that everyone wished for peace'.[9]

That same year marked the 1,000th anniversary of the Magyars coming to the Danubian plain, and Budapest prepared to celebrate from spring until autumn. By now, Elizabeth had withdrawn almost completely from public life, and lost interest even in Hungary and its politics, rarely going beyond the castle grounds when she still visited. She was persuaded to return in May 1896, when she and Francis Joseph opened the Millennial Exposition of Hungarian achievement in the Budapest town park. They also attended a thanksgiving mass in the coronation church later that week, while in June, they were together for the opening of a new wing of the royal palace in Budapest and for a solemn procession in which the Holy Crown of St Stephen and the coronation regalia were borne across the Danube to the Parliament House and back to the Crown Room beneath the palace dome. Nevertheless, whenever appearing in public, she kept her face shielded behind a black fan.

At around the same time, the matter of the imperial succession was resolved. The increasingly devout Archduke Charles Ludwig, heir to the throne, had recently made a pilgrimage to the Holy Land. In his religious zeal, he had drunk a cup of water from the River Jordan, and on 19 May, soon after returning to Vienna, he succumbed to typhoid.

Of the emperor's three brothers, only the youngest, Ludwig Victor, was left. Despite efforts once made by his mother to arrange a marriage between him and the empress's youngest sister, Sophie, he remained a lifelong bachelor. Devoted to theatre and the arts, bisexual, and occasionally photographed as an adult in women's dresses, his behaviour was tolerated at court until he was involved in a brawl at the public baths in Vienna, after which he was known irreverently as 'the Archduke of the Bath'. Such a character was bound to attract gossip and it was said that the emperor banished him from the city, joking that he should be given a ballerina as his adjutant to keep him out of further trouble. While relations between the brothers cooled for some time as a result, Francis Joseph never restricted his public duties or appearances, and accepted his little foibles. He spent most of his adult life at Klesheim, his castle in Salzburg, where he was a generous employer to the servants on his estate, although he often returned to Vienna to visit the family. He had been Rudolf's regular hunting companion, while Gisela and Valerie also enjoyed his company. As the youngest sibling of a monarch, he had a degree of liberty that his eldest brother must have envied many a time, but nobody ever saw him as a future emperor.

Charles Ludwig's tubercular eldest son, Francis Ferdinand, was now the hope of the Habsburgs. Second in line to the throne was his brother, Otto, a debauched nonentity whose marriage to Princess Maria Josepha of Saxony had not curbed his excesses or scandalous behaviour, and which would end in death from syphilis ten years later.

On 27 August 1896, the emperor and empress attended a gala dinner at the Hofburg in honour of Tsar Nicholas II and Empress Alexandra. Though still dressed in mourning, the empress put Alexandra, thirty-four years younger, completely in the shade. Yet it was an ordeal for her, and it would be her last public appearance before she retired from public life on medical advice. Despite suffering from anaemia, she still insisted on a punishing diet, and some days, she ate no more than a few oranges. She became dizzy on long walks, which were clearly too arduous for a woman almost sixty years of age, and fainted when her hair was being done. Her lady-in-waiting, Marie Festetics, was increasingly alarmed by her obsession with becoming stout, warning her that she was too pale, and that as she ate so little, she risked severe malnutrition or a stroke. A medical examination, to which the empress submitted with reluctance, hinted at possible heart trouble. Although the emperor had long since given up trying to make her see reason, he never ceased to worry about her health.

Husband and wife paid what would be their last visit together to Cap Martin in March 1897. Elizabeth was increasingly depressed and weary, and he warned Katherine that when they arrived, she might be shocked by the empress's appearance. The visit was completely ruined for him by anxiety about her, and on their return to Vienna, he told Count Eulenburg, the German ambassador, that she was 'in such a state of nerves that our life together was seriously deranged.'[10]

Next she visited Biarritz, San Remo, where she briefly considered having another villa built, and Switzerland, where a new doctor ordered her firmly to eat properly. For a short time, her health improved, until tragedy struck yet again. On 4 May, at a charity bazaar in Paris, a set of curtains caught fire, the hall burst into flames, and at least 100 people were burnt to death, with more than twice as many injured. Among the dead was her youngest sister, Sophie, Duchess of Alençon, who refused to leave the building until all the girls working with her had been rescued. She was only identified after her dentist examined the teeth from her charred remains.

Elizabeth was beside herself at the news, and soon afterwards, her Greek teacher Frederick Barker (now part of her entourage) said she was so weak that she could hardly move herself from one room to another. Her thoughts and conversations were increasingly preoccupied with mortality. Her intention, she said, was not to survive the emperor, but to die alone, without her husband or children at her deathbed, as that would be too painful for them.[11]

Francis Joseph's golden jubilee was in 1898, but it seemed unlikely that she would be fit enough to take part in any celebrations. When he and Valerie joined her at Kissingen in the spring, they were horrified by the state of her. Once such a rapid walker, now she found it an effort to drag herself around. She told her daughter how she longed for death, refusing 'to believe that there is a power so cruel that, not content with the sufferings of life, it would tear the soul from the body in order to go on torturing it'.[12]

During the summer, husband and wife spent another fortnight together at Ischl. Any hope the emperor had of her being able to accompany him in any jubilee appearances was dashed when Dr Widerhofer warned him she must resign herself to being a complete invalid for the rest of her life or else submit to a thorough cure at Bad Nauheim, and she was too ill to argue. An official bulletin announced that she was suffering from anaemia, inflammation of the nerves, insomnia, and a certain dilation of the heart, which gave no cause for serious anxiety but would require her absence for thorough treatment abroad.[13] On 16 July, husband and wife parted, both fearing they might never see each other again. He stayed at Ischl until the end of August, then went to Schönbrunn before going to Hungary for army manoeuvres. He wrote to her every other day, and on 10 September, soon after his return to Vienna, he wrote to Katherine that at last he had good news from the empress, who was enjoying the invigorating air of Switzerland.

One day earlier, she had arrived at the Hotel Beau-Rivage, Geneva, brushing aside warnings that the city was notorious for harbouring some of the most dangerous revolutionaries in Europe. She was perfectly safe there, she said, and nobody would want to attack an old woman like her. For once, she was in unusually high spirits, even doing justice to her luncheon. Earlier that week, she and Barker had been strolling around

FERDINAND I, EMPEROR OF AUSTRIA.

Above left: Francis I, Emperor of Austria, who reigned as emperor of Austria from 1792 to 1835 and as last Holy Roman emperor until 1806.

Above right: Ferdinand, emperor of Austria from 1835 to 1848.

Right: Archduchess Sophie and her eldest son, Archduke Francis, the future emperor, after a portrait by Joseph Stieler, *c.* 1833.

Emperor Francis of Austria with Archduchess Sophie and her son, Francis at Laxenburg, after an engraving by Charles Scoliksen, 1833.

Above left: Archduke Francis Charles, brother of Emperor Francis and father of Emperor Francis Joseph.

Above right: Emperor Francis Joseph, at around the time of his accession.

Right: Archduke Francis Charles and
Archduchess Sophie in their later years.

Below: Schönbrunn Palace, Vienna.
(*Sue Woolmans*)

Emperor Francis Joseph and Tsar Alexander II at Belvedere, Weimar, October 1857.

The imperial family, 1860.

Back row: Emperor Francis Joseph; Maxmilian; his wife, Charlotte; Ludwig Victor; and Charles Ludwig.

Front row: Empress Elizabeth with Rudolf on her lap; Gisela; and the emperor's parents, Sophie and Francis Charles.

Above left: Archduke Maximilian in uniform as an admiral of the Austrian navy, later the ill-fated emperor of Mexico.

Above right: Empress Carlota of Mexico, after a painting by Franz Xaver Winterhalter.

Below left: Empress Elizabeth with her dog, Shadow, *c.* 1861.

Below right: Emperor Francis Joseph in the robes of the Order of the Golden Fleece.

Above left: Empress Elizabeth on horseback.

Above right: Crown Prince Rudolf, *c.* 1865.

Left: Katherine Schratt.

The wedding of Gisela and Leopold of Bavaria, 20 April 1873, at Vienna.

Ischl, Kaiservilla. (*Sue Woolmans*)

Above left: Archduchesses Gisela and Valerie, *c*. 1885.

Above right: Francis Ferdinand in the uniform of a captain of the No. 4 Dragoon Regiment, *c*. 1888. (*Sue Woolmans*)

Left: Crown Prince Rudolf and Crown Princess Stephanie, *c*. 1887.

Crown Prince Rudolf's hunting lodge, Mayerling.

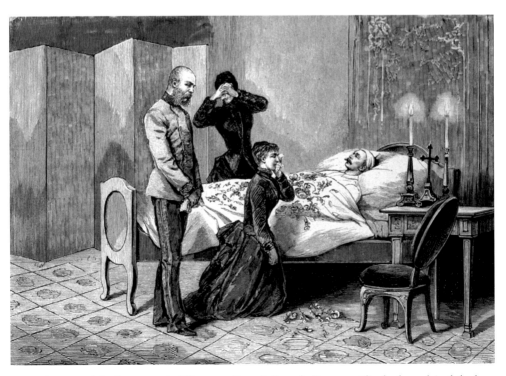

A romanticised portrayal of Emperor Francis Joseph, Empress Elizabeth, and Archduchess Stephanie at the deathbed of Crown Prince Rudolf, 1889.

Emperor Francis Joseph on military manoeuvres.

Above left: Empress Elizabeth, after a portrait by Leopold Horovitz, *c.* 1892.

Above right: Emperor Francis Joseph and three of the children of Archduchess Valerie, *c.* 1894: Francis Charles Salvator, Hubert Salvator, and Elizabeth.

Above left: King Francis Joseph and Queen Elizabeth of Hungary at the millenary celebrations, Budapest, June 1896, after a painting by Julius von Benczur.

Above right: Emperor Francis Joseph and Empress Elizabeth at Kissingen, spring 1898, one of the last photographs of her before her assassination.

Below left: Emperor Francis Joseph, *c.* 1900.

Below middle: Archduchess Elizabeth and her husband, Prince Otto von Windischgraetz, *c.* 1902.

Below right: Emperor Francis Joseph in lederhosen at Ischl.

Prince and Princess Leopold of Bavaria (Archduchess Gisela) and their sons, Georg and Conrad, *c.* 1906. (*Sue Woolmans*)

Emperor Francis Joseph talking to the pilot of an Etrich-Taube monoplane, Wiener Neustadt airfield, September 1910.

The wedding of Archduke Charles and Princess Zita, with Emperor Francis Joseph on their left, October 1911.

Above left: Archduke Francis Ferdinand, Sophie, Princess Hohenberg, and their children, Sophie, Maximilian, and Ernest, *c.* 1912.

Above right: Archduke Charles and Archduchess Zita with Archduke Otto and Archduchess Adelheid, 1914.

Above: Archduchess Valerie, Archduke Francis Salvator, and their nine children, 1914.

Below: Archduke Francis Ferdinand, Sophie, and their daughter, Sophie, riding to the flower festival at the Vienna Prater, June 1914. (*Sue Woolmans*)

Below: The funeral of Emperor Francis Joseph, Vienna, 30 November 1916.

Above left: Emperor Charles, Empress Zita, and Crown Prince Otto at Emperor Francis Joseph's funeral. (*Mark Andersen*)

Above right: Charles and Zita, king and queen of Hungary at their coronation, Budapest, December 1916.

Below: Empress Zita with her children and Archduchess Maria Josepha, her mother-in-law, at Lequetitio, Christmas 1927. (*Mark Andersen*)

Above: Empress Zita with her children at Lequetitio, on the occasion of Crown Prince Otto's coming of age, November 1930. (*Mark Andersen*)

Below left: Crown Prince Otto, 1930. (*Mark Andersen*)

Below right: Crown Prince Otto and Archduchess Regina, soon after their wedding in 1951. (*Mark Andersen*)

outside and sat down to admire the view. As she peeled a peach and offered him half, a raven swooped down, seized it in its beak, and flew away. Knowing that the Habsburgs viewed the raven as a bird of ill-omen, Barker suggested she forego her visit to Geneva, but she assured him that she had no fears.[14]

On the afternoon of the 10th, she planned to take the ferry for Territet. As she and her lady-in-waiting, Countess Sztáray, walked to the landing stage, they were confronted by a scruffily dressed man and stepped aside to let him pass. To her horror, the countess saw him raise his fist and strike the empress. She fell backwards, knocking her head on the pavement, and was helped to her feet. A hotel porter and cab driver had alerted the police, but although frightened, she insisted that she was well enough to continue her journey. After crossing the gangway to the ferry, she suddenly turned white and asked the countess to give her her arm. A man came up to help, and from a distance, they heard somebody calling out that 'the assassin' had been apprehended. Only then did the countess realise just what had happened.

Elizabeth was taken into an upper deck of the ferry, which had just started. Another passenger, a former nurse, offered her some water and sugar in alcohol, and she opened her eyes as she tried to sit up, asking drowsily what had happened. A moment later, she sank back into unconsciousness. When her bodice was unbuttoned, a bloodstain could be seen on her chemise, from a small wound on her breast. She had been stabbed with a metal file. Countess Sztáray sent for the captain and begged him to return to shore at once, as she could not let the empress of Austria die without a doctor and a priest present. On reaching land, she was taken on an improvised stretcher back to the hotel. Doctor and priest were summoned, but all they could do was confirm that she had passed away, far away from her family as she had fervently wished for.

Meanwhile, Francis Joseph was at Schönbrunn in his study, writing to her how glad he was to hear 'at the better state of mind reflected in your letter and at your contentment with the weather, the air and your quarters with the terrace, which must afford you a wonderful view over the mountains and the lake.'[15] When his adjutant, Count Paar, clutching a telegram from Geneva in his hand, urgently requested an audience with him, he realised that it must be bad news. Paar said the empress had been seriously injured. The emperor begged him to find out further details by any method possible. Just then, another aide brought a second telegram. With tears rolling down his cheeks, the emperor took it from him to read the news that the empress had just passed away.

The man responsible was Luigi Lucheni, an Italian builder's labourer and self-professed anarchist with an abiding contempt for monarchy and aristocracy. He had vowed to kill the next crowned head who came his way, and his target was to have been Philippe, Duke of Orleans, claimant to the French throne, who was supposed to have been visiting. The duke did not arrive, so when Luccheni heard that the empress of Austria was about to come to Geneva, he determined to strike her down instead. After giving himself up to the police without trying to flee, he was put on trial and sentenced to life imprisonment. Twelve years later, he hanged himself in his cell.

All remaining jubilee festivities in Austria were immediately cancelled. Katherine was also on holiday, but when she heard the news, she travelled back to Vienna to be with the emperor and comfort him, as did Gisela and Valerie, mourning, yet finding solace in the knowledge that their mother had now found the eternal rest she craved.

She had said that she wanted her body to be laid to rest on Corfu, but there was only one place for an empress to be buried. On 12 September, she was moved to the Habsburg chapel of the Capuchin church, and the state funeral took place five days later. Ironically, the only other crowned head present, Emperor William II, was the one whom she had so disliked. At the end of the ceremony, Francis Joseph fell to his knees at the coffin and sobbed for several minutes.

For the rest of his life, he rarely if ever talked about his wife or his son to anybody outside the immediate family. Staff and courtiers around him would be informed that her name must not come up in conversation in his presence. He kept his favourite Winterhalter portrait of her on an easel by his desk in his study, and each year on the anniversary of her murder, he went down to the vaults alone to say a long prayer over her coffin.

The empress's death meant the end of the old relationship between the emperor and Katherine. Elizabeth had foreseen that it would cause her difficulty, and in her last months, she entreated her daughters to treat 'the friend' kindly if she should predecease her husband. Gisela and Leopold, who had accepted it without question, honoured her request, but the pious and disapproving Valerie and Francis Salvator thought otherwise. Katherine was disappointed that she had not been mentioned in the empress's will, although the emperor made amends by presenting her with a jewel she had often worn. She was even more upset when the empress had told her she would be one of the first recipients of a new medal, the Elizabeth Order, being issued to commemorate the golden jubilee. When Katherine's name was not included and she tactfully reminded him of Her late Majesty's promise, he told her sadly that now the empress was dead, he could not possibly bestow the order on her without risking gossip. This and other small incidents all put a strain on their relationship. Valerie reluctantly invited her to come and visit her and Francis Salvator at their home at Wallsee, in accordance with the empress's wishes, but Francis Joseph advised her to refuse. Furious with them all, she lost her temper and openly criticised Valerie. The emperor was equally angry, and after an argument, she suddenly left for three weeks in Monte Carlo without telling him in advance. Once tempers had cooled, they began to correspond again, but it was clear that nothing could ever be the same again between them.

On 18 August 1900, the emperor celebrated his seventieth birthday at Ischl. The streets of the town were hung with black and yellow flags, bonfires were lit on the mountains nearby, and several deputations came to offer His Majesty their congratulations. Gifts were brought to the Kaiservilla, including some from Katherine. However, ten days later, Valerie found her father looking particularly sad. When she asked him to come out for a ride that afternoon with her and the children, he told her that he could not, as he was going to visit Katherine for the last time. She had made up her mind that afterwards she would leave him, probably for ever. Much as she had disliked the relationship, and had hoped and prayed for it to end, Valerie was very concerned; one look at his weary tired face, so close to tears, reminded her how much the companionship had meant to him in his loneliness, and what a void would be left in his life. As expected, it proved a painful meeting, and afterwards, he wrote to Katherine of his hopes that she would tell him everything one day when her nerves were better: '… which with God's help will happen in not too long a time, and I will again be receiving your dear, *dear* letters'.[16]

After the death of Elizabeth, Francis Joseph usually spent Christmas at Wallsee with Valerie, Francis, and their ever-growing family. He loved to help decorate the tree and distribute presents. On the next day, he would go to Munich and stay with Gisela, Leopold, and their four children, who always postponed their Christmas festivities until he arrived. Both daughters were touched to see how happy he was in such surroundings, so unlike the elderly careworn gentleman he appeared the rest of the time. It pained them to think that he had been denied such contentment throughout his married life. After Valerie and the grandchildren spent a few weeks with him at Schönbrunn in the spring of 1902, he wrote to Katherine how much he had enjoyed being with them: 'The older one gets the more childlike one becomes, and so I am coming closer and closer to them and their company'.[17]

Valerie hoped he would take a second wife and find the contented home life he never had before—to say nothing of an officially recognised union with a princess or archduchess and not a mistress. If he did, the court at Vienna might become the focus of high society once again, and the Habsburgs might even have another male heir to the throne. The Austrian government had similar ideas and were thought to be about to recommend remarriage once court mourning was over. Their first choice was his widowed sister-in-law, Archduchess Maria Theresa, who at forty-two might be able to bear him a son, while Valerie had in mind one of the unmarried Orléans princesses.

The emperor was aware of such thoughts, but at the age of seventy, he was too set in his ways and had no intention of taking another empress. He lived for his work and was accustomed to the humdrum routine that he had followed for so long. Actively hating change, he would not hear of any alteration being made to his rooms in the Hofburg. When the royal palace at Budapest was completed, he took little interest in the new apartments and insisted on staying in his old quarters in an older part of the castle. Baron von Margutti opined that it was his unflinching devotion to duty that made him 'less an individual than a mere machine, a process which increased as the years went by'.[18]

'He no longer understands the times'

Between Emperor Francis Joseph and his nephew, Archduke Francis Ferdinand, since 1896 also his heir, relations were civil but never close. They became even more distant after the sovereign was informed of a most unwelcome discovery. The wife of his second cousin, Archduke Frederick, Duke of Teschen, the redoubtable Archduchess Isabella, had fondly imagined that this most eligible of bachelors was courting her eldest daughter, Archduchess Maria Christina. One summer day in 1899 after a tennis party at their castle at Bratislava, a servant found Francis Ferdinand's gold watch, which he had left behind. Hanging from it was a locket containing a miniature picture, not of her daughter, but of her lady-in-waiting, Countess Sophie Chotek, his occasional doubles partner at tennis. Aged thirty-one, she came from a good family of Bohemian nobility, ennobled by the Habsburgs in the sixteenth century. They had a long history of service to the empire, her father being the diplomat in Brussels who had helped to negotiate the marriage between Rudolf and Stephanie. Yet she was not of sufficient rank to become the next empress of Austria-Hungary.

A furious Archduchess Isabella dismissed her at once and informed the emperor. At first, he was prepared to regard it as a mere infatuation, but his nephew said he and the countess had been passionately in love for five years and he intended to marry her. It seemed grossly unfair to him that if any member of the family was attracted to someone, some minor blemish in their lineage invariably ruled out marriage. Instead, they were constantly marrying their relatives, and half the children of these unions were 'cretins or epileptics'. At least one member of the imperial family had taken to heart the unfortunate mistake made too often by previous generations, and understood the consequences of inbreeding. Quite apart from this, most of the eligible princesses, he thought, were 'ugly underdeveloped ducklings' of seventeen or eighteen. Now in his late thirties, he was too old for them and had neither 'the time nor the inclination to attend to the education of a wife'.[1]

His stepmother interceded with the emperor, telling him that his relationship with the countess had changed her difficult, unhappy stepson for the better, and that she would make him an excellent wife. Despite this, the emperor summoned his nephew for an interview, told him firmly his behaviour was most regrettable because it had caused a rift with his cousins, which it was his duty to repair, and that he must break off all contact with the countess. Francis Ferdinand declared he would not and formally requested permission to marry her. The emperor said he forbade such a marriage, but finding his nephew obdurate, he gave him a week to consider the matter. Next, the archduke consulted his physician, Dr Eisenmenger, whether any children of his were likely to inherit his tuberculosis. He was reassured that the disease was rarely passed on, that measures could be taken to protect his family in the unlikely event of his doing so, and that his health would clearly benefit from a happy marriage.

Faced with trying to win the emperor's support and waiting, or the possibility that Sophie might be sent away from Austria so they would never see each other again, Francis Ferdinand decided life without her would be intolerable. At one stage, he allegedly declared that if he was not allowed to marry her, he would either go mad or kill himself. He had reached the end of his physical strength, and said dramatically that he could no longer be responsible for anything.[2] The emperor may not have believed him, thinking he was being melodramatic, but the last thing he wanted was another heir to the throne taking his own life, and the threat might have helped to persuade him he was serious. He told his nephew that he could only marry the countess if he renounced his succession to the throne. That, the archduke argued, was impossible as his place had been conferred on him by God. At this, the emperor grudgingly assented to the marriage, insisting it could only be a morganatic union. When told it would be theoretically possible for Sophie to become queen of Hungary when Francis Ferdinand succeeded him, ironically in view of the archduke's well-known antipathy to the Magyars, he decided that all possible pressure must be put on him to call off the marriage. Should he marry without permission, he would be expelled from the Habsburg family, leaving his philandering and venereally-infected younger brother, Otto, as heir.

At the family dinner on New Year's Day 1900, Francis Joseph raised his glass silently to Charles, the twelve-year-old son of Otto, as if the old gentleman recognised the boy as his real heir. Valerie, watching Francis Ferdinand's face carefully, thought he looked very grave.[3]

Most of the family stood solidly by the emperor. His stepmother, Maria Theresa, broke ranks in supporting the couple and begging him to make an exception in order to ensure his happiness, but nearly everyone else said that if the future emperor was to marry a lady-in-waiting, it would endanger the future of the dynasty. In April 1900, matters were settled, on the understanding that as long as any constitutional problems resulting from a morganatic marriage could be settled, the emperor would reluctantly give his consent. The countess could never become an empress, and any children of the couple would be excluded from the succession. On 12 June, all male members from the Most Serene Arch-House of Habsburg were summoned to the Hofburg for a family council, presided over by the emperor and his Lord High Chamberlain, Prince Alfred de Montenuovo. Francis Joseph told the assembled company that his successor's marriage plan was well known to everyone present, and that it contravened the family statute. As it was so dear to his nephew's heart, he would grant his wish as far as possible. For the sake of order, and to minimise the harmful consequences of such an action for the monarchy, he needed to have the consent of all members of the house and their signatures on a clarifying appendix to the family statute. Torn between loyalty to the family and to his own future, Francis Ferdinand reluctantly signed as well.

Eleven days later, the emperor received his nephew in a private audience. He was uneasy as he had been unable to prevent such an unsuitable matrimonial alliance, while Francis Ferdinand was annoyed at being forced into a morganatic union. Nevertheless, his mind was made up, and he was accordingly asked to sign and swear to a renunciation of certain rights for his wife and any children. He was assured that Sophie would receive the title of Princess Hohenberg on their marriage.

At another ceremony in the Hofburg on 28 June, the emperor, fifteen senior archdukes, and a select group of court officials heard the heir renounce under a solemn and binding oath all claims of his proposed wife and children for the rights of status or inheritance that would normally be accorded to 'a marriage between equals'. On 1 July, the couple were married at the chapel of Reichstadt, a castle in Bohemia given to Archduchess Maria Theresa by the emperor. Neither he nor any of the archdukes were present at the celebrations. A simple service was performed by the village priest and two Capuchin monks, with no address, and no reception afterwards, only a wedding breakfast for the immediate family. During the meal, a telegram arrived from Ischl, confirming that the morganatic consort of the groom was to be styled Princess Hohenberg and with the title Her Grace.

The couple spent their honeymoon at Konopischt, a fortress some 30 miles from Prague, which Francis Ferdinand had bought in 1887 and converted into his home. One of his abiding passions was horticulture, with over 200 varieties of rose blooming in the gardens. Later he opened his grounds to the public on certain days and would wander happily among the visitors, sharing their enjoyment of everything around them.

Though he disapproved of his heir's morganatic marriage, Francis Joseph bore him and his wife no personal ill-will. He gave them the finest of Vienna's baroque palaces, the Upper Belvedere, as their official residence in the capital. Two months after the wedding, he officially received Sophie for the first time, and afterwards wrote to *Frau* Schratt that the occasion went off very well. His nephew's wife, he remarked, was 'natural and modest, but appears to be no longer young'.[4]

Unlike those of the emperor and his ill-fated son, this was one Habsburg marriage made in heaven. A week after the wedding, the archduke wrote to his stepmother in gratitude for her support in helping to make it all possible for them. Sophie, he told her, was 'a *treasure* and that I cannot describe my happiness.... I'm doing famously, much less nervous and feeling so healthy. It is though I have been born anew.'[5] Princess Zita of Bourbon-Parma, who would later marry his nephew, Charles, and become the last empress of Austria-Hungary, saw much of them together and was sure that Sophie had proved the ideal partner for such a highly-strung man. She knew just how to handle him, make him relax, and calm him whenever one of his angry outbursts was coming, by gently pressing his arm with a soothing 'Franzi, Franzi'.[6]

Within four years, three children were born to them. A daughter, named Sophie after her mother, was born in July 1901; a son, Maximilian, in September 1902; and a second son, Ernest, in May 1904. Sophie's fourth confinement unhappily ended with the birth in November 1908 of a stillborn son, leaving her severely weakened for a while. Their doctor strongly advised against any further pregnancies.

The petty humiliations of Habsburg protocol did little to disturb their domestic life. Nevertheless, Francis Ferdinand was infuriated by the treatment meted out to her for daring to marry above her station. At family dinners, if invited at all, she was seated at the bottom of the table and served last. She was not permitted to accompany her husband to any state functions, stand near him if the national anthem was being played, or even sit in the same box as him at the theatre. Sentries were withdrawn from the gates of their Vienna residence, the Belvedere Palace, when he was not present, even though his wife and children remained behind. They circumvented this by spending as little time as possible there, confining their visits largely to the new year season when they were expected to attend the customary court dinners and other functions. After that, they took a large suite at the Alpine resort of St Moritz, where Francis Ferdinand would enjoy his skiing holiday, and then return to Konopischt.

Sophie always behaved with great dignity and patience, and never allowed herself to be provoked. The one occasion on which it proved too humiliating for her was at a court ball when she realised that Montenuovo had deliberately arranged for a man to give her his arm. Rather than entering a packed ballroom alone, she decided to leave quietly and go home instead. She was highly gratified when some foreign royalties, notably German Emperor William II, went out of their way to flatter her, and were prepared to honour her as an empress consort-in-waiting.

Guests who enjoyed their hospitality at home must have wondered if their host at Konopischt was the same bad-tempered, intolerant archduke of popular legend, of whose shortcomings they had been warned. He admitted he had a hasty temper and was not good at controlling it, but his outbursts were generally followed by profuse apologies and requests for forgiveness. To one of his senior military aides, he once remarked, perhaps partly in jest, that he regarded everybody he met as being a scoundrel at first sight, and then allowed them to change his mind if they could. Loathing flattery, he respected those who told him the truth and were prepared to challenge his views if necessary in calm and reasoned discussion.

Not everybody at court completely trusted Sophie, and it was inevitable that some in the imperial hierarchy would strongly resent her presence. Dr Godfried Marschall, Suffragan Bishop of Vienna, believed she had ambitions above her station and was scheming for the archduke to allow their children to take their rightful place in the succession behind him as the next emperor. Yet few others, if any, were prepared to speak out openly or find fault with a princess against whose character little could be said with conviction. Some found her unusually cautious with money, but lack of extravagance was hardly a fault, and after the late empress's obsession with building new houses and palaces for her own pleasure, it was a fault for the better. She and her husband were unfailingly generous to their servants, who were always devoted to them.

One member of the family who clearly resented Sophie's presence was Archduchess Elizabeth, daughter of Crown Prince Rudolf. She had always disliked Francis Ferdinand, presumably because he had become heir apparent in place of her father, and was disinclined to show any kindness towards his wife either. To her was attributed some responsibility for spreading spiteful rumours and scurrilous tales at court about her, and after once being forced to acknowledge Sophie's presence when they both attended an aristocratic reception, she complained bitterly afterwards that '*she* leaned across to me!'[7] Ironically, her mother, Rudolf's widow, was unfailingly supportive of the couple. The widowed Crown Princess Stephanie knew what it was to be an outcast at court for reasons beyond her control, and she was also trying to obtain approval for what was regarded as her own 'unsuitable' second union. She had married Count Elemér Lónyay, a Hungarian aristocrat, in March 1900, three months before Francis Ferdinand and Sophie were able to become husband and wife. While he thought it insulting to his son's memory, the emperor raised no objection, although others saw her action in a less kindly light. Among them were her father, who promptly cut her out of his will, and her daughter, who broke off all personal contact with her.

Patience, forbearance, and a refusal to be provoked brought their own reward. At length, public opinion began to side with Sophie and her husband and against the petty slights and vindictive behaviour of Montenuovo. In March 1905, the emperor at last ended a letter with the words, 'I send warm greetings to the Princess.'[8] Later that year, she and the children were raised to the style of Serene Highness.

The behaviour of Francis Ferdinand and Sophie had been flawless throughout, in stark contrast to that of his younger brother. The unfaithful, venereally diseased Otto disgraced himself once too often the night he threw a party for some of his male companions, and their drunken conversation turned to the subject of women and their charms. Suddenly he staggered to his feet and invited them back to his wife's bedroom, where she had been asleep. 'Now you shall see how beautiful my wife is,' he announced, as he tore the bedclothes away and she tried to hide under the bed. One of her aides gallantly intervened, tried unsuccessfully to save her from this humiliating spectacle, and then angrily telephoned the emperor to report the incident. The latter sent for Otto and scolded him in no uncertain terms.[9] When the court of Saxony learnt how abominably her husband had treated his wife, a member of their house, there was considerable coldness between them and the Habsburgs. Otto was ordered to leave the marital home, although on certain court occasions, he and his wife had to appear together for the sake of appearances. During his final years, as syphilis took its toll, he had to wear a leather nose, underwent a tracheotomy, and spent his last few months being cared for by one of his mistresses before dying at the age of forty-one.

The youngest brother, Ferdinand Charles, was little better. Having become estranged from Francis Ferdinand for marrying beneath him, he failed to practise what he preached by becoming romantically involved with Bertha Czuber, the daughter of a Viennese professor. Although attractive, intelligent, and of good character, unlike Sophie she lacked aristocratic blood. He had the temerity to ask Francis Ferdinand for his support in marrying her, received a blunt refusal in reply, and retired into seclusion in the Tyrol, denying that Bertha was his mistress. A few years later, he astonished the family by admitting he had secretly married her morganatically. He was expelled from the House of Habsburg, struck off the army list, stripped of his orders and medals, and banished from the empire. 'Herr Ferdinand Berg', who thus officially ceased to exist in the eyes of the family, died from tuberculosis at the age of forty-seven in 1915.

The emperor had to face the fact that his two younger nephews had sinned against the family's good name. In sharp contrast, their elder brother and heir to the throne had married beneath him but otherwise led an irreproachable life as a perfect husband and father. As for the heir's morganatic wife, despite intense and persistent provocation from those around her, she displayed the patience of a saint in never putting a foot wrong, causing a scene, or persuading her husband to make a grab for power. Even so, he 'could not forgive the match', and never ceased to reproach himself for having allowed the marriage to take place.[10]

Though he might find her rather too ready to know what was good for him, the emperor still enjoyed the company of Valerie and her husband, and doted on their children. When they came to stay with him in Vienna, the youngsters would play on the floor in his study while he was at his desk, tumbling around happily on the carpet, or drawing on the used envelopes and crayons he gave them. When more serious matters claimed his attention, he would tell them gently that he had to return to his work.

The children may have been happy at Schönbrunn, but for guests and foreign diplomats, Valerie's presence did little to relieve the atmosphere of gloom. Count Eulenberg, a close confidant of the Emperor William and Katherine, dreaded invitations to dine at the palace, as he thought Francis Joseph had such a stultifying effect on his daughter. In her husband's company, she was an agreeable host, but when her father was around, she was so overcome with shyness that she rarely opened her mouth. As the emperor was hardly the most amusing of men, the result was an evening of utter boredom, which could hardly finish too soon for host or guests. Even Valerie thought as much as she sat for hours knitting, yawning, or sighing, until her father's patience was exhausted and he would rise to his feet, saying, 'And now I must really get to work.'[11]

There were no such problems with the more outgoing Gisela, a lively conversationalist whose husband, Leopold, had become the emperor's favourite hunting companion. She had inherited her father's thrifty habits, and until electric lighting was installed in the Hofburg, the chandeliers were supplied daily with fresh candles, regardless of whether those from the previous day had been lit or not. Gisela could always be relied on to pack up partly used or even unused candles and take them back to Munich for her own use.

When Katherine renewed her contact with the emperor in the spring of 1902, he was almost beside himself with joy. He wrote to her that she would find him much aged and 'feebler in mind', although he was in better shape than he might admit. When she returned to Vienna, she resumed the old habit of entertaining him to breakfast. He still took an interest in her appearances on stage, although rather less than formerly.

Even in his seventies, he could still spend long hours in the saddle on his autumn manoeuvres without suffering undue strain. Such routines were to him a vital part of the empire's role, a chance to judge the qualities of his army, and to warn him and them of what might be needed in the future. Gradually, his interest in army manoeuvres diminished, as modern warfare did not interest him. Having been brought up in the old tradition of being in the midst of his men, riding close to them in the ranks, he found something disconcerting about trench warfare.

Throughout his life, he insisted on high standards of efficiency and dress, and every serving officer had to be turned out properly in accordance with military standards. His servants knew he must always have the right clothes laid out if possible, though occasionally this was not possible. Shortly after being appointed to the imperial household, his valet was asked to produce a pair of trousers for a particular uniform. After rummaging through the boxes without success, he was advised by a footman to tell him that the missing garment had been eaten by moths. When told, the emperor shook his head and said how dreadful it was that they had not even left the buttons.[12]

Such standards were also rigorously applied in domestic life. One night when he was unwell, his physician was sent for in a hurry. The man decided there was no time to waste in putting his smartest clothes on, so he came to the emperor's room at once. On looking up at him as he entered the bedroom, the aged yet obviously not so ill sovereign barked crossly, 'Frock-coat!'

Although he now rarely travelled outside the borders of his empire, Emperor Francis Joseph maintained regular contact with other European sovereigns. King Edward VII of England, who succeeded his mother, Queen Victoria, in January 1901, was a regular visitor to Austria. King and emperor had little in common in personality or outlook, but always had great mutual respect. Both, it was said, strongly desired the maintenance of peace in Europe, even if only because the king loved peace and the emperor because he was afraid of war. At a court ball during the Boer War of 1899–1902, Francis Joseph declared in the presence of foreign diplomats that his sympathies were completely with the English.

King Edward felt himself forever in his debt as a result, paying his only visit to Vienna as sovereign in August and September 1903, the first time an English king had been in Austria for over 700 years. At a banquet at the Hofburg on his first evening, the king delighted his host by announcing his appointment as a field marshal of the British Army. Such appointments concerning foreign rulers were generally notified to those rulers' capitals and cleared with military authorities at home in advance. King Edward knew such a gift would be more effective if bestowed unexpectedly. The emperor was thrilled, and for the rest of the evening, he talked of little else. Early next day, he sent personal telegrams of greeting to all fellow field marshals on the British Army list. The emperor's personal staff had rarely seen their master unbend so much.

At the same time, King Edward wanted to speak with the emperor about the plight of the widowed crown princess, who had been treated by some at court as a virtual outcast since her husband's suicide and her second marriage in 1900. While he had always been more sympathetic to her than the empress, the emperor treated her with coldness. King Edward asked him to look upon his former daughter-in-law more gently in future. When she was seriously ill later that year, he enquired regularly after her state of health, sent her doctors, medicine, and food from the imperial kitchens, and visited her personally several times, and when she recovered, he was clearly delighted.

Stephanie's relationship with her daughter was beyond saving, but the younger Elizabeth did not hesitate to tarnish the Habsburg name with scandal. In January 1902, she married Prince Otto von Windischgrätz, and within less than two years, she discovered that he was having an affair with a Prague actress, Louise Ziegler. In December 1903, she visited Louise, confronted her with the accusation, and shot her with a revolver. According to some sources, she recovered from her wounds, but others said she was badly injured and died not long after. The emperor asked his ministers to hush everything up, and evidently with more success than during the pathetic aftermath of Mayerling.

Despite the good relations between emperor and king, the latter never managed to persuade the elder man to come to London. A visit was provisionally scheduled for June 1904 but cancelled for various reasons, not least of all on the grounds of health and fatigue on his part.[13] Nevertheless, the Prince and Princess of Wales, later King George V and Queen Mary, came to Vienna in April that year. The British heir found everyone very kind and pleasant, 'but my goodness this Court is stiff and they are frightened of the Emperor.'[14] The Princess was less critical; she thought it 'all delightful tho' tiring, everyone so kind & the Emperor charming'.[15]

In Austria and Germany, King Edward was suspected of trying to detach the emperor from the Austro-German alliance. When he visited the emperor in August 1908, he asked him to try and use his influence to persuade Emperor William of the danger of escalating naval rivalry between Germany and England. It was no more than part of his general effort to enlist a friendly fellow-monarch's help in trying to defuse international tension. Yet Francis Joseph, who was uninterested in naval matters, declined to become involved.

The emperor had his doubts as to Francis Ferdinand's suitability as heir to the throne. The archduke could be charming in his own family circle, as a devoted husband and father, or as a host showing people around his treasured rose garden. Away from home, he was brusque, lacking in grace, and not afraid to show the violent prejudices—anti-Semitic, anti-Magyar and anti-Italian—that could lead to him being regarded as a political liability. In these spheres, the reasonable outlook and good influence of his wife had limited effect. Yet he showed himself more methodical than Rudolf had been in preparing himself for the throne. He built up a personal intelligence service at the Belvedere, and in January 1906, he persuaded the emperor to accept it as a military chancellery. It grew into a team of fourteen officers who prided themselves on having greater knowledge than the emperor's own advisory body.

In an era when royal and aristocratic youngsters were brought up largely by nannies, tutors, and governors, saw little of their parents except at afternoon tea or formal family gatherings, and were afraid of their fathers whose behaviour towards them was often remote and verged on tyranny, the domestic life of Francis Ferdinand, Sophie, and their children was particularly close. Their father usually had his breakfast with them in their nursery, while their mother nursed and bathed them herself when they were very small. When official functions meant they were separated, the parents telephoned them every day or kept in touch by telegram. In later years, daughter Sophie would recall fondly that their father took them with him on every possible occasion when they travelled away from home, and that their mother was 'the heart, the peace-making centre of the family'. Their parents hoped they would enjoy the lives of private individuals and country squires, or in the case of his daughter, as the wife of one, rather than making grand princely or ducal and unhappy marriages of convenience. For 'little Sophie', who always said that they were never spoiled and brought up 'to know that we weren't anything special,' Maximilian, and Ernest, it was a particularly warm, secure, and happy childhood, and remained thus until cruelly rent asunder by the events on that cataclysmic day in June 1914.[16]

The emperor was sometimes exasperated with his energetic, bustling nephew, but he knew it was important for the man who was his heir to be adequately prepared by having access to official papers, and copies of all official documents and despatches were sent regularly from the war ministry to Belvedere. Francis Ferdinand always remained as interested in military affairs as the efficient if unpopular Archduke Albrecht, who had died in 1895, and in naval matters, ever ready to don an admiral's uniform and launch new battleships or visit the fleet. Yet his uncle still found him aggressively authoritarian, and looked askance at what was almost becoming an alternative court in Vienna, where ambassadors were welcomed while carefully keeping in touch with the man expected to ascend the throne before long.

Uncle and nephew shared a common bond in their aversion to Hungary. They were both present at celebrations in Budapest in June 1907 for the fortieth anniversary of the imperial coronation that followed ratification of the *Ausgleich*. After the special church service, they talked about the proceedings. Francis Ferdinand remarked what an effort it was for him to come to Hungary, as he never liked being there, and the emperor told him quietly that he agreed. Yet whatever his personal views, he was always punctilious about respecting Hungarian susceptibilities. Being there may have brought back unhappy memories of Elizabeth and her passionate support of the Magyars, and he may have been unable to forget and forgive their taking up arms against Habsburg rule during the early months of his reign. Even so, whenever he was in the country, he never wore any uniform other than that of a Hungarian field marshal or his own 1st Hussar Regiment, and he always donned it before leaving Vienna, so he would be thus attired on his arrival at Budapest, and he always wore the ribbon of the Grand Cross of the Hungarian Order of St Stephen. At informal receptions after court banquets at Budapest, he always spoke with the Hungarian guests in their own language, even if he knew they were fluent German speakers as well.

Francis Ferdinand did not hesitate to conceal his distrust of the Prussians. Once a German officers' deputation came to Vienna, and he shook hands and spoke to everyone present except the detachments of Prussian regiments, whom he walked past without comment. It earned him a sharp reprimand from his uncle afterwards, but it did not prevent him from his particular interest in reviving the time-honoured and now lapsed alliance between Austria, Germany, and Russia. They had been united in the Holy Alliance of 1815, and the *Dreikaiserbund* of 1873, and the heir was convinced that a re-establishment of the old brotherhood would help to strengthen the monarchic principle, as well as guarantee peace throughout Europe. The main barrier was an agreement made between Russia and republican France. Francis Ferdinand had initially been impressed with the young Tsar Nicholas II, and was sure he could create a warm personal relationship with him that would surely lead on to friendship and political stability between their respective empires.

Although Francis Joseph was the senior European monarch in Europe, the eldest and the longest reigning, it was hard for him (or anyone else) not to be overshadowed by Emperor William II in Berlin. A personal connection bound them together in that Gisela had inherited the Achilleion at Corfu from her mother, but it was a reminder of times best forgotten. In 1907, she sold it to William, who visited it every April with his family and suite until after the outbreak of the First World War. Sometimes he sailed back from Corfu to Trieste, breaking his journey in Vienna with a display of enthusiasm that the more elderly sovereign came to dread. While William treated him with all due deference and respect, the assertion in his memoirs that Francis Joseph treated him almost like his own son was an exaggeration.[17] The older man found his contemporary tiresome at times, resenting his arrogance and the impression he strove to give that he was an authority on everything. Francis Joseph had never forgiven William for his effrontery in finding fault with Austrian troops during his visit to Vienna in the autumn of 1888. He commented once to *Frau* Schratt that the mere thought of the emperor's forthcoming visit to Vienna was giving him indigestion. A small shooting party would be a pleasant, cosy affair until the emperor arrived with his large suite, 'and then it will be more awkward and strenuous'.[18]

Yet Francis Joseph still respected William, particularly for his coming to terms with the handicap of a stunted left arm and hand, which never prevented him from riding or shooting, albeit with assistance. He admired William's role in the general development of Germany's economic and military prowess during his reign, and remained unerringly loyal to the Austro-German alliance, though he may have regarded the younger man with suspicion, knowing that William and his friend, Count Eulenburg, regarded the elderly senior ruler in Vienna as long past his prime and far too old to make any pretensions to leading the Triple Alliance. Francis Joseph may have had a more charitable view of Emperor William's peaceable intentions than his contemporaries. When his entourage had discussed a controversial, even bellicose telegram from the sovereign in Berlin to Paul Kruger, President of the Transvaal, in the spring of 1901 during the Boer War in South Africa, he disagreed with those who thought William was trying to issue a challenge to England, saying he knew 'only too well that the German Emperor's one thought is always the maintenance of peace'.[19]

In personality, both rulers were very different. As German Chancellor Prince Bernhard von Bülow observed, William always wanted to be at the centre of attention, while Francis Joseph kept himself 'so far as his duties as ruler allowed him, well in the background, and never spoke from the stage'.[20] Moreover, William went out of his way to treat Francis Ferdinand and Sophie with all due honours, receiving the princess as if she was royalty, a civility that did not please Francis Joseph.

In 1908, Austria celebrated the diamond jubilee of the father figure beloved and revered by all. Festivities were planned carefully so as not to tire him, and so every few weeks, some ceremony took place. The first was on 7 May, when Emperor William led a deputation of German kings and princes to Schönbrunn to greet the emperor. It was as if each of them freely acknowledged that despite the transfer of economic, political, and military supremacy from Vienna to Berlin, for the Germans, there was still only one emperor.

One family difficulty remained unresolved. It was believed that the emperor might celebrate his anniversary by revoking the law that excluded the children of Francis Ferdinand from the succession. That he did not do so did not concern the heir unduly. Much as he might once have longed his elder son to succeed him as emperor one day, at length, he realised the advantages of being disinherited. The Habsburg crown, he once said, was no better than a crown of thorns. Far more rewarding for the family was the emperor's raising of Sophie from the rank of princess to that of duchess of Hohenberg in October 1909, a year later.

An initiative by the dual monarchy in 1908 would cost the empire dearly. With changes taking place in the Balkans, the emperor believed the best way of ensuring peace in the area was to work closely with St Petersburg, preserving the old Austro-Russian entente. The time had come for the annexation of Bosnia and Herzegovina, and on 6 October 1908, the emperor signed a proclamation addressed to the people of both provinces saying that, as they deserved an autonomous constitutional government, he had decided that Austria would extend 'sovereign rights' to both provinces. They would be his only territorial gains during his long reign. He had not anticipated the result, for the timing of such a move displeased several of the other crowned heads in Europe. Emperor William was offended at not having been taken into his old ally's confidence beforehand, while in England, King Edward feared that stability in the Balkans would be compromised. The annexation turned Serbia into a sworn enemy of the dual monarchy, intent on vengeance. Over the next few years, more observers would come to believe that the scene was set for the final battle between Germans and Slavs, and that it could be the start of a greater war than Europe had ever witnessed before.

In March 1909, after pressure from Russia, Serbia agreed to recognise the annexation and to pledge good neighbourly relations with Austria, and the crisis was officially over. Those who dreamt of and aspired to a 'Greater Serbia', the anarchists, officers, lawyers, academics, and civil servants, were content to bide their time. Moreover, the annexation had strengthened rather than weakened the Austro-German relationship. William II believed he had halted Austria's slide into isolation, and did not intend to release the Habsburg emperor from the bonds of Hohenzollern friendship. On a visit to Vienna, he made a speech telling the people of Austria that he had stood shoulder to shoulder beside their emperor. It irritated Francis Joseph, who looked uneasily on the military stance of his Prussian ally whom he had considered such a staunch man of peace.

The end of diamond jubilee year had been marked by demonstrations in Bohemia against the Habsburgs, and nearly a fortnight of martial law in Prague. In February 1910, General Marijan Varešanin, Governor of Bosnia, proposed that a senior member of the dynasty should visit Bosnia and Herzegovina. The emperor was keen to undertake the journey himself, and in March, it was announced that he would go at some time between 30 May and 5 June. Rumours of a conspiracy reached the Austro-Hungarian embassy in Paris during May, with a police informer claiming he had heard southern Slav anarchists talking of a plan to kill the emperor at Mostar, capital of Herzegovina. The authorities were sure that any attempt on his life was more likely to be made at Sarajevo than in any other town. Closer surveillance of travellers entering the town was ordered, and extra uniformed police were stationed in the streets.

Francis Joseph was not bothered by such threats, which he dismissed as one of the hazards of his trade. His only reservation was that the summer heat and dust might be too much for him. He made the journey, arriving safely at Sarajevo on the afternoon of 30 May, the train stopping at several stations in Bosnia in order to give his new subjects a chance to see him, albeit from a safe distance, staying in the Bosnian capital for four nights, driving through the city in an open carriage four times. When he returned to Vienna on 3 June, he wrote to Katherine Schratt that it had gone better than he had expected. One of the senior military commanders, General Michael Ludwig von Appel, called it 'a triumphal progress' and suggested that the heir, Francis Ferdinand, ought to come to Sarajevo and bring his wife.

Not long afterwards, five shots were fired at Varešanin as he rode back to the Konak. He was unhurt and his assailant, Bogdan Žerajić, killed himself with his last bullet. It was found that he had been shadowing the emperor during his visit and had been trailed by three detectives in Sarajevo all the time. A friend testified to the fact that while he was at Mostar railway station, he was so close to the emperor in his distinctive white uniform, an easy target for would-be assassins, that he could almost have touched him. He did not do so, he said, as he was so overawed by the dignity in the elderly gentleman's face. He targeted Varesarin instead and, failing to hit his quarry, killed himself as an act of martyrdom. A schoolboy, Gavrilo Princip, visited Žerajić's grave and swore he would avenge his death.

Now in his eightieth year, the venerable Francis Joseph was highly respected by his subjects and other rulers. Theodore Roosevelt, a former president of the United States, was received by him in private audience in April 1910, when he allegedly called himself 'the last monarch of the old school' and 'the protector of my people against themselves.'[21] Roosevelt was left with the impression of a gentleman, if not a very able man, who was broadminded enough to respect republican forms of government. He could appreciate that the United States of America was a federation of peoples functioning effectively without any need for a unifying dynasty. Such a concept might work perfectly well for nations of the new world, but not necessarily for Europe, particularly not the old system of the dual monarchy that rested on divine sanction. Sometimes he admitted self-deprecatingly to others that he was something of an anachronism, and politicians were heard to complain that when they suggested proposals to him for modernisation, they were countered by preconceptions dating back to the Schwarzenberg era.

It was a state of affairs regretted by the commentator Joseph Naernreither, who wrote in 1913 of the 'wall of prejudices' that cut the emperor off from any independent-thinking political personalities. All fresh political ideas, he said, were kept from the sovereign by the ring of courtiers, military, and medical personnel that surrounded him. 'The powerfully surging life of our times barely reaches the ear of our Emperor as distant rustling,' he commented. 'He is kept from any real participation in this life. He no longer understands the times, and the times pass on regardless.'[22]

On the other hand, it was arguable that years of experience and fundamental common sense gave him a deeper, more detached insight into human problems than younger ministers or generals could comprehend. Yet in his last years, he knew he was an elderly man out of time, out of touch, and lacking the energy to provide the leadership his empire needed. He was in some ways still the same emperor he had been during his early years, proud of the Habsburgs' position in history, afraid of losing wars and therefore provinces. In an age when the peoples of his empire wanted national equality and representative government, he still hankered after the acquisition of more provinces. The only territories he had added to his dominions were Bosnia and Herzegovina, thus assimilating South Slavs into the empire, a move fiercely resisted by Germans and Magyars alike. Thirty years earlier, Crown Prince Rudolf had predicted that Balkan expansion would prove a mistake, fearing that it was tantamount to putting one foot in the grave.[23] Those who shared his views might not have been surprised when events around Bosnia were one day to start the war ultimately destined to destroy the empire.

For many years, Francis Joseph had celebrated his birthday on 18 August each year by hearing low mass early in the morning in the villa at Ischl, where he continued to spend part of the summer. Afterwards, the family and members of his suite came to congratulate him in person, and after a family dinner in the afternoon, his son-in-law, Prince Leopold of Bavaria, proposed his health. He would reply to this with his own toast, as he emptied his glass of champagne, to the health of his family and welcome guests. In August 1910, there was a larger gathering than usual, with more than seventy members of the dynasty making a special effort to join him in celebrating his eightieth birthday.

Each year on the birthday, every member of staff received a bottle of wine and a loaf of bread. Once, the director of the Chancellery Office, known behind his back as 'the master of economies', announced that he intended to withdraw this privilege as the servants did not use the wine to drink their master's health, but sold it instead. There was such a storm of indignation that the idea was quietly dropped.

While he was a staunch lifelong Roman Catholic, the emperor was equally tolerant of other faiths and had no time for religious bigotry. Prejudice against Protestants had no place at his court or among his personal suite. On all his journeys within the empire, in addition to attending services at Catholic churches, he always made a point of visiting those of the Protestant and Greek faiths, as well as mosques and synagogues, and often went to their services as well.

His eldest grandchild, Elizabeth, daughter of Gisela and Leopold, fell in love with Baron Otto von Seefried zu Buttenheim, a cavalry lieutenant in the Bavarian army and a Protestant. It would not be received well by the family, she feared, because of differences in rank and religion. Yet she was not an archduchess, and her grandfather saw no reason to withhold his consent to their marriage as she was a fairly junior member of the family. He gave them his blessing, granted the baron a commission in the Austrian army, and the match proved a happy one. This leniency was not extended to every member of the imperial family. Where dynastic interests were not at stake, he could be kindly, patient, and courteous. Where he thought they were being jeopardised, he could be inflexible, even callous, as the case of Francis Ferdinand had made evident.

Up to the age of eighty, the emperor's health was good, though old age brought on bronchial catarrh and asthma. Since his mid-seventies, he had regularly suffered from such attacks, ascribed by his entourage to the cold water with which he had himself rubbed down on rising each day.

His physician, Dr Joseph von Kerzl, advised him to omit this routine, but in vain. In the spring of 1911, he had a severe cough and was ordered to remain in bed. He did so, but still insisted on having the state papers brought to him each morning. Nevertheless, Francis Ferdinand was warned of his uncle's condition in case it should lead to anything worse.

In the last week of May, Sir Fairfax Cartwright, British minister in Vienna, reported to Under-Secretary of State for Foreign Affairs Sir Arthur Nicolson that while the emperor was in Hungary 'all manner of rumours are current with regard to his health'. While there seemed no cause for alarm, his persistent hoarseness and cough were a cause for concern among his medical advisers. They advised him not to return to Schönbrunn, which was too exposed to wind and dust, but instead take up residence in a nearby villa at Wiener Wald, surrounded by fields and forests. They also wanted him to abandon his old routine of spending summer at Bad Ischl, on the grounds that it was not good for him. By the autumn, he seemed much better, although at his time of life, he could no longer be expected to attend tedious, almost interminable court balls, let alone pay state visits to foreign capitals.

'A higher power has restored the old order'

In October 1911, the emperor went to Schloss Schwarzau, seat of the Duchess of Parma, 40 miles from Vienna, for the marriage of his great-nephew, Archduke Charles, to Princess Zita of Bourbon-Parma and propose the toast at their wedding breakfast. As this young man would probably be the next sovereign but one, he took the greatest interest in his future.

Charles was the son of Archduke Otto, Francis Ferdinand's younger brother, who had died in 1906. As Francis Ferdinand's descendants were barred from the succession, Charles was second in line to the throne. The late Duke of Parma's family had included several feeble-minded children, admittedly by his first marriage, and as Zita belonged to a deposed Italian royal house, he felt she might be an unsuitable bride for a Habsburg archduke who was likely to succeed to the throne. Initially, he had hoped his granddaughter, Elizabeth, eldest child of Valerie, would be chosen. The idea was instantly dismissed by Archduchess Maria Josepha, Charles's mother, who was all too aware of the potential consequences. She went to Francis Joseph and pleaded that, as both were related twice over, it would be most unsuitable for them and probably even more unfortunate for any children they might have.

Charles and Zita had originally met as small children, and did not see each other again for over ten years. While on a family visit during military service as a young adult, he saw her again, and a passing acquaintance soon became much more. Their engagement was announced in June, just a few days before he was due to leave Austria on his first important representative mission abroad, at the coronation of King George V. During the weeks prior to their marriage, the family noticed that Charles was clearly very happy with his princess, and that on the day of the wedding, 21 October, the emperor seemed in the best of spirits. Nobody had seen him in such a jovial mood for some time, and they would never do so again.

While group photographs were being taken after the ceremony, it was unusually chilly. Nobody had provided the monarch with a cloak, and afterwards, he went down with a severe chill that developed into bronchitis. Coughing heavily and feverishly, his health gave cause for concern again that autumn. Not until the following spring did he seem his old self once more, no longer complaining about the consequences of 'that wretched day at Schwarzau'.[1]

Francis Ferdinand and Charles had developed a close bond. The younger man regularly expressed his devotion to his uncle, who in turn said that when he became emperor, he would allow Charles regularly in the Hofburg so they could work together. The closeness continued after Charles's marriage, and at first, Zita seemed equally devoted to her husband's uncle and aunt. Despite this, Zita later allowed herself to be influenced by gossip from others that suggested that Francis Ferdinand and Sophie had previously tried to lead the young bachelor Charles into leading a frivolous life. If rumours were to be believed, they hoped he would follow in his father Otto's footsteps, end up a debauched wreck long before his time, die young, and thus leave the way clear for Maximilian Hohenberg to succeed his father as emperor one day. It was his uncle's fault, the pious Zita believed, that Charles had been led from the straight and narrow as a young man, had not led a bachelor life of complete purity, and was not a virgin on their wedding night.[2]

This was not the only problem Zita had where her uncle by marriage was concerned. Many at court wondered whether the archduke would still be prepared to abide by the terms of his oath regarding the disqualification of his sons from the imperial succession when he came to the throne, and as wife of the man who would be the emperor in waiting, she had more to fear than most. Francis Ferdinand gave Charles his word that he would honour his undertakings to the letter, but Zita still distrusted him, considering him not just a devoted family man, but also 'a very powerful and determined personality'. She was particularly suspicious after he once made a chance remark to her about a particularly industrious land agent, telling her that he could not understand anybody working as hard as that unless it was for the sake of his children. Although he had not intended to plant any misgivings in her mind, it was enough to make her anxious about what His Imperial Majesty Francis Ferdinand might do once he was answerable to nobody else. Others believed that, as a devout Catholic, he had made his solemn and sacred pledge before God, and that alone was enough to ensure he would never go back on it. His secretary, Paul

Nikitsch-Boulles, was sure that he envied the children their tranquil future, with no prospect of succeeding to the imperial throne. He saw nothing in their education that was designed to prepare them for such an eventuality, and he looked forward to his sons enjoying a future existence as country squires, while his daughter would be much happier with a socially suitable partner than in a royal or imperial marriage of convenience.

With Sophie, Zita always enjoyed a close relationship, although this once caused a problem for the elder woman. At a court ballroom, Zita once took Sophie's hand in greeting and kissed it, as a mark of respect. Sophie immediately pulled her hand away as if it had been stung, and begged Zita never to do so again in public. She explained this was just the kind of situation that people who wanted to cause difficulties for her were always looking out for.[3]

In the summer of 1911, Charles had been chosen to represent the Habsburgs at the coronation of King George V and Queen Mary of England. The idea had been that of Francis Ferdinand, who would normally have been expected to undertake the duty, as he had done at the funeral of King Edward VII the previous year. Largely because of the problems that would arise from the presence of Sophie and what precedence she should or should not be given at the English court, he recommended that Charles should go instead. In spite of this, it was alleged that he was jealous of his nephew for having been chosen instead and caused a scene. It was as if he could never escape the taint of malicious gossip put about to blacken his name for no good reason.

The Hohenberg children were kept in ignorance as far as possible about their parents' difficulties connected with their mother's anomalous position at court. 'Little Sophie' recalled years later that they never asked their parents about the problems they faced, and they never sat down and explained things to them. The situation, she said, was left unmentioned as though it did not exist, but they were well aware that it did and were always nervous about being taken along to court because they sensed that they were 'somehow in a special category'.[4] They did not even meet the emperor until 1912, by which time Sophie was aged eleven, and then it was quite by accident. Renovations were being made at the Belvedere, and they were staying at the Hofburg. One day, the archduke had to inspect the guard in a courtyard and they all wanted to watch. They then heard a commotion, saw the emperor shuffling down the passage, and fled back to their rooms in terror. Later that day, the archduke asked his uncle if he might present his children. The emperor agreed, and as they came in, bowing and curtseying before him, he looked at them and said wryly, 'I think we saw each other this morning, didn't we?' It was the only time they ever came face to face while their parents were alive.[5]

In October 1912, King Nicholas of Montenegro declared war on the Ottoman Empire. Fighting was over within two months, and an armistice was agreed on 3 December, with peace talks opening at St James's Palace, London, a few days later. Proclaiming that he had always been unlucky in wars, Francis Joseph was determined to keep Austria out of the conflict. He was at odds with the more military-minded in Vienna, led by General Oscar Potiorek, who had succeeded Varešanin as governor of Bosnia and Herzegovina in May 1911 and was pressing for mobilization and the despatch of more troops to the provinces in case of rebellion. Francis Joseph rejected his request each time, on the grounds that it would be seen as provocative and inflammatory.

On 28 October 1912, the ministerial council decided to request a gradual increase in troops, calling up reservists while taking care not to intensify the crisis by ordering full-scale mobilization. The greatest priority was given to Bosnia-Herzegovina and southern Hungary, but by the end of November, the despatch of additional troops in Galicia, needed to fight the Russian army, was causing alarm in Cracow and Lvov. At first, Francis Ferdinand favoured the idea of suing for peace, but after the armistice was signed, he was perturbed by reports of unrest in Belgrade and considered preparing a pre-emptive strike. For a long time, he had been critical of general staff planning in the army. Conrad von Hötzendorff, who had been appointed imperial chief of staff in November 1906 largely on the archduke's recommendation, was a vociferous advocate of modernising the armed forces. After differences of opinion with Foreign Minister Alois von Aehrenthal, particularly over Conrad's enthusiasm for a preventive war against Italy, he was dismissed in 1911. Aehrenthal was in poor health and, after his resignation, followed by his death in February 1912, Francis Ferdinand recommended to the emperor that he should be reinstated as chief of general staff. This was accordingly done, although both soon felt that he had a tendency to try and interfere in foreign policy affairs to an unnecessary extent.

Leopold von Berchtold, the new foreign minister earlier that year, was concerned about the mood in Belgrade, as well as pro-war hysteria in much of the press. On a private visit to Francis Ferdinand at the Belvedere, he found the heir keen for an immediate attack on Serbia and Montenegro. Later that day, at Berchtold's request, the emperor presided over a meeting of ministers at Schönbrunn. Neither Hötzendorff nor War Minister General Alexander Krobatkin were present, so it was not technically a war council. In Krobatkin's absence, the case for military action was presented by Francis Ferdinand, while Berchtold said they ought to reserve judgment until they knew the outcome of the conference at St James's Palace that was about to open in London. When the Austrian finance minister argued that the imperial economy could ill afford the cost of such a campaign, the emperor decided they should support the peace talks in England, with no military action contemplated at present.

Francis Ferdinand and Berchtold agreed with him. Hötzendorff and Krobatkin thought otherwise, arguing that only a short victorious campaign against Serbia and Montenegro would give the dual monarchy authority to impose an acceptable settlement in the western Balkans. At the end of the month, Berchtold sought another audience with the emperor and found him a steadfast supporter of peace. Bulgaria's refusal to cooperate at the conference table led to more fighting in the Balkans from February to April 1913, after which the diplomats resumed peace talks in London. The Austrians were largely outvoted at the conference, and Francis Joseph authorised Potiorek to proclaim a state of emergency in Bosnia and Herzegovina, thus putting the army on a war footing in both provinces.

The strain imposed on Francis Joseph by this perpetual state of crisis was considerable. By now, he generally visited the Hofburg only for official business and increasingly rare ceremonial occasions, and he was rarely seen in public. A few days at Wallsee spent with Valerie and her family in the winter of 1912–13 gave him a brief respite, but at this time in his life, he was increasingly weary of the situation beyond the borders of the empire. During the first ten years or so of his reign, he and the empire had been repeatedly involved with conflicts of one kind or another, and as a young man brought up as a soldier, he took it all in his stride. Now, in the evening of his days, he had to resign himself to the fact that the potential for conflicts was rarely absent.

Once again, he was finding comfort in the company of Katherine Schratt, now a widow of nearly sixty. She spent some of her time abroad, gambling at Monte Carlo and driving around in an automobile, much to his consternation. Whenever she was in Vienna, they saw each other again, and some people even thought they had secretly married. The emperor was far too conscious of his own imperial dignity to contemplate even marrying an actress. However, the octogenarian ruler and his middle-aged companion clearly benefited from each other's company. When his doctor ordered him to stop smoking strong cigars, one of his few remaining indulgences, in order to keep his bronchitis at bay, Katherine found him milder ones instead. On summer evenings, she would invite him to a private dinner party at her house.

With his heir, the emperor still disagreed on various matters, and some of his entourage thought he only had to know the heir's view on a subject to make him want to do or order quite the opposite. Having an elaborate network of unofficial informers who could be relied on to keep him in touch with military affairs and with the aspirations of different minority groups throughout the empire, Francis Ferdinand was more well-informed than his uncle on various imperial matters, as he was not dependent on what a small circle of advisers chose to tell him.

One subject on which he held strong views for a time was that of Serbia and what he thought an obsession on the part of some to fight a preventative war against the restive kingdom after the annexation of Bosnia and Herzegovina, with their predominantly Serb populations. It was a policy he shared with Hötzendorff, whose appointment he had eagerly supported as new chief of the general imperial staff in 1906 and prevailed upon the emperor to appoint him, convinced that he was the man needed to help modernise the archaic, poorly equipped army. Within a few years, the archduke realised that Hötzendorff needed restraining, because of his obsession with the idea of declaring war on Serbia in order to weaken and subdue her. This, the heir to the throne realised, would draw Russian into the conflict and result in European war. Even if Austria and Germany were to win such a conflict, which he thought 'totally out of the question', it would be a tragedy for the Austrian monarchy. At a dinner in February 1913, he pointedly celebrated the emperor's reluctance to approve Hötzendorff's plans for war, raising his glass in a toast to peace. Privately, he warned his uncle that war between Austria and Russia would only encourage revolution in both countries and 'thereby cause both Emperor and Tsar to push each other from their thrones'. For these reasons, he considered war would be utter lunacy, along with Hötzendorff's requests for mobilization.[6]

Much as he might resent his sovereign's old-fashioned obedience for tradition down to the last letter, the heir held his uncle in great respect. Had the communication between them been better, Francis Joseph might have persuaded him to modify his prejudices against the Magyars, and managed to convince them of their strengths as well as their weaknesses. Both men had many things in common, not least their tastes and prejudices, their middlebrow views on literature and music, and their dedication to the army, yet they were very different in personality. The tired, elderly emperor hankered after a quiet life in his declining years, particularly after so many tragedies in his ill-starred family life. He hated scenes, something the archduke would readily resort to with his temper if necessary in order to get his own way, and the emperor soon learnt that the best way to avoid unpleasantness was to send for his nephew as little as humanly possible. Zita thought they were too different in temperament, the atmosphere was never relaxed, and 'there was always electricity in the air when they were together'.[7] An additional source of difficulty and potential friction between both was the customary one regarding a sovereign and his sometimes impatient heir-in-waiting. With his active, well-informed staff, Francis Ferdinand did not hesitate to place or at least nominate certain friends and associates in the key military and civilian posts of the empire. It placed a strain on their relationship, and Francis Joseph's successor 'must have appeared at times like his undertaker'.[8]

The duchess of Hohenberg's lack of precedence at court still irritated her husband. In May 1911, Sir Fairfax Cartwright was told there had recently been some unpleasantness between sovereign and heir on the matter of her precedence at a court ball. According to gossips, the archduke had reportedly 'behaved in so violent a manner' that the emperor said he feared for his nephew's mental stability, and it might be necessary to exclude him from succession to the throne. This may have been a contributory factor in the emperor not sending the archduke to London to represent him at the coronation of King George V, but Archduke Charles instead.

Two years later, when Emperor William's daughter, Victoria Louise, was marrying Ernest Augustus of Hanover, later Duke of Brunswick, in Berlin, and the presence of Francis Ferdinand was specifically requested, Emperor Francis Joseph asked that this be rescinded, ostensibly on the grounds that if Sophie went as well, she might make too favourable an impression on the other guests. It was a strange reason for withholding consent, and if true, suggested that Montenuovo was ever more fearful of her popularity (and that of the archduke in Germany) and of the adverse effect it might have on his aged master's reputation. Disappointed by this turn of events, the German emperor did his best to atone by being more solicitous than usual when he was a guest at Konopischt that autumn, going out of his way to flatter his hosts. By this time, Emperor Francis Joseph had in his own small way made amends in August 1913 by appointing his nephew inspector-general of the monarchy's armed forces, a post only held once previously, by his cousin, Archduke Albrecht.

The year drew towards a close with a private visit abroad for the archduke and his wife that was little short of a major triumph. In November, they arrived at London for a short visit to England, firstly to visit King George V and Queen Mary and Windsor Castle, and then the duke and duchess of Portland at Welbeck Abbey in Nottinghamshire. At the former venue, on the king's instructions, no princesses were asked to join the party, so that Sophie could be granted precedence after the queen. It was a tactful gesture that ensured the guests would be at their ease throughout their time there. Queen Mary found them both very pleasant and easy to get on with, and believed it was due to his wife's influence that the archduke was no longer very anti-English as he had once been. On the contrary, he was very enthusiastic about his visit, about England in general, and thoroughly gratified by the kind reception he had received everywhere. Before they left England, the king and queen said they would come and visit them at Blühnbach, the archduke's autumn retreat, in September 1914.

The threat of war remained while Serbia was basking in success after a small but significant victory over Bulgaria during her short military campaign in the summer, and was clashing with Montenegro over territorial issues. A secret society, the Black Hand, had been established among army officers in Belgrade in 1911 with the aim of uniting Serb minorities in the Habsburg and Ottoman empires with those in Serbia itself. Once more, the emperor's warlike spirit was aroused. Losing patience with the Serbs, he thought the time had come to administer a swift pre-emptive strike. Francis Ferdinand urged caution, largely on the grounds that the army was in no condition to undertake a campaign, but the emperor's view prevailed. He authorised Berchtold to send Serbia an ultimatum, handed on 18 October to Nikola Pasic, prime minister and foreign minister in Belgrade, giving them eight days to evacuate Albanian territory or face the consequences. Realising there would be no military help from Russia, Pasic gave way and the ultimatum was complied with. The Black Hand viewed him as a weakling whose commitment to the cause of Serbia was questionable, but the day of reckoning would soon come.

Yet it was generally assumed that the emperor would see his days out without witnessing any further major European conflict. His first English biographer, Gribble, who published a life of him early in 1914, noted in his final chapter that the emperor hoped there would be peace in his time, and he would probably get his way: 'There prevails throughout Europe, as well as throughout Austria, a sentimental feeling that he has suffered enough, and that it would be cruel to disturb his last days with war or civil commotion.'[9]

Despite differences with the heir, the emperor was slowly warming towards him and his wife. At the Vienna court ball in February 1914, which unbeknown to those present would be the last-ever such event, the emperor unbent sufficiently to ask Sophie to come and sit with him for a little while. Above all, he was impressed with the way in which Francis Ferdinand had discharged his military duties.

The first few months of 1914 were particularly successful for the imperial heir and his wife, combining business with pleasure to some extent. In the spring, they welcomed the duke and duchess of Portland to Konopischt, repaying their hospitality of the previous autumn. The archduke and his family then went to stay at Miramar in Trieste, and the German emperor arrived on board the yacht *Hohenzollern*. In order to meet him, Francis Ferdinand was appropriately attired in the uniform of a grand admiral of the German navy. It was not a uniform he particularly liked, and admitted that it made him feel a fool, but he assured one of his aides it did not matter, as the German emperor was 'always dressed up himself in the worst possible taste'.[10]

A few weeks later, at the beginning of June, Francis Ferdinand and Sophie attended a function in the Prater, the Viennese pleasure park. For the first time, Sophie was allowed to join her husband in the imperial box, and a captivated press made much of the occasion as well as describing her dress, black jacket, and hat in great detail. Even more remarkably, Archduchess Isabella, Sophie's former employer who had been so horrified to learn of her romantic involvement with the heir some fifteen years earlier and had been her bitter enemy for so long, executed a remarkable *volte-face* when she wrote to Francis Ferdinand about a dance in Vienna that she and her husband were planning, and she would be so pleased if both of them would like to come.

Everybody recognised it would be expedient to treat the future emperor with all due consideration, for there was a widespread feeling that he would reign before long. In April, the emperor had been seriously ill with chronic bronchitis, and daily bulletins on his health were issued by Dr Kerzl for over a month until he was out of danger. In spite of this, few people expected him to live for much longer.

There was one major duty for the heir to undertake before long. One of his first decisions after being appointed inspector-general, taken after consultation with Hötzendorff, was to hold summer manoeuvres that year in Bosnia, and he would be obliged to attend them. In March 1914, it was announced that the archduke would be at manoeuvres in the Bosnian mountains in June, and then pay a state visit to Sarajevo with the duchess of Hohenberg. Three years earlier, he had considered a similar journey but had second thoughts after being warned that the Serbs would probably make an attempt on his life. Members of the Black Hand were urging all patriotic Serbs to take 'holy vengeance' on the Habsburg dynasty, and he was told he would be threatened if he went. While insisting that it was his duty, sometimes he gave the impression he would rather not tempt providence by going to Bosnia.

Whether he was in a position to make the visit at all was for a while in some doubt, and he was ready to cancel the tour altogether if the emperor's health worsened and he should succeed to the throne. In Belgrade, the conspirators started to whisper among themselves that they might not need their weapons after all, for if the emperor was really unwell, his heir could not come to Bosnia. Even when daily bulletins were discontinued, the sovereign was still unable to carry out his normal work of reading and approving reports of ministerial council meetings within the usual fortnight.

The emperor had fully recovered by the end of May. He and the heir met a couple of times in the first days of June for their regular audience, and Francis Ferdinand was still wondering over whether to visit Bosnia or not. With the asthma, which he found was worsening with age, he was also anxious about the intense midsummer heat there. Moreover, once again, there were reports of a conspiracy to kill him. While he had long since learnt to live with the threat of physical danger and attempts on his life, and could take these in his stride, sullen crowds were for him a far greater annoyance. When he mentioned his doubts to the emperor, the latter advised him to do as he wished and did nothing to dissuade him. He even agreed that the duchess of Hohenberg could accompany him, more or less as an equal, although in accordance with Habsburg protocol, she was still obliged to travel separately from her husband and by a different route.

It was the last time uncle and nephew ever came face to face. The emperor remained at Schönbrunn while his heir and family spent a few days at Konopischt, where he entertained Emperor William II, with whom his friendship was deepening. With the emperor came Admiral Alfred von Tirpitz, his secretary of state for the navy, who shared the archduke's passion for horticulture and wanted to come and see the rose gardens. The meeting of these three men would shortly give rise to extraordinary rumours concerning a 'Konopischt pact'. According to James W. Gerard, America Ambassador in Berlin, Sophie's ambitions for their children were largely responsible for the war that broke out a few weeks later, and the German emperor, 'playing upon her ambitions', persuaded her husband to agree with them.[11] Their common strategy, asserted British journalist Henry Wickham Steed, foreign editor and subsequently editor-in-chief of *The Times*, was an agreement reached by both men to divide the continent of Europe into joint spheres of influence after the war in which their allied empires would be victorious. There would be prizes for the two sons of the next Austrian emperor, with Maximilian being crowned king of an independent Poland, and Ernest of Hungary, Bohemia, and Serbia.[12]

Towards the end of the month, the emperor was planning to leave for Ischl, while Francis Ferdinand set out for Bosnia. The circumstances surrounding his invitation to attend army manoeuvres in June 1914 were never made completely clear. Hötzendorff later said he was first aware of the impending visit in mid-September 1913, when the archduke personally told him and mentioned he was planning to take Sophie with him. Later, the chief of staff said he was unaware of the plans until the end of September, when Potiorek first discussed arrangements with him. As inspector-general, it was assumed that the archduke would be expected to be there. Moreover, he had been given clearance by the emperor for Sophie to come with him and be accorded full honours at military ceremonials.

More recent research has suggested that he was going to Bosnia merely as an observer, that he would not be attending the exercises as inspector general, and that he had no official role in them.

There has been speculation as to why the archduke went to Sarajevo at all. It was not, as has been thought, because he sought acclamation for himself and for his wife as well, continuing to prove that she had an important role as his officially recognised consort, in a gesture that would facilitate her being empress once he succeeded his uncle to the throne. The reason was that Potiorek, who took up his appointment as governor-general in 1911, insisted that he must. Initially, his plan was for the archduke to attend manoeuvres on 26 and 27 June, and also come to Sarajevo. Francis Ferdinand reluctantly agreed to a short informal visit to the city without any official public appearances. This did not satisfy Potiorek, who insisted on something on a grander scale, perhaps to give his status official approval. He would undertake full responsibility for security if the visit was a formal one with planned public appearances, but if the archduke insisted on making it a more or less sudden unofficial visit, he could not promise adequate protection. After consultation on both sides, the archduke reluctantly agreed to spend a few hours in the capital one morning, despite Potiorek's insistence that it ought to be an all-day affair.

The date of the visit remained to be chosen, and Sunday 28 June seemed the only possible choice. Ironically, this was Serbia's national day, a day of national mourning and vengeance, the anniversary of the Battle of Kosovo in 1389 at which the Turks had destroyed medieval Serbia; and, more recently, the first anniversary of vengeance fulfilled, namely, Serbian victory in the Second Balkan War. It was thus a day on which every patriotic Serb vowed revenge against those whom they regarded as unwelcome foreign intruders. As he had lived in Serbia for several years, it is impossible to believe that Potiorek was unaware of the date's significance. On the other hand, he knew that Bosnia was a hostile environment with such a volatile situation that he himself rarely appeared on the streets of Sarajevo, and when he did, he was protected by strict security. It was therefore astonishing that he now assured the archduke he would be perfectly safe in the city on the Serbian national holiday. Rumours of Serb agitation had led to strict security on Emperor Francis Joseph's visit in May 1910 with nothing left to chance, and with the strictest precautions imaginable having been taken prior to and during the occasion. It established a precedent that was completely ignored four years later. When Edmund Gerde, chief of police, objected that arrangements were insufficient, Potiorek dismissed his fears, stating that it was the responsibility of the military and therefore none of his business.

Francis Ferdinand had long known that he was and always would be a target for assassins, and accepted it as something to which he had been born. He disliked being shadowed by detectives and saw it as a necessary evil, especially as their presence had a reassuring effect on his wife. Everyone, he used to say, was in God's hands. In spite of this, he had a premonition that the plans were fraught with danger, and that he might not return alive from Sarajevo. He may have received or been advised of warnings that he would be a marked man. In May, he and Sophie had invited Charles and Zita to the Belvedere for a small family dinner. After Sophie had gone to put the children to bed, Francis Ferdinand took advantage of her absence, turned to Charles and said gravely that he would soon be murdered. In his desk were papers that would concern him, and when it happened, he was to take them. A horrified Charles protested that he must be joking, but Francis Ferdinand replied that he was serious.[13]

Despite his apparent nonchalance at being a target for anarchists, he tried to put forward reasons for getting out of the visit altogether, firstly on grounds of the emperor's health, and after the latter's recovery, because the heat in Bosnia might prove injurious to his lungs. On 7 June, the emperor and heir had a meeting at which he put forward the latter as a valid excuse and asked to be relieved of the trip. The emperor made it clear he wanted the archduke to go.[14] All the same, security precautions were curiously relaxed, and Margutti was aghast to receive printed programmes that week giving every detail of the couple's itinerary. Informing the public, and therefore the terrorists, about every step of the archduke's schedule, he insisted, 'was really playing with fire'.[15] During the emperor's visit in 1910, a complete garrison had lined the streets, several hundred suspected subversives were taken into custody, and many more were placed under temporary house arrest. This time, the troops remained on manoeuvres some distance away, and the only infantry battalion in Sarajevo was kept in barracks.

Francis Joseph planned to leave for Ischl in the middle of July, the routine he had followed for the last few years. He had told his aides that he had no intention of altering the date, as there were so many claims on his attention with state affairs. They were surprised when he announced at less than a day's notice that he intended to go on 27 June. For him to change his plans like this was almost unprecedented. The only reason, they thought, was that he wanted to be away from Vienna when his heir returned from Bosnia, so he would not have to have a face-to-face meeting with him. It seemed that the emperor was still less than well disposed towards his nephew and successor, and had been irritated by plans in the programme treating the duchess of Hohenberg as a future empress. Too old and weary to insist on getting his way anymore, he simply preferred to avoid confrontation.

During the next few days, Francis Ferdinand was noticed to be remarkably ill an ease when the forthcoming expedition was mentioned, as if he had a foreboding of disaster. While he was with the family at their estates at Blühnbach, they took a carriage drive through the park. As they did so, he pointed at the surrounding forest, remarking that all this land would be part of Ernest's inheritance. With hindsight, it was a strange if perfectly true comment.

On 23 June, he and Sophie said farewell to the children and left Konopischt for the last time. One of his final gestures was to call the master of his household, Francis Janaczek, present him with a gold watch in recognition of the service he had given him over the years, and hand him the keys of his desk at the Belvedere, with instructions to give them to Archduke Charles should anything happen to him. Husband and wife were due to travel to Vienna, but at the station, the axle on their private railway carriage burned out and they had to move to an ordinary first-class compartment. The archduke muttered crossly that it was a fine start to their journey. First, their carriage was running hot; then there would be a murder attempt in Sarajevo; and, if that did not happen, next there would be an explosion on board the *Viribus*, the battleship on which he was due to sail from Trieste. Ominously, another failure dogged him before the train left for Trieste, as the lights failed in his private carriage and an apologetic stationmaster had to escort him to his seat, surrounded by flickering candles. He quipped that it was just like being in a tomb.

The military exercises in Bosnia were over by midday on 27 June, and the archduke then sent the emperor a telegram to let him know that the bearing and efficiency of the army corps had been outstanding. Next day, he confirmed, he and his wife would be visiting Sarajevo.

On the morning of 28 June, a day of blazing sunshine and heat, the motorcade of seven vehicles began its progress through the Serbian capital. In the first were local police officers, and in the second were the town mayor and his party. Francis Ferdinand, Sophie, and Potiorek followed in a six-seater behind them with Count Francis von Harrach, the bodyguard and owner of the vehicle. Their programme included a military inspection at the barracks, an official reception in the city hall, and a visit to a folk museum.

Nedeljko Čabrinović and his fellow conspirators from the Black Hand were armed, waiting, and watching. A few minutes after the motorcade had started, Čabrinović noticed a uniformed police detective and asked casually which vehicle was the archduke's car. On being given the answer, he took the bomb from his jacket, aimed it at his target, and missed. The car behind them was wrecked, while the occupants and several onlookers were slightly injured. Čabrinović attempted to swallow his capsule of cyanide, spilt most of it, and was overpowered and arrested by the police as he tried to jump into the river. At this stage, it would have been wise for the police to clear the streets of spectators, search the town, reinforce the security guard around the archduke from some of the large numbers of police and soldiers in the city, and amend the official programme that had been announced in all the newspapers—or else cancel it altogether.

None of these things were done. Francis Ferdinand arrived at the city hall angry and unnerved after this narrow escape. As the mayor began his prepared speech of welcome, the archduke interrupted him, asking what kind of welcome it was for him to pay them a visit and be greeted on his arrival with bombs. Sophie leant forward, whispered a few words into his ear, and touched him gently on the arm. He regained his composure, allowed the mayor to continue, and replied with a terse message of thanks; he then enquired after those who had been wounded, with a view to visiting them later in hospital. He sent a telegram to the emperor, telling him not to take too seriously any reports about the bombing incident as he was unhurt. When told that Čabrinović had jumped into the river but been dragged out and arrested by police for questioning, he remarked cynically that they would be less likely to lock the fellow up than award him a medal.

A change of itinerary was discussed, and when two of the archduke's aides asked Potiorek to alter the arrangements, he asked them testily whether they thought Sarajevo was full of assassins. He reluctantly agreed that a planned visit to the National Museum should be postponed, or even cancelled altogether, as a punishment to the citizens by depriving them of any further sight of the esteemed couple. As the attempt on the heir's life had failed, he thought it unlikely there would be another and assured them there would surely be no harm in driving along the Appel Quay to for the official luncheon at the Konak, his residence. When someone suggested it would be tempting providence to continue through the crowded streets until soldiers from the garrison could be positioned along the route to protect the archduke and his wife, Potiorek insisted it would be unnecessary, and the archduke himself diplomatically refrained from objecting.

The route was suddenly altered, and nobody thought to inform the driver of the leading car until he was ordered to change direction. As he stopped to reverse and the cars came to a halt, another member of the Black Hand, Gavrilo Princip, stood on the corner watching them. He had been thrown into a panic by Čabrinović's failure and was sure he would also be arrested. Now he saw the Habsburg target and his wife before his eyes. Drawing a loaded pistol from his pocket, he walked into the street, aimed, and fired twice. A crowd surrounded him until he was arrested and led away by an officer.

The archduke was sitting bolt upright as a stream of blood spurted from his mouth. Sophie cried out in horror and then collapsed. Harrach thought she had fainted from fear, and then saw that she had been shot as well as her husband. She died almost immediately. Her husband tried to prevent her from falling, as he entreated her to live for the sake of their children until he lost consciousness. Murmuring pathetically 'it is nothing' several times, he slumped forward in his seat. By the time the cars reached the governor's residence, he was also beyond help. Their bodies were carried into Potiorek's suite, where several physicians and surgeons confirmed that they were dead. Two priests were summoned to read the last rites, and the Archbishop of Sarajevo led prayers for the deceased. As they dropped, preparations for the official luncheon in the dining room could still be heard below.

Within hours, a telephone call was received at the Kaiservilla at Bad Ischl. Count Paar had been on duty when tragic news arrived from Mayerling in January 1889, and again from Geneva in September 1898. History was about to repeat itself. Paar's record of the emperor's reaction to the news that 'a higher power has restored the old order which I unfortunately was unable to uphold,' has passed into history, though the phrases may seem too stilted to be credible.[16] The archduke may have besmirched the august name of the dynasty by persisting in a morganatic marriage, and it had always rankled with the emperor. Yet he had never ceased to respect, even applaud his nephew's abilities, and had almost certainly appreciated that he would have discharged his duties honourably and capably once he ascended the throne.

At Chlumetz, Sophie, Max, and Ernest were sitting down to luncheon when their tutor, Otto Stankowsky, was suddenly called away from the table. Returning to the dining room very pale, the children assumed he had bad news about his mother, who was ill. Having decided a relation ought to break the appalling news to them, he said nothing. When their aunt, Henriette, arrived later that afternoon, with tears in her eyes, she told them that there had been an attack on her parents and both were wounded. Little Sophie said they must go and visit them in hospital, and was advised that they should pray for them instead. Not until early next morning did their tutor and their uncle, Carl, Count von Wuthenau-Hohenthurm, the husband of their maternal aunt, Marie von Nostitz, tell them 'the dreadful truth' as gently as they could. 'The anguish was indescribable, and also the feeling of total bewilderment,' Sophie later recalled, 'All our lives, we had known nothing but love and total security. Now, suddenly, we simply couldn't imagine what was to become of us.'[17]

In less than forty years, several European crowned heads, consorts, and heirs had fallen victim to assassins. In addition to Empress Elizabeth in 1898, the list included Tsar Alexander II of Russia in 1881; King Humbert of Italy in 1900; King Carlos of Portugal and his heir, Luis Felipe, Duke of Braganza, in 1908; and King George I of the Hellenes in 1913. King Alexander and Queen Draga of Serbia had been hacked to death alongside several relations, servants, and ministers in 1903, and three years later, royal guests from throughout Europe narrowly escaped a terrorist's bomb in Madrid during the wedding procession of King Alfonso XIII and Queen Ena of Spain. At first glance, the double assassination seemed little more than just another chilling reminder of the risks that royalties had to take when appearing in public.

Many in high places were aware that the deaths would have a major impact on events in the empire, even if they could not foresee the precise course of events over the ensuing weeks. During the height of his powers, Bismarck, who had died in 1898, had warned that it needed 'only some damned foolish thing in the Balkans' to set Europe ablaze.[18] A few thought the assassination of the heir and his wife was 'a happy dispensation for Austria', while others were sure that had they lived, the next emperor would have brought an end to the stagnation of his uncle's regime. Stephanie, now Countess Lónyay, was convinced the couple had been sent to their deaths. She later said that the assassinations could not have happened without the government's knowledge. The emperor, she insisted, was well aware of the risk his nephew was taking, but he 'simply looked on'.[19]

Valerie hurried to the palace so she could be with her father at his time of need, finding him in better spirits than she had expected. Although he spoke of the orphaned children 'with tears in his eyes', when she told him that Charles would 'do well', he looked at her and said solemnly that it was 'one great worry less'.[20] It came as no surprise to her that he was not personally stricken, and too honest to make any pretence of emotion or bereavement, but he felt deeply for his great-nephews and great-niece. For the first time in their lives, he asked for them to be brought to him, and he explained as gently as he could what had happened to their parents. In his old age, he had become increasingly fond of younger members of the family, and now he made an effort to try and spend more time with those who had suffered more deeply than anyone else from this terrible blow.

Archduke Charles was at luncheon with his wife, Zita, and family at Reichenau, about 30 miles south-west of Vienna. After an unusually long pause following the first course, a servant came out, not with a food tray but a telegram from the late archduke's aide, Baron Rumerskirch. Zita saw the colour drain from his face as he opened it and read the message. They had both counted on being called to the throne in perhaps twenty or thirty years of time, always assuming that Emperor Francis Ferdinand, or Francis II, would not find a way to alter the succession in favour of his sons.

Once the worst of the shock had passed, Charles telephoned the emperor's staff in Bad Ischl to confirm the news. The emperor was returning to Vienna at once and Charles, now heir to the throne, was asked to come and meet him at Hietzing, the station closest to Schönbrunn Palace. When they met, according to Zita, who was not actually present but only told later, it was then that the older man burst into tears for the first time since hearing the news. He had been spared nothing, he said as he turned to the young new heir to the throne, 'but at least I can rely on you.'[21]

The coffins of the murdered couple were brought back from Sarajevo to the coast by rail, then by sea to Trieste aboard a battleship, and by rail again to Vienna, on the evening of 1 July. Their close friend, Emperor William II, his brother, Henry, and King Albert of the Belgians were all planning to attend the funeral in person, until it was announced that the emperor's poor health precluded him acting as host to European sovereigns and their representatives. It was followed by advice from the authorities in Sarajevo, who had learnt that about a dozen conspirators had been dispatched from Belgrade to carry out further assassinations, and it would be very unwise for the German emperor to come.[22]

Although not specifically mentioned at the time, there was another pressing reason for not inviting foreign potentates or their representatives. To do so would present them—particularly emissaries from England, Russia, and Italy—with an opportunity to discuss the Austrian response towards Serbia after the outrage. Neither the minister-presidents nor senior ministers of the dual monarchy intended to be drawn on the matter without sufficient time to consider.

The obsequies in Vienna were limited to a single day. Interment would be in the family crypt at Artstetten, Francis Ferdinand's estate in Lower Austria, which he had built five years previously, aware that his wife would never be allowed to rest beside him in the imperial vault beneath the church of the Capuchins. There was to be a lying-in-state and a service in Vienna. Prince Montenuovo, the archduke's nemesis and ironically the product of a morganatic marriage himself, was in charge of the arrangements, and he ordered that Sophie's coffin should not be brought to the service but instead left at the station. The woman who had literally died for her country had no insignia on her coffin, apart from the gloves and fan of a lady-in-waiting. It took the personal intervention of Archduke

Charles, furious at this petty attitude to her even after death, before it was agreed the couple would be honoured with a joint service.

Next morning, the chapel was opened to the public for a few hours. At midday, a large crowd was still waiting to be admitted, but the doors were firmly closed to them. That afternoon, a requiem was held, lasting barely an hour, attended by ministers, generals, members of the diplomatic court, and family, with the emperor remaining impassive throughout. Francis Ferdinand's secretary watched him carefully throughout and saw no sign of emotion or sorrow on his face, as he looked carefully at the mourners present. When the service was over, he turned quickly without another glance at the caskets and left the chapel.

That evening, the hearses bearing the coffins left the Hofburg for their last journey to Amsterdam, with no military parade and only a minimal escort. The minister of war had ordered an ever-reluctant Montenuovo to agree that commanding officers of units in the Vienna garrison might turn out their troops to line the route, and over 100 members of the aristocracy joined the cortege at the Hofburg to walk bareheaded behind the hearses to the station. It was not only out of respect to the murdered heir, but also a snub for the court chamberlain and his third-class burial for the man who was evidently more popular than he ever thought. The coffins reached Artstetten early next morning, after having almost been thrown into the Danube while crossing the ferry. A simple service was held in the village church, attended by the children, the dead man's stepmother, Maria Josepha—who stayed away from court for the next few months in protest at the shabby treatment towards him and his wife in death—as well as Charles, Zita, and other close friends, staff, and servants.

Berchtold, who had been a close friend of Francis Ferdinand and generally one of the less belligerent of the emperor's advisers, decided after the assassination that a tough response, including possible military action against Serbia, was called for. Austria must act decisively to reaffirm her status as one of the great powers. His advice, and growing evidence of complicity by the Serbian government in the shooting, persuaded Francis Joseph that strong measures were called for. The assassination had evidently not been a spontaneous act but a carefully planned operation, involving not only nationalist conspirators but also military officials in Belgrade. He needed to know from Count Tisza how the Hungarians might react to any military confrontation. Tisza agreed that forceful diplomatic pressure on Serbia was needed, but certainly not war.

Francis Joseph was of the same opinion. However, on 2 July, he wrote to Emperor William II, declaring that those responsible in Belgrade must be punished and that Serbia must be eliminated as a political force. The letter was entrusted to a personal envoy, Count Alexander Hoyos, and presented to the emperor in Berlin on 5 July, a week after the murders. The same day that he wrote the letter, the emperor remarked to Heinrich von Tschirsky, German ambassador in Vienna, that the future looked black: '... if only we could detach England altogether from her French and Russian friends!'[23] Hoyos stayed in Berlin for two days of discussion with senior policy makers, and his comments suggested that Berchtold was more eager for war than the emperor. They may have created the impression in Berlin that if a general European war was inevitable, it should come sooner than later, at a time when Germany could rely on the dual monarchy to honour the full terms and spirit of their military alliance. On 6 July, Berchtold was advised that Austria-Hungary could rely on German support in any action taken against Serbia.

On the morning of 7 July, Francis Joseph resumed his holiday at Bad Ischl. During the crises leading to war in Europe in 1859, 1866, and 1870, he had been in regular communication with his generals and ministers. Now, while they were in Vienna discussing Serbian action and what support they might expect from their fellow European powers, he was some distance away with only a small personal staff, presumably acknowledging that the time when he could influence events or maintain control had long since passed. The baton had been handed over to his chief ministers and the military commanders. Nevertheless, the emperor's authority to take the decisive step was essential. Berchtold went to Bad Ischl on 8 July to consult him on the wording of a communique to Serbia, expecting it to be rejected and lead to a localised war. Tisza had already recommended restraint, and on discussing the matter with Berchtold, Francis Joseph agreed that he and his ministers must present a united front. He was sure that there could be no satisfactory solution without a positive guarantee that the Pan-Serbian movement would be suppressed on the initiative of Belgrade.

Berchtold convened a council of ministers on 19 July. They agreed that a *démarche*, a strongly worded statement of view combined with a list of formal demands (not an ultimatum, as generally supposed), should be presented to Belgrade and complied with within forty-eight hours. These included a formal assurance that the Serbian government would condemn and forbid all Serb propaganda directed against Austria-Hungary, publish a declaration to this effect on the front page of the official journal on the following Sunday, express regret that Serbian officers and officials had participated in anti-Austrian propaganda, undertake to suppress all Serbian publications inciting hatred and contempt of Austria-Hungary, and accept the assistance of representatives of Austria-Hungary in stamping out 'the movement against the territorial integrity of the dual monarchy and [taking] part in initial proceedings on Serbian territory against persons accessory to the Sarajevo crime'.[24] If these were not complied with, there would be a suspension of diplomatic relations, providing for mobilisation within a week if necessary. Francis Joseph and Paar discussed the matter at Bad Ischl, both confident that if war was to break out, it would be a local affair, and that Serbia would yield under pressure.

On 21 July, Berchtold presented the emperor with a copy, believed to have been approved and revised by Emperor William and Baron Heinrich von Tschirschky. Two days later, it was sent to the Belgrade government and rejected. When the emperor was informed, he was disappointed but said that breaking off diplomatic relations did not necessarily mean war. After consulting Berchtold, with a heavy heart, he signed the order for mobilisation against Serbia and Montenegro on the evening of 25 July. Later, he saw Katherine Schratt, and told her sadly that he had done his best but feared this was the end. To Hötzendorff, he said that 'if the monarchy must perish, it should at least perish with decency'.[25]

Hötzendorff had already given every impression of wanting to push Austria into war with Serbia. On 22 June, he had warned Berchtold that the dual monarchy was surrounded by hostile powers on all sides; its continued existence depended on a positive deed, regardless of cost, and great sacrifices would have to be made.[26] It was a supreme irony that the assassination of the archduke and his wife should have brought about the 'positive deed', and that they were in a manner of speaking the sacrifice that gave the chief of staff his excuse for war.

Once war was officially declared by Serbia on 28 July, Francis Joseph was assured that Serbia was too weak to resist and would be overrun within two or three weeks. Next day, he issued orders for the court to return to Vienna. In a proclamation to his subjects, he said how much he had wanted to devote his remaining years to working for peace and to protecting his peoples from the burdens and sacrifices of war. This was no longer possible, now that after many years of peace 'the machinations of a hostile Power' had compelled him to take up the sword in order to preserve the honour of his monarchy, 'to defend its integrity and its power, and to stand guard over its possessions'.[27]

9

'Then it will be the end'

Having signed the declaration of war against Serbia, and with it the death sentence of the old order in Europe, Emperor Francis Joseph left Bad Ischl on 30 July. Russia ordered general mobilisation that same day, and twenty-four hours later, the governments of Austria-Hungary and Germany put their armies on a war footing. On 1 August, fighting broke out along Germany's eastern frontier, followed by an invasion of Luxembourg and Belgium. Two days later, Germany declared war on France, and one day after that, Britain on Germany. Reluctantly, and under German pressure, Francis Joseph did likewise on Russia on 6 August. With regret, he took off his Order of St George, presented to him by Tsar Nicholas I in 1849 and which he had worn with pride ever since. He was equally dismayed when Britain joined France in declaring war on Austria-Hungary on 12 August, even though there was no conflict of interest between Vienna and the western powers, the Austro-German alliance apart.

The emperor now ceased to be anything more than the titular ruler of the Austro-Hungarian Empire. There was no possibility of his taking personal command of his troops; he wished he could be with his army, but knew he was too old. All military power was concentrated in the army high command, led by Hötzendorff as chief of general staff. A British correspondent in Vienna at the time noticed that the crowds enthusiastically supported war against Serbia, little knowing what they had let themselves in for. The Austrian papers realised that the man in the street thought the Serbs would be taught a good lesson if only a small fleet of Danube monitors could be despatched to within shooting distance of Belgrade. Defeating a small insolent Balkan state was one thing, but with the Russians on their side, it was a different matter entirely.

As emperor at a time of national conflict, his roles were limited to the customary tasks of administrative routine in studying the papers and reading reports from the battlefronts in Galicia and Serbia. They offered him little encouragement, and he knew that the war was going badly for the dual monarchy. Francis Ferdinand's persistent warnings that the army was grossly inferior to those of the other continental powers, especially in artillery, had been largely disregarded, and the lessons of 1866 never learnt.

As heir to the throne, Charles was attached to the Austro-Hungarian headquarters, but as the next emperor, for him to be posted anywhere where his life might be at risk was out of the question. After a few weeks, he asked for and was given a new role as the link between the emperor and his forces. When not visiting the battlefields, he stayed in Vienna, generally at the Hofburg, receiving copies of all reports submitted by ministers to the emperor himself. The latter devoted part of each day to instructing his heir in the arts of government and the benefit of advice accumulated over his sixty-five years on the throne. Each night or morning, Charles was handed files to deal with. Next day, he reported on the decisions he had taken or recommended, and the emperor would question him on his reasons and comment on his conclusions.[1]

When Charles brought his little two-year-old son, Otto, in to see his great-great-uncle, the boy was a comfort to the elderly sovereign in his last years. Katherine had given the emperor a small casket containing a music box with a toy nightingale emitting the sound. It stood on the study table beside his cigars, and he enjoyed listening to it so much that he would often wind it up for company when he was alone. Otto also loved it, and when he came to visit, the sovereign had to wind it up repeatedly to keep him amused, until he had to suggest that the bird was becoming hoarse from singing too long.[2]

The emperor was also very close to Zita, and during his visits to her apartments, he spoke to her with a candour he rarely displayed to anybody else. He told her he had never really recovered from the events of 1848, and that the work he had carried out for over sixty years since then had been his attempt to impose order on chaos. Believing nationalism was the plague of their century, he had striven to halt its progress. His fears had grown with each passing year, as he saw the empire threatened by nationalist movements and the growth of parliamentary pressure, its future depending 'on alliances with all their uncertainties and weaknesses'.[3] She knew he was horrified by the war, and that he believed that a conflict that had been intended as one of revenge for an act of terrorism in Serbia had become one driven by the worst excesses of nationalism.[4]

Hötzendorff proved an unreliable commander. Despite assuring the Germans that in the event of war with Russia most troops would be sent to Galicia, an undertaking repeated by Francis Joseph to William

II in a personal message, he still ordered maximum concentration against Serbia. It meant needless changes in strategy that cost the dual monarchy dearly, resulting in defeat by Russian forces at the Battle of Lemberg in September. General Potiorek had hoped that Serbia would be vanquished by 18 August, the emperor's eighty-fourth birthday, but by then, his men were no longer making any progress against Serbian troops.

Francis Joseph was kept informed on matters to do with the policy and conduct of the war by General Bolfras, head of the military chancellery. Irritated by confidential reports of desertions from the Czech regiments and dissatisfied with the conduct and strategy of his general staff, he said he wished the Austrian army was under German leadership. When Zita congratulated him in mid-August after news of an Austro-Hungarian victory against the Russians, he told her sadly that in the past, his wars had begun with victories, only to end in defeats. People would say he was old and could not manage any longer, 'and after that revolutions would break out and then it will be the end'.[5]

By now, he spent most of his time at Schönbrunn, and Montenuovo had ordered the park next to the palace to be closed to the public for security reasons. There might be popular demonstrations against the war and perhaps even the imperial crown, and it was important that the sovereign saw or heard nothing of them. The Viennese readily believed rumours of his having become senile or even died, with the news being kept secret from the public. Always frugal in his personal habits, he could do little more in the way of self-sacrifice. From the first day of the war, he had stopped eating white rolls, ordering that only black bread should be served at his table, even when children or guests were invited. Only when he suffered serious digestive problems did his physician persuade him to have white bread, if not white rolls, again. Christmas 1914 at Schönbrunn was a wretched affair, far removed from the cheerful festivities at Wallsee in earlier years, and not even the presence of his daughters and grandchildren could cheer him up.

In November 1914, Italian Minister for Foreign Affairs Antonino Castello, a strong advocate of the triple alliance, had died. His successor, Giorgio Sidney Sonnino, thought otherwise, and the emperor foresaw that Italy would shortly renounce her neutrality and join their enemies. In March, the emperor presided over a ministerial council, for the last time, to discuss the Italian situation. Sonnino was demanding territorial gains from the dual monarchy as the price of continued neutrality, and a treaty signed in London in April offered Italy more land in the event of an allied victory over Germany. Italy declared war on Germany and Austria-Hungary a month later.

This ever-widening conflict was proving very different from the localised campaign against Serbia that Francis Joseph thought he was endorsing with reluctance the previous summer. While Emperor William and his generals intended to continue the war at all costs, by the spring of 1915, he was so keen to prevent further bloodshed that he appealed to Pope Benedict XV to act as a mediator in Berlin, and after this failed, to act in a similar capacity in Petrograd and try to conclude a separate peace with Russia. As part of any settlement, he was prepared to relinquish Bosnia, Herzegovina, and Galicia. Military circles were pessimistic about any initiative from Vienna, as long as the Austro-Hungarian forces remained so committed to the Berlin war strategy, with Austria having long been very much the junior partner in the alliance.

In June, German and Austrian troops won a significant victory by recapturing the strategic fortress of Lemberg on the eastern front. A three-day battle forced a retreat by Russian forces, which had captured it the previous autumn, and with this, Russia's threat to invade Hungary receded. Four months later, Tsar Ferdinand of Bulgaria entered the war on the side of the central powers. Francis Joseph remarked that 'the Bulgarian' was only doing so because he thought they would be victorious. By the end of November, the Austro-Hungarian, German, and Bulgarian armies had overrun Serbia. The emperor acknowledged this had been achieved largely with the help of other powers, particularly under the German leadership that he so admired. Yet the dual monarchy was increasingly dependent on German military and economic resources in general, and gradually losing any independence of action.

On 18 August 1916, the emperor's eighty-sixth birthday was celebrated with a solemn Mass in the chapel at Schönbrunn, followed by a luncheon at the war ministry with the military cabinet. All those present were under no illusions as to the progress of the war, but tried to bring some cheer to the occasion, and joined in enthusiastically when Krobatkin proposed his sovereign's health. Yet Russian successes in Galicia and the Bukovina were bringing the dual monarchy closer to defeat. On 27 August, Romania entered the war on the side of Italy and France and quickly overran Transylvania, much to the shock of the Austro-Hungarian forces. German troops managed to halt the Russian front and the Romanian advance, but at the inevitable price of ever greater German dominance. In September, the emperor had to agree to a joint high command of the central powers, headed by Emperor William and his commanders, Generals Hindenburg and Ludendorff, who were now in complete control of all German and Austrian forces.

The emperor believed his prime minister, Count Stürgkh, was keeping bad news from him about conditions in Vienna, particularly the shortage of basic provisions. He knew that a starving nation would not put up with much more and foresaw that the intensified submarine warfare that Germany intended to pursue would bring the United States into the war on the side of Britain and her allies. Declaring he could not let his empire go to hopeless ruin, he pledged himself 'to end the war next spring whatever happens'.[6] It was a resolution his successor would try his utmost to carry out.

On 21 October, Friedrich Adler, son of the socialist leader and a professional journalist, walked up to Stürgkh as he was lunching in a Viennese restaurant and shot him dead. He gave himself up, was found guilty of murder, and sentenced to prison. Around this time, there were riots in Vienna, with food shops plundered and ransacked, and a crowd marched to the gates of the palace. When the emperor saw them and asked to know what was going on, his valet, Eugen Ketterl, told him reluctantly that they were protesting against lack of food. He learnt that children were being sent home from school, some fainting through weakness, and that his household would not let him drive through the streets, because they wanted to prevent him from seeing queues standing for hours to buy from dwindling stocks still left in the shops. It made him angry that he only found out such details from his valet, instead of being informed by his ministers. Next day, he told them firmly that if people were really suffering from famine and poverty, it was their duty to make peace at any cost, even without consulting their German partners if necessary. Blind adherence to the time-honoured alliance must not take precedence over the welfare of his subjects, otherwise anarchy would break out and revolution could overwhelm the empire while the armies were at war.

Bad news on all fronts left him weary and despondent. Until his last few weeks, he told his entourage that he was well, simply because he refused to be ill. Yet by the autumn of 1916, he could conceal his failing health, a recurrence of bronchitis, no longer. Fits of coughing and fever alarmed his doctors, and early in November, pneumonia was also diagnosed. He coughed badly at night, but the doctors were reassured to find that his heartbeat and breathing were still regular. Margutti continued to bring him his documents each day, and read him some aloud, but thought that he could no longer understand them properly. It was agreed that on 2 December, the sixty-eighth anniversary of his accession to the throne, he would issue a proclamation increasing the rights of sovereignty exercised by Charles, who would subsequently share joint charge of affairs of state with him. Many wondered whether he would live that long.

Despite being advised to go to bed, he insisted he would cough less if he was sitting upright, and he still had work to do. Yet on 20 November, he finally admitted he was very tired and went to bed early, having asked to be woken at his usual hour in the morning. A telegram was sent to Charles, who was in eastern Saxony visiting the eastern front, to warn him the end was approaching. He and Zita returned to Schönbrunn soon before midday on 21 November to find the emperor a little better than he had dared to expect. When told that the heir was accompanied by his wife, he sent a servant to ask them to wait outside for a few moments as he would never dream of receiving a lady in casual attire. As he was getting weaker and had a temperature, he was persuaded to make an exception for once. When they walked into his study, they were surprised to find him still sitting at his desk, studying documents about army recruitment. Putting them aside, he chatted to them about how pleased he was to have received the Pope's blessing and about their recent victories in Romania.

Those around him knew his time had almost come. Reading their thoughts, he admitted that although he had taken the throne in difficult times, he was leaving it under even worse ones, much as he would have liked to spare Charles such a fate. He had every confidence in his young successor: '... he is made of the right stuff, and will know how to cope'.[7] Katherine Schratt found him unable to follow conversation or answer her much of the time. Gisela and Valerie wanted to visit him together, but hesitated in case he should draw the obvious conclusion that they were coming to join a deathbed vigil. Instead, Valerie arrived on her own, staying in the palace so that she and Erszi could be on hand to help look after him, and Gisela came later.

That evening, he finally admitted that the effort was too much for him. At around 7 p.m., he laid his pen down on his desk for the final time and let Ketterl help him to bed. Outside, large crowds assembled near the cathedral, the newspaper offices, and at the gates of Schönbrunn. Soon after darkness fell, Valerie left for the station at Vienna to meet one of her daughters off the train, only to be recalled immediately by one of the palace staff.

Before being left to sleep, the emperor told everyone that he had not finished his work, and he must be woken again next morning at the usual time. Ketterl made him a cup of tea and helped him to sip from it, as he muttered feebly, 'Why must it be just now?'[8] A court chaplain was summoned to administer the last rites, and Valerie read the prayers for the dying. Another fit of coughing turned into the death rattle as the emperor sank back against his pillows. Family, court dignitaries, and others gathered round as his heart gradually ceased to beat. Ketterl dressed him for the last time in his field marshal's uniform, and pinned his medals on his breast. Charles and Zita had been sent for, and arrived just too late. As everyone filed out of the death chamber, nobody seemed to know what to say or do. There was complete silence for a few moments, and then Prince

Lobkowitz, a senior member of Charles's household, walked up to him with tears in his eyes and made the sign of the cross on his forehead as he said 'May God bless Your Majesty!'[9]

One of Charles's first actions as emperor was to respect the close friendship enjoyed by the deceased, and led Katherine Schratt to the bedroom of the deceased where she laid two white roses on his chest. Having last visited him two days earlier, she knew it was probably the last time she would see him alive.

As the rules of court ceremonial laid down that an emperor could not be buried until nine days after his death, his body lay in state at the palace for three days. On 28 November, Emperor William came to Vienna, joining Emperor Charles in prayer beside the bier, but for security reasons did not stay for the funeral two days later. Before the ceremony, the coffin was taken along a route from the Hofburg chapel to the Cathedral of St Stephen, so the citizens of Vienna had a last chance to salute him. A short service was attended by Emperor Charles, Empress Zita, and the four-year-old heir, Archduke Otto, who were joined by King Ludwig III of Bavaria, King Frederick Augustus III of Saxony, Tsar Ferdinand of Bulgaria, and German Crown Prince William. The procession followed the funeral chariot on foot in procession to the crypt of the Capuchin church. Two days later, a final requiem was said in the Hofburg chapel, attended by the imperial family and court dignitaries. It was the sixty-eighth anniversary of the day that Emperor Ferdinand had laid aside the imperial crown in favour of his eighteen-year-old nephew.

The emperor had sometimes said that he was spared nothing. Nevertheless, he had survived to a healthy old age, and unlike several of his closest relations, he died from natural causes. Above all, he had been spared the final downfall of the Habsburg dynasty.

'I renounce all participation in the affairs of state'

When he ascended the throne, Charles was aged twenty-nine. Having been left an almost insurmountable task, his instinct and his conscience told him that the war must be brought to an end as soon as possible. He was as desperate for peace as his great-uncle had been (and, unlike him, would probably have hesitated to sign the mobilisation order two years earlier), and forced completely against his nature to lead his empire in a conflict he detested because of the sheer waste of human life.

Some of the empire's elders were convinced that their cause was already doomed. He valued good relations with Germany, and had the utmost respect for Emperor William, but knew he was no more than a figurehead for the Prussian military establishment, committed against his better judgment to the cause of total victory at any cost. He also appreciated that German victory would mean domination of the dual monarchy by Berlin, and that any major military success by the Germans could mean the end of Austria as an independent power. His accession manifesto, published on the first full day of his reign, began by praising Francis Joseph's 'wisdom, insight and fatherly care' for the peoples of his empire, promising to continue his legacy, and vowing to do everything possible to banish as soon as possible 'the horrors and sacrifices of war', and to win back for his peoples 'the sorely-missed blessings of peace'.[1] The Germans noted that there was no mention of pursuing the war until victory was achieved, only until peace was made.

On the same day that his manifesto was published, he received a visit from Hungarian Prime Minister Count Tisza to discuss Charles and Zita's coronation as king and queen in Budapest. The new ruler, he emphasised, would have no real authority in Hungary until he was crowned, and he recommended that the ceremony should take place on the earliest possible date, 30 December. This would make it too soon for Charles to attempt any constitutional changes, and at the coronation, he would be required to swear an oath that he would not 'alienate the boundaries of Hungary and her associated countries, nor anything belonging to those countries under any title whatsoever'.[2] The status of Hungary within the empire could not be easily changed once he was crowned and sworn in. With the war still in progress and Magyar soldiers comprising a major part of the armies, Charles had no choice but to agree.

The coronation celebrations were attended by their ally, Tsar Ferdinand of Bulgaria, who said afterwards that they were among the most splendid and beautiful he had ever seen. The new king and queen, accompanied by their eldest son, Otto, attended the customary banquet afterwards, but at a time of war, they decided that to host any balls and dances afterwards would be in poor taste, and they returned to Vienna by train immediately afterwards.

Even before the coronation, the new emperor and empress had demonstrated where several of their priorities lay. While the most important thing was to secure peace, they were also fully committed to the cause of ameliorating the conditions under which so many of their subjects lived, and would indeed live once the fighting was over. One of their senior ministers, Joseph Baernreither, was entrusted with plans for a thorough reform of social services throughout the empire. Charles was greatly concerned at the impact that struggling with conditions in the trenches would have on the health of returning young soldiers. Many of them were no more than boys, and if they survived unhurt, they would come back as grown men. He believed a new ministry ought to be created dealing with health, housing, invalid care, and other problems that the nation would face after the end of hostilities. Meanwhile, Zita was much preoccupied with setting up children's charity funding organisations and new youth welfare initiatives.

During the war, the emperor and empress were adamant that there was no question of their living in anything approaching the lap of luxury while the rest of their people were having to put up with increasing hardship. The conservatives at court and their castles in the countryside were astonished when Zita ordered all horses in the royal stables to be harnessed to coal carts to help with deliveries of fuel to Vienna households. Glittering balls at court and great receptions had already been a thing of the past for some time; now white bread and chocolate were struck off the list of essential provisions and, except when foreign dignitaries were invited to lunch or dinner, menus were plain, if not Spartan. The emperor and empress shared simple tastes. On an average working day, the former ate nothing at all between a solid breakfast of warm meat and vegetables and a light supper in the evening. His favourite drink was a glass of Schilcher, a plain table wine from the Burgenland, which he preferred to all the bottles in the palace cellars.

They had not been back in Vienna before long when Zita became aware of a whispering campaign directed against her. Charles's youth and inexperience gave him the appearance of a political dilettante, and her composure and confidence the impression of an intriguer. Born at Pianore Villa in Tuscany, the daughter of a prince who had been duke of Parma until his territory was annexed to Sardinia-Piedmont, she had Italian and French blood and was nicknamed the 'Italian schemer'. It was reported that she was often present at her husband's audiences with his ministers and his military briefings. While she might look as if she was doing nothing more than sitting in the same room sewing, there was suspicion that a royal consort should be there at all on such occasions. Charles wanted her to be kept informed of what was happening in the war, and he ordered that she should be sent a daily report from the military *attachés* about developments at the front. German Ambassador in Vienna Count Otto Wedel sent regular reports about her to Berlin. He told Erich Ludendorff, quartermaster of the German general staff and one of the men in Berlin most responsible for the conduct of the war, that despite her personal charm and friendliness, her popularity was on the wane, and that the people of Austria 'do not entirely trust the Italian and her brood of relatives'.[3]

Zita was not beyond making occasional efforts to influence her husband, but far better at concealing it and keeping her opinions secret than Empress Augusta Victoria in Germany and, more particularly, Empress Alexandra in Russia. She was also very perceptive about the personalities of others. From the start, she had grasped that if they had a friend in Germany, it was Emperor William, but knew he was completely under the thumb of his generals. To her, he was a dreamer who believed in final victory, which was why 'he handed over everything to Hindenburg and Ludendorff'. She also had the wisdom not to try and impose her views on the conduct of the war too strongly. There was one exception early during the reign, when she tried to intercede with Charles on the treatment on captured enemy prisoners. After she had finished speaking, he told her politely that she really must leave these matters to him, as he was the soldier and she was not.[5] It was a lesson she learnt at once, and did not try it again.

Despite this, she did score one tactical victory with some subtlety. On a visit to Homburg in April 1917, she and the emperor were present at a reception attended by the sovereigns with various generals and ministers. While standing with Empress Augusta Victoria, she remarked how it would be if the French and English knew such a meeting was taking place and decided to bomb the building. Seeing the look of horror on the German empress's face, she reassured her by saying she was sure the English would not do so as there were ladies present, followed with the remark that she had been carefully building up to—namely, that she had been told German pilots were bombing the palace of Queen Elizabeth of the Belgians. The incredulous empress called Hindenburg over and asked Zita to repeat the assertion to him. He expressed disbelief and said he had never heard of any such attacks, but he would look into the matter at once. Immediately afterwards, the bombing stopped and the queen was safe.

Even if she did not have any direct influence on how the war was run, she soon had some say in how it ought to end. Almost as soon as her husband ascended the throne, she attempted to use her powers of persuasion in cultivating the idea that it would be possible to abandon Germany in order to achieve it. Her objections to the conflict, like his, were strongly humanitarian. They were based on what she had seen in her visits to the hospitals and heard from those who had served at the front, and political as she was concerned about how the supremacy of Germany would be exercised if they won and what the fate of the monarchical system would be in Austria if they lost, as well as moral, as she believed it was a sin for so many lives to be wasted. To some of her contemporaries, such a way of thinking was both treasonable and heretical. It did not stop her from believing that it was her duty to her husband and to their people to try and exert some influence over him in saving the Habsburg monarchy by leaving Germany, and German dreams of victory at all costs, to face the war alone.

Within weeks of his accession, Charles and his newly appointed foreign minister, Count Ottokar von Czernin, were alarmed if not altogether surprised by the German decision to reintroduce unrestricted submarine warfare. They had received prior warning when Czernin was told during his first official visit to Germany in the first week of January 1917. After several months of stalemate in the trenches of the Western Front the previous year, Hindenburg and Ludendorff were convinced that sinking neutral and enemy freighters alike off the western coasts, thus cutting off food, fuel, and military supplies to England, would bring victory a step nearer.

Believing that military deadlock would eventually lead to an armistice and an acceptable peace treaty between both sides, Charles, Czernin, and Zita were strongly opposed to the idea. They were shocked at the thought of civilian lives being lost, especially those of neutral countries, and suspected with good reason that it would almost certainly hasten entry of the United States into war against them. Nevertheless, the Austro-Hungarian Empire was very much the junior party in the alliance, had no say in the matter, and the emperor and minister recognised that it would be impossible for them to seek a separate peace or abandon the German alliance. To attempt to do so would invite disaster, and there was no way in which they could actively argue against the U-boat campaign as Germany's mind was clearly made up. At this stage, Charles still sought a general peace settlement. Only as a last resort—should Germany refuse to join peace talks whose outlines he had already agreed in advance with the entente—was he prepared to consider denouncing the alliance with Berlin outright and taking Austria out of the war independently. He did in the end agree to this, but only once it was too late to save the dynasty.

At a lunch party on 26 January 1917 during an official visit by Charles and Zita to Emperor William's headquarters, Admiral Henning von Holtzendorff remarked to Zita that she sounded as though she was against the war. She answered that she was, just like every other woman 'who would rather see joy than suffering'. Plainly annoyed, the admiral asked her what did suffering matter, as he worked best on an empty stomach; it was a case of the people tightening their belts and 'sticking it out'. She replied coldly that she did not like to hear such talk when people were sitting at a fully laden table and immediately cut short the discussion.[6]

Like her husband, she abhorred the idea of submarine warfare, dreaded American intervention, and did not trust the Germans. Like her husband, she also realised that the empire could not go through another winter like the previous one, and that the many ethnic and nationalist rivalries in the empire were making it impossible to coordinate a unified military strategy for much longer.

Charles was ill at ease with the Germans, as a nation and in their dedication to victory. Zita recognised that he had problems with the Prussians because he thought they had very little sense of humour, whereas he 'always saw the funny side of anything'.[7] He and Zita's brother, Sixtus, both feared and mistrusted the German hegemony that threatened continental Europe, and to them, the best means of countering it would be a revival of the eighteenth-century Franco-Austrian alliance, leading to a new alignment of Europe enabling Austria to shed her traditional alliance with and be liberated from Germany, a dictatorial, bullying ally, and join a looser, broader alliance with France and Britain. A couple of years earlier, Sixtus had spoken to Pope Benedict XV about his belief that peace could be achieved if only Austria-Hungary could be freed from unwilling reliance on Germany. While he appreciated the virtues of being realistic about their chances, the Pope refrained from trying to discourage him. His next mission was to approach one of the entente powers who might be receptive to a Habsburg peace offer.

Sixtus's Bourbon ancestry carried some weight in France, where there was still some sympathy for the former French dynasty. His sister's status as wife of the next Austrian emperor made him worthy of interest to several French politicians, who were intrigued by the possibility that Austria-Hungary might try and leave the war early, leaving a beleaguered Germany to fight on her own and face probable defeat. One was Charles de Freycinet, former French prime minister, who invited Sixtus to meet him in Paris while on leave from the Belgian army in the autumn of 1916, shortly before the death of Francis Joseph. A subsequent interview with Prime Minister Aristide Briand gave Sixtus hope that some negotiation between Paris and Vienna was possible now that Charles had inherited the throne. On 21 January 1917, the latter contacted his military *attaché* in Switzerland and asked him, in great secrecy, to make contact with Sixtus. Eight days later, Zita's mother, Maria Antonia of Portugal, Dowager Duchess of Parma, travelled by train to Neuchâtel in Switzerland, carrying a private letter from Zita formally inciting Sixtus and their younger brother, Xavier, to come to Vienna incognito for a meeting.

All of them were united in bringing an end to the conflict as soon as possible. Sixtus and Xavier were aware that whatever Charles might say to those in Berlin who only heard what they wanted to hear, he was just as anxious for peace as well. The longer the slaughter on the battlefield dragged on, the more it imperilled the future of the Habsburg monarchy.

After the meeting, Zita learnt of the conditions being made for peace. One was that the provinces of Alsace and Lorraine should be returned to France. Another was the full restoration of Belgian independence and her colonies in the Congo. Austria would guarantee to respect the independence of Serbia and agreed that the Ottoman city of Constantinople was to be ceded to Russia, fulfilling centuries of Romanov ambition to retake the ancient citadel of the Orthodox faith. She took the proposal to Charles and they worked on it together. Charles agreed to all the French conditions apart from the one regarding Serbia. While conceding its right to exist as a separate nation, he would commit himself to nothing that allowed it to expand.

Czernin had regular meetings with Zita to discuss some of the peace proposals, but there were additional suggestions about which she was not informed. He was particularly careful not to anger Germany and made it plain that he would prefer a negotiated peace between all the belligerent countries. Believing that nothing more at this stage was being proposed than the opening of diplomatic channels, he was unaware that Charles had committed himself to the restoration of Alsace and Lorraine. When he was with Czernin, the emperor paid lip service to the theory of the alliance with Germany, but in private, he had already told Zita that he fully agreed they would support France and use all means in their power to bring pressure to bear on their ally. Emperor William dismissed any idea of peace without annexations as out of the question: '... that is something I cannot ask my Army and People to accept'.[8] He was scathing about Charles's secret feelers put out to the entente and plan to 'abandon' his allies, saying that he was working on a policy of 'when I go to the Germans, I agree to everything they say, and when I return home, I do whatever I please.'[9] To a colleague, he had once spoken patronisingly of Charles, 'Who does this young man think he is?' In vain did Charles warn him that they were fighting against a new enemy that was more dangerous than the entente, 'against international revolution which finds its strongest ally in general starvation'.[10]

Count Tamás Erdödy, a Hungarian aristocrat and former childhood playmate of the emperor, was used as a go-between. He took the information in writing to Neuchâtel with him on 21 February, with some of Czernin's thoughts and memoranda personally annotated by the emperor. Sixtus was told to burn everything personally after he had read it, but he felt he needed a copy to show the French as proof of the Habsburgs' commitment to ending the war, so he translated some of the emperor's letters and Czernin's papers into French before destroying the originals. The translations were handed to President Poincaré at the Elysée Palace on 5 March. As Charles had left personal comments on the proposals, the president was sure that this must be something significant. He advised Sixtus and Xavier to accept Zita's invitations to Vienna and keep the government fully informed.

In the last week of March, the brothers donned disguises and came to stay at the count's house in Vienna. After a joyful reunion one evening with Charles and Zita, much of it spent catching up on family news over the last few months, Czernin appeared and Zita discreetly withdrew. Xavier was the only one who left a written account of what was discussed at the meeting. A proposal that Constantinople should be given to Russia was dropped, now that revolution had overthrown the Romanov Empire, and Czernin agreed there was no reason why this should feature in any peace talks. He objected to proposals regarding Alsace-Lorraine, on the grounds that it was not for Austria to promise returning land that did not belong to her to another nation and would provoke anger in Berlin. The discussions ended inconclusively, with the brothers determined to try and win the minister over to their view. They arranged a meeting with Czernin at Erdödy's house on the next evening, 24 March, at which he promised to obey his sovereign's commands, but kept talking about the might of Germany and the harm it could inflict on Austria-Hungary if negotiations went wrong.

Meanwhile, Charles was planning to proceed with or without his minister's approval. With Zita and her brothers present, at Laxenburg

Castle, he drafted a firm written commitment to the conditions of peace that Sixtus could take back to Paris with him, including a promise to stand by a French re-annexation of Alsace and Lorraine. Sixtus left with the document and returned to Paris. While the letter was being written, telephone conversations were being held with Czernin to clarify some of the finer points of diplomatic language. The calls proved that Czernin knew the document was being drafted and inferred that commitments to restoring Alsace and Lorraine were being made despite his reservations. His conversation with the brothers, promising to follow the emperor's lead on the issue, suggested that he knew of their intentions.

Despite this, Czernin was unaware that a central part of France's conditions was that there would be no proposal regarding a possible peace for Germany, and the deal being offered was only for Austria-Hungary. His insistence that they could not resolve the Alsace-Lorraine issue without German involvement had arisen as he believed that Sixtus was bringing a message that accorded with his views on how best to end the war, a series of compromises between all the powers, and with this Charles agreed. Had Czernin known they intended to abandon Germany at the first available chance, he would not have been party to any of the meetings. As a semi-constitutional monarch, Charles had to act with approval of at least some of his cabinet ministers, and in his zeal to broker a peace deal, he was not keeping Czernin fully informed. Charles's repeated requests to get his signature on some of the documents suggests that he saw his minister's role as merely a constitutional requirement that could be used to later legitimise the imperial initiative in negotiating with an enemy power. He had always understood that peace with the allies would come at the price of abandoning the traditional alliance with Germany.

Earlier in March, riots in St Petersburg, the abdication of Tsar Nicholas II, and the Bolshevik Revolution had all signalled the beginning of the end of Russia's participation in the war, although it was not until the Soviet government signed the Treaty of Brest-Litovsk with Germany almost a year later that one enemy power on Austria's eastern front was removed. Even so, prospects were still ominous for the Austro-Hungarian Empire, especially as the Italian campaign was a heavy drain on military resources. Charles decided to launch a new peace initiative, and as his brothers-in-law, Sixtus and Xavier, were also passionately in favour, he contacted French President Raymond Poincaré and Briand. Both Poincaré and Briand assured him they did not seek the destruction of the Habsburg monarchy, only the return of Alsace-Lorraine, in German hands since the end of the Franco-Prussian War in 1871, and unconditional guarantees of Belgian and Serbian independence. Pressed by Sixtus, Charles agreed to these conditions in writing, assuring them that he would take up the issue of French demands for the restoration of their territory with his allies. However, with a change of administration in France, Briand's government resigned on 20 March. The new prime minister, Alexandre Ribot, proved less enthusiastic about negotiating with Charles and his representatives for a separate peace.

The advent of the new provisional government in Russia, which was less committed to pursuing the war, convinced the German High Command that a victorious end to the war was in sight. Czernin was still adamant that any separate peace by Austria would amount to betrayal of their ally. Charles knew time was running out, especially now that the United States of America under President Woodrow Wilson had declared war against Germany on 6 April (although not on Austria-Hungary until 7 December). He feared that a combination of hunger and war weariness would lead to revolution. When he told Emperor William that if an all-out U-boat campaign was launched and the Americans entered the war all hope would be gone, William assured him confidently that it would be done so swiftly that England would be brought to her knees before America had a chance to do anything.

Later that spring, Sixtus returned to Vienna for more talks, which ended without agreement. Discussions in Paris with British Prime Minister David Lloyd George were amicable enough but merely underlined the fact that no immediate response to Charles was possible. While he was eager to consider any proposals to secure peace, he emphasised that Italy would need to be consulted first, and as she had entered the war largely with hopes of territorial gains at Austrian expense, the plan seemed doomed. In May, Charles wrote to Sixtus reiterating his opposition to any form of peace in which Italy did not participate, but expressing hope for an Italian peace overture in which she might be prepared to compromise on her annexation demands. The understanding reached in Austria-Hungary with France and England on many essential points, he was sure, would help them to overcome any remaining obstacles in the way of an honourable peace.

In Germany, there were also demands for an end to the war, and on 19 July 1917, a Peace Resolution was passed in the *Reichstag*, calling for a peace of understanding and permanent reconciliation of peoples, and emphasizing that forced territorial acquisitions and political, economic, and financial oppressions were irreconcilable with such a peace. It was ignored by the German High Command on the grounds that the empire should redouble the war effort, as the only way to avoid social and political revolution was by total victory.

No progress was made during the summer. In September 1917, Ribot was succeeded as French prime minister by Paul Painlevé, who only held power for two months before his resignation brought Georges Clemenceau to office. The latter, a fervent nationalist, was resolved to achieve victory over France's enemies just as strongly as Germany sought total conquest on the other side.

In April 1918, after the treaty of Brest-Litovsk signed by Germany and Russia took the latter out of the war, Czernin delivered a speech criticising Clemenceau, whose policies, he said, were the major obstacle to the quest for peace. A furious Clemenceau retaliated by publishing Emperor Charles's letter of 24 March 1917. The German reaction was one of utter fury. Charles and Zita, 'the Italian schemer', were bitterly denounced. To add to Charles's woes, he had ignored a recent warning from his personal physician, Dr Delug, that he needed a complete rest of at least six weeks on account of his general health and in particular his heart. At such a crucial time, any prolonged period of taking it easy was plainly out of the question, but physically he was about to pay the price.

On 13 April, he awoke, feeling extremely unwell after what was later diagnosed as a mild heart attack. Czernin was demanding to come and see him at the palace in order to sign a document, which he called a 'Declaration of Honour' to be sent to Austria's allies, denying that any of the letters to Sixtus had been issued in an official capacity, and that at no point in any discussion had Belgium or Alsace-Lorraine even been mentioned. He needed it, he insisted, for himself and the honour of his family.[11] His reaction was extraordinary, not least his overwrought declaration that it would be all over for Austria, Germany would invade, he would take over as the 'Iron Chancellor', and then a few minutes later that if the document was not signed he, the emperor, and the empress would all have to commit suicide.[12]

From his sickbed, Charles had no choice but to sign the patently dishonest letter in the hope of calming him down. Even then, he was so worried as to what Czernin might do next, he feared he could be a danger for the whole empire, and phoned the President of Police in Vienna to ask if he could be arrested before he did anything drastic. He was told politely that the police could only arrest him after he had done something. Charles had already resolved to dismiss his plainly unstable minister but was saved the trouble. Czernin's position was no longer tenable, and after an ill-tempered cabinet meeting a day later, he offered his resignation, which was immediately accepted.[13]

Yet the result of recent events was to force Austria-Hungary into even more dependence on her German ally, and even more irrevocably committed to Berlin's war strategy. Emperor William was mortified to learn that his ally had willingly endorsed France's demand for the return of Alsace-Lorraine. Worse still, his capitulation before the entrenched power of German and Magyar opinion had destroyed whatever faith the entente powers ever had in the young emperor, and with it the monarchy's chances of salvation through a compromise agreement with the western powers. German military victory would come at a cost; Charles and Czernin's successor, Stefan von Burián, were asked to agree to a political alliance, a military treaty, and a customs union if they were to dispel doubts raised by the Sixtus letter. Germany now planned to dominate Austria-Hungary economically as well as politically.

On 11 May, Charles visited Emperor William privately at Spa. It was a cordial enough occasion on a personal level, but Ludendorff was also present, and clearly intent on taming his independently minded and dubious ally. A secret joint memorandum, with Charles in no position to argue against, was drawn up. It provided for the construction of a close, long-term treaty between both emperors; the conclusion of a special military pact, or *Waffenbund*, between the empires; and a programme of coordination with the ultimate aim of creating a single, unified economic bloc. The result was effectively to reduce Austria from an independent nation to a semi-vassal state of Germany in all but name. General Arz von Straussenberg, Charles's chief of staff, was obliged to sign with barely any discussion a document providing the main instrument of German domination. Any hopes that Austria may have had of attempting to broker an independent peace with the western powers were now null and void.

By late summer, the tide was turning against Germany and her allies. It would have been little consolation to Charles had he known in June 1918, when the last great military gamble of Hindenburg had brought German troops to within 40 miles of Paris, Marshal Joffre said gloomily on behalf of the French that if only they had made terms with Austria the previous year, Germany would have had to give in. A few weeks later, the situation was reversed. On 8 August, the Fourth British Army opened the Allied offensive in the Battle of Amiens and, in a speedy advance on the first day of fighting, took around 16,000 soldiers from the defending German Second Army as prisoners. The once ever-optimistic General Ludendorff lost his nerve, declared at supreme headquarters that it was the 'black day' of the German army, and at last admitted that their cause was lost.

On 14 August, Emperors Charles and William met at Spa to discuss the implications and faltering progress of the war. It was the last occasion on which they ever came face to face. All they could do was have futile discussions on renewing the search for peace. Yet Charles was under no illusions. He had been deeply concerned for a long time, knowing how much the morale of his people depended on blind faith that their German ally would work miracles on the battlefield. The German High Command had made so many boasts about imminent victory, at least until 'black day', and Charles had received very different reports from his own liaison officers. He always suspected that when the German collapse came, it would be sudden, and the news of 8 August came as no surprise.

Even after the emperors had parted for the last time, Charles suspected his senior ally would continue to hope for some degree of success in stemming the enemy advance, and perhaps try to prolong the war—and their chance of winning—through a neutral intermediary such as Queen Wilhelmina of the Netherlands. Charles and Burián decided to issue a joint public appeal to the world for a peace conference. Issued in Vienna on 14 September, it was too vague and too general in its phrasing, and any hopes that it might persuade the authorities in London, Paris, and Washington to call a conference were quickly dashed.

On the evening of 25 September, a telegram was brought to Charles announcing that the Bulgarians had surrendered. Faced with the threat of Allied armies marching on Sofia, Tsar Ferdinand had decided to sue independently for peace. This, in the words of Burián, 'knocked the bottom out of the barrel'. The triple alliance of the Austro-Hungarian, German, and Ottoman empires that Bulgaria had joined two years earlier, and thus made a quadruple alliance, had now ceased to exist. Ferdinand, whose notorious touchiness, lack of tact, and unreliability had made him one of the least popular sovereigns of his time, saved his dynasty by abdicating in favour of his elder son, Crown Prince Boris. As he still owned two castles in Austria and six in Hungary, he considered that one of these would be the right place to settle in exile, and he travelled on the royal train towards Marchegg in Lower Austria. It was a singularly ill-chosen time. Count Berchtold was sent to intercept the train and, on orders from Charles, to order him to return to his native state of Coburg. Bulgaria, the smallest and weakest member of the Central Powers' alliance, was nevertheless responsible for guarding the south-eastern flank of the Austrian Empire.

It was a sign that defeat was looming for Germany and her allies. On 4 October, the three remaining members of the Central Powers' alliance, Austria-Hungary, Germany, and Turkey, each sent parallel notes to President Wilson, calling for an end to the fighting and the opening of peace talks on the basis of his Fourteen Points. The message from Vienna reminded him of its previous attempts to do so.

On 9 October, Germany received a partial response from Washington, demanding the immediate evacuation of France and Belgium as a precondition for any further progress. Berlin promptly accepted these conditions, but Austria received no response. As a result, one week later, Charles issued a manifesto promising to turn the empire into a federal state 'in which each racial component shall form its own state organisation in its territory of settlement [and] shall guarantee to each national state its independence'.[14] He honoured his coronation oath by stipulating that these new reforms should in no way effect the integrity of the lands of the sacred Hungarian crown, but the time had passed.

Another twelve days after that, the Habsburg empire started to come apart. The Czech national council assumed control of the governor's residence in Prague and declared Czechoslovakian independence from Austria and Hungary. The Croats, who had previously been so loyal to the monarchy, followed likewise a day later. During the next few days, they were followed by the Slovenians, the Poles in the northern part of the empire, and the Ukrainians and Romanians on the eastern frontier. Hungary, hoping to save her own borders in the event of defeat, had her cabinet formally absolved of their oaths of loyalty to the House of Habsburg so they could at least claim to be behaving honourably when they abandoned it. Next day, all Hungarian troops serving in the Habsburg military received an order from their new government to lay down their arms and return home. Within less than a week, the Austro-Hungarian Empire had entered history.

Charles then renounced the German alliance, something he had longed to do almost ever since ascending the throne. On 26 October, he sent a telegram to Emperor William, informing him as a 'dear friend' and despite his closest fraternal and friendly feelings of brotherly alliance that it was his duty 'to save the existence of those states whose fate has been entrusted to me by divine providence'. Within the next twenty-four hours, he intended 'to seek a separate peace and an immediate armistice'. His conscience as a sovereign would not allow him to do otherwise.[15]

While crowds roamed the streets of Vienna, the emperor spent sleepless nights waiting by the telephone for news from the Allies of a peace offer. Still he clung to the belief that it must surely come, even though it was clear the Allies could not make an offer unless every major power, including the United States, supported it. President Wilson had made it clear that he did not look kindly on the defeated monarchs and their persistence, as he saw it, of obstructing nations that sought their independence and self-determination.

By this time, conflicting accounts of the fate of the Romanovs in Russia had spread throughout Europe as part of the Bolsheviks' policy to spread misinformation about what had actually happened. Some accounts said accurately that ex-Tsar Nicholas, his wife, and children had all been killed, while others intimated that only the former sovereign was dead, and his wife and children had been moved to a place of safety. Nevertheless, the fear of knowing what a revolutionary mob could do once unleashed was enough to strike fear into the hearts of Charles and Zita, who were already parents of five small children under the age of six and knew that what had almost certainly happened to the imperial Russian family at Ekaterinburg could inspire other revolutionaries to attempt the same elsewhere. There was unrest in Vienna, but some troops and garrisons were loyal to the emperor and empress, with little if any of the sheer hatred felt in some quarters in St Petersburg against their sovereign and his consort less than two years before. A number of admirals, generals, and courtiers called at Schönbrunn to pay their respects to Charles. In particular, Hungarian Admiral Nicholas Horthy vowed tearfully that if they were forced to abdicate, he would never rest until he had restored His Majesty to the thrones of Vienna and Budapest.

The long-feared moment could not be postponed indefinitely. In Germany, on 9 November, Imperial Chancellor Max von Baden declared that Emperor William had no alternative but to abdicate and leave Germany forthwith, settling in neutral Holland where he would spend the rest of his twenty-two years. Charles and Zita received the news without surprise. Zita later recollected succinctly that for a ruler they knew was 'under the thumbs of his generals', it appeared a natural end to his reign: '... they had just packed him off'.[16]

Two days later, Chancellor Heinrich Lammasch and Minister of the Interior Edmund von Gayer visited Charles with a document that would technically remove him from office. Both politicians presented it to him as renunciation rather than abdication. By signing it, he would agree to set aside his political rights on a temporary basis, relinquishing his power but not his crown until the peace settlement had been negotiated, with the monarchy going into abeyance rather than being abolished. Technically, it was a manifesto agreed jointly by members of the last imperial cabinet and socialist ministers of the new republic, requiring the emperor to recognise in advance any new constitution that might be decided upon and to relinquish all participation in affairs of state. It proved to be the last action by the last ruler of the Habsburg dynasty.

As they entered the emperor's study, Lammasch was overcome with fear that Charles would not sign, and thus encourage a civil war led by the more hard-line socialists as had happened in Russia. He therefore grabbed Charles and begged him to sign it. Charles angrily shook him off. Zita did not fully understand what they were proposing and assumed the document was outright abdication. She flew into a rage, and according to Charles's secretary, Karl Werkmann, revealed her Bourbon ancestry as she declared with emotion (as had the Tsarina the year before) that a sovereign could never abdicate. He could be deposed by force, but she would rather fall at her husband's side than abdicate. Their son, Otto, would be left, and even if all of them were killed, there would still be other Habsburgs.[17] When the ministers continued to press her, she insisted that their people would be reduced to the utmost misery: 'Who will be concerned for the country if it is no longer led by the one man who is above party interests, and cares only for the future of all?'[18]

When the emperor explained to her that it was merely a temporary renunciation, she calmed down. As he was convinced that this was the best solution for Austria as regards negotiating with the Allies, and seeing there was no way to rule in defiance of political consensus without the army and without the empire his family had ruled over for centuries, he signed. In the declaration to which he put his name, he declared that ever since his accession, he had always tried to lead his people out of the horrors of a war for which he was blameless. Not wishing to stand in the way of anybody, he now undertook to recognise in advance whatever decision German-Austria might make about its future form. As the people had taken over the government, 'I renounce all participation in the affairs of state.'[19]

Officers from the Swiss and Dutch embassies arrived at the palace with an offer to escort the emperor and his family safely out of Austria and to guarantee his private properties, but Charles politely refused on the grounds that since he had not been deposed, he considered he and his family had no reason to leave Austria. Instead, they would move to their private hunting lodge at Eckartsau, north-east of Vienna. That day, the emperor, empress, and their children went to the chapel to pray that they would return to the palace one day. After going to say goodbye to those who were left, they were driven away and arrived at their lodge without incident.

On 13 November 1918, Charles issued a proclamation relinquishing his right to take part in Hungarian affairs, and releasing all officials in the country from their oath of loyalty to him. He deliberately avoided using the term abdication, in the event that the people from either of the old dual monarchy nations should suddenly recall him.

'An eminently lovable if weak man'

Although everyone had managed to leave Schönbrunn safely, it was a miserable and isolated Christmas for the former emperor and empress and their children. Zita checked through their remaining food supplies, including a trunk full of small gifts they had used on state visits, so they had some presents to give the servants. A Spanish influenza pandemic was sweeping much of the world, and all the children fell ill. At one stage, Charles Ludwig, not quite eighteen months old, was close to death. Charles, aged beyond his years by strain and heart trouble, was also very unwell. He got up from his bed for Christmas Eve, but was still so weak that he had to remain seated in an armchair while presents were being distributed, and he was quite exhausted afterwards. That same night, they heard that toasts to the emperor were being drunk by loyal supporters throughout Vienna. As the new German-Austrian chancellor, Dr Karl Renner, summed it up, the new state was 'a republic without republicans'.

Matters were not improved by unfounded rumours about the state of Charles and Zita's marriage, evidently put about by those seeking to undermine their reputation for political ends. In February 1919, reports in the American press stated that he was contemplating seeking divorce from his wife 'on the grounds that she assisted Italian victories'.[1] Those who knew the couple well, and knew of their utmost dedication to the Catholic faith, recognised this for the empty slander that it was.

By the spring of 1919, Charles was under pressure to leave Austrian soil or give up the crown altogether. In Vienna, the socialist movement had a formed a pro-communist Red Guard, and there were fears for the family's safety. Prince Sixtus feared the revolutionary government in Austria might fall into the hands of the extreme left, and recalling the imprisonment and callous murder of the former Tsar Nicholas II, his family, and their last remaining servants, it was imperative that the family should be escorted to safety. He asked for and was granted an audience with King George V at Buckingham Palace. Talking to the king and queen, he pointed out that the fate of the Romanovs had set a chilling precedent, especially if a communist revolution was to break out and succeed in Austria as well. The king had never ceased to reproach himself for not offering the tsar and his family sanctuary after his abdication. Even though Charles had been emperor of an enemy power, albeit a reluctant one, a sense of monarchical solidarity impelled the king to try and do the honourable thing, and he promised to do what was necessary.

Lieutenant-Colonel Edward Strutt, a Catholic aristocrat who had been a student in Austria and a friend of Archduke Francis Ferdinand, was entrusted with the task of getting the emperor and his family out of Austria without delay and into Switzerland at once. An ever-cautious official at the War Office in London warned him that 'the British Government can in no way guarantee your journey'.[2] At his first meeting at Eckartsau with the former sovereign and his consort on 17 March, Strutt was impressed with the emperor whom, he thought, had 'a good-looking, well-bred but weak face', and that his appearance described his character, 'an eminently lovable, if weak, man, by no means a fool, and ready to face his end as bravely as his ancestress, Marie Antoinette'.[3]

When the possibility of their going to Switzerland was mentioned, Charles was adamant that the new republic that had been proclaimed in Vienna had no right to exist as it violated the terms by which he had signed his act of renunciation, and under such circumstances, he could not leave. Strutt had been advised that both partners in the new Austrian coalition government, one being the conservative and formerly pro-monarchist Christian Socialist party, had decided to confront their former ruler with three alternatives. If the emperor and empress would abdicate all rights, they could live in Austria as private citizens; if he refused to abdicate, he would be exiled; if he refused to abdicate and leave, he would be interned. Strutt was then shown in to meet Zita, whom he considered felt the humiliation of their changed circumstances more deeply than her husband did.

After further discussions with Zita, Strutt proposed that her husband should leave without abdicating, and perhaps return home once the situation had calmed down. The long-term future of republicanism in Austria did not look assured, as many were unhappy at the prominence given to the radical left in the new regime, and the idea that the revolution had somehow created a republic without republicans captured something of the government's fragility. Zita proved more difficult to persuade than her husband, as she strongly disliked the idea of being seen to flee.

At length, Strutt produced the reason against which there could be no argument, namely that a dead Habsburg was no good to anyone, whereas a live one with a family could be. At this, she smiled and said she would do all she could to help. They would leave under Strutt's orders and management, and trust that the emperor would not have to abdicate. He agreed, reassured by the knowledge that that he was leaving as emperor and 'not as a thief in the night'.

As chancellor of German-Austria, Karl Renner had confirmed on behalf of the new government that the former sovereign could go into foreign exile without having to assent to a formal deed of abdication, now changed his mind—or else submitted to pressure from colleagues—and declared that he must renounce all rights to the throne before leaving Austrian soil. Strutt was prepared for this and had come up with a clever ruse. He had secretly drafted and signed a message to the War Office on an official British Mission telegram form to the Director of Military Intelligence in London, saying that the Austrian government had refused permission for the emperor's departure unless he abdicated, and instructing him to give orders to re-establish a blockade and stop all food trains from entering Austria. He himself was not empowered to send such a message to his superiors, but Renner was not to know. When he read the message, he admitted defeat, reluctantly admitting that the emperor could go without conditions.[4]

On 25 March 1919, after attending Mass for the Feast of the Annunciation, the imperial family boarded the imperial train, reassembled in all its glory with three saloon carriages, a kitchen and a dining car, two luggage trucks, and an open truck for the cars for one last journey. As the family left the church, an emotional crowd burst into the imperial national anthem. Veterans gathered to escort their former ruler to the train, and as it pulled off from the platform, Strutt heard a groan of dismay emanating from those who had come with sadness to watch them leave.

After travelling across Austria, at Feldkirch, near the border with Switzerland, Charles signed a document known to posterity as the Feldkirch manifesto, revoking the documents he had signed renouncing his participation in the affairs of government and declared he had been unlawfully deposed. It was to demonstrate that he had merely undertaken an act of voluntary self-banishment and was claiming that the republican government was 'null and void' for him and for the House of Habsburg. A decision was taken not to publish it, but to distribute it privately to select recipients such as the Pope and King Alfonso XIII of Spain.

On the following afternoon, they crossed the Swiss border. For a few weeks, they settled at Château Wartegg, near the Austrian border, and in May, they moved to Villa Prangins on Lake Geneva.

In April 1919, the Austrian parliament had passed legislation officially expelling the Habsburg dynasty and confiscating all the official property via the Habsburg Law or, in full, the 'Law concerning the Expulsion and the Takeover of the Assets of the House Habsburg-Lorraine'. Charles was banned from returning to Austria again, while Otto and other male members could only do so if they renounced all claims to the throne and accepted the status of private citizens. Towards the end of the month, a four-man delegation representing the republics of Czechoslovakia, Yugoslavia, Poland, and Austria, each of which had confiscated all the fixed assets of the dynasty and frozen its bank and investment holdings abroad, offered a final comprehensive settlement of 184 million Swiss francs to be paid on condition that the former emperor undertook not to set foot in the territories of the old monarchy for twenty-five years, and to renounce all sovereign claims for himself and his heirs. To this, he, or a spokesman representing him, replied that any question of renunciation could only be settled between himself and his peoples, and the Habsburg crown 'could not be treated as an object of barter'.[5]

Meanwhile, his last Hungarian prime minister, Mihály Károlyi, had taken advantage of the situation to proclaim a Hungarian democratic republic with himself as provisional president.

In March 1919, he was ejected from office by a Social Democratic-Communist coalition that made Hungary a Soviet republic, under the Communist leader Béla Kun. His harsh rule alienated large numbers of people, and he was overthrown in August. Archduke Joseph Augustus took power as regent for Charles, but he was forced out when the Allies refused to recognise him. In March 1920, Nicholas Horthy, the last commander of the Austro-Hungarian navy, was named regent of Hungary. He assured Charles of his unimpeachable loyalty, of his conviction that a monarchical restoration would happen before long, and that he would report fully to him on all Hungarian political developments. Charles trusted him, having little choice to do otherwise.

As the months passed, it became clear that Horthy was not so loyal after all. Maybe he was reluctant to relinquish his powers; perhaps he was genuinely concerned that a return to monarchical government would antagonise nationalist elements in Hungary and elsewhere and leave the country as an international pariah. Whatever his reasons, his support for the emperor rapidly faded. When Charles sent proclamations to Budapest by secret courier for the regent to publish in his name, they were received and then ignored. Specific orders to him to prepare the way for the king's return, and to suggest a suitable time, were answered evasively, if at all. The regent also ordered the officers of Hungary's armed forces to swear him a personal oath of allegiance, with no mention of either king or dynasty. For

Charles, this was the moment at which he realised that Horthy's fidelity was open to question.

In spite of this, he had never given up hope of reclaiming his throne and regarding Hungary as the more promising constituent part of the former empire, with or without the regent's support. By September 1920, he felt he could not afford to delay his return beyond the following spring. One factor that encouraged him was the apparent support of France. As prime minister before resigning in 1917, Aristide Briand had been an ardent supporter of Emperor Charles's initiatives for separate peace talks. Four years later, and back in power, he was one of several politicians who saw the value of countering Italian ambitions in the Balkans and in having a friendly Catholic nation in the Danube as a balance to Protestant Prussia. Others in France disliked Horthy's military dictatorship in Hungary and were convinced that a liberal monarchy in its place was to be preferred, and they also distrusted the radical leaders in the new Czechoslovakian republic. Much as he might try and deny it later, or at least play down his supportive role, Briand was for a while seen as a determined and friendly sympathiser towards the Habsburg monarchy. Nevertheless, he was reluctant to make any French partisanship too public until or unless Charles's restoration bid succeeded. His policy was at best a vague statement of non-intervention pending the outcome of Charles's mission. If it was a failure, he assumed, the rest of the world would be none the wiser as to his encouragement.

Despite warnings by many of his supporters and by Horthy himself that the time was not right, Charles believed the mere news of his reappearance and the regent's willingness to hand over power would revive Hungarians' love for their king. He was also sure he could count on French support if he succeeded, and that there would be no armed intervention from Hungary's neighbours. At the time, the Hungarian diet was dominated by two right-wing monarchist parties, the Christian Union and the Smallholders.

Shorn of his moustache and carrying a forged Spanish passport, Charles arrived undetected at Szombathely on 26 March and went to the palace of Count János Mikes, a prominent legitimist. The news spread quickly among local loyalists, and by early next day, Charles had assembled a few trusted individuals who would form part of his privy council, if all went according to plan. One was Colonel Antal Lehár, younger brother of the composer Franz, who willingly placed himself and his soldiers at Charles' disposal, but warned him of the risks. When Charles contacted Prime Minister Count Pál Teleki to talk about details, he found him unenthusiastic. Teleki thought he should have waited and urged him to return to Switzerland, otherwise civil war might break out. Eventually, they agreed that Charles should seek an urgent meeting with Horthy.

He arrived at the palace unannounced early on the afternoon of 27 March, as Horthy was about to sit down to dinner. Both men withdrew for a private and, at times, emotional discussion lasting for about two hours. In thanking him for his services, Charles said the time had come for him to hand over his powers as regent back to him as king of Hungary. Horthy told him he was courting disaster, and he implored him to leave at once and return to Switzerland before it was too late and the Powers learnt of his presence in Budapest. Charles said he had come too far to turn back empty-handed, and he spent the rest of the meeting trying to break down Horthy's resistance. Having made numerous concessions and offers, including that of military commander-in-chief and naval admiral-in-chief, both of which were refused presumably as the regent recognised that to retain power allowed him to take any post he wanted, he reminded Horthy of his pledge of loyalty at Schönbrunn in November 1918, and of the sworn oath of obedience to the Habsburg monarch from which he had never been released. Horthy reminded him that this oath was no longer valid, having been superseded by one he had more recently sworn to the Hungarian nation. Shocked by his recalcitrance, an exhausted Charles insisted that he was abiding by his position and would give him five minutes to think it over. During this break, Horthy reiterated his fear of civil war and bloodshed, said that the king's cause would not prevail, and was sceptical about his claim of Briand's assurances of support.

A tentative three-week truce was reached. Horthy expected Charles to leave Hungary and either march on Vienna or retire to Switzerland, while Charles hoped that, whether he invaded Austria or not, Horthy would work towards his restoration within the three weeks. Charles was driven to Szombathely, but it was clear that he had little support, with some calling for his immediate expulsion or even arrest. When Horthy contacted the French high commissioner in Budapest to ask what the truth was with regard to Briand supporting his return, he and the French government insisted they had never encouraged the former emperor to return to Hungary, Briand publicly denying a deal had been made.

With the army still loyal to Horthy, Charles reluctantly left by train on 5 April, reaching Hertenstein in Switzerland the next day. His proclamation that he was Hungary's rightful ruler appeared in Hungarian newspapers on 7 April, and a perturbed Swiss government placed strict limits on his political activity. Charles thought the Great Powers would not oppose a restoration and that, despite the vote in parliament, the Hungarian people longed for his return. In fact, there were no demonstrations of support in Hungary, except on a small scale in the traditionally royalist western counties. While he was treated respectfully at Szombathely, officers wavered in their support and the people generally treated him with indifference. Teleki resigned on 6

April, and eight days later, Horthy appointed as his successor Count Stefan Bethlen, a legitimist at heart but one who understood there was very little if any chance for a restored monarchy at the time.

Meanwhile, Charles and Zita were warned they would not be welcome in Switzerland much longer. They were forbidden to return to Prangins or their old castle at Wartegg, and with the approval of the local canton, they stayed for a while at the National Hotel in Lucerne. With their limited means and the lack of privacy, it could only be a temporary measure. Shortly afterwards, Hertenstein Castle, where the rent payable would be about half the cost, was offered to them. Charles took a lease on it for one year, but the Swiss authorities made it clear that he had outstayed his welcome.

Negotiations were conducted with representatives of several different countries throughout Europe. In London, Foreign Secretary Lord Curzon firmly denied any truth in reports that they were willing to admit the family to England. Sweden followed likewise, and overtures were made to King Alfonso XIII and his foreign minister, the marquis of Lema. The Spanish government said they could not be expected to guard the former emperor as Napoleon had been at St Helena, and moreover, if the family came there, Charles would need to provide financially for the family. It was taken for granted that any ex-sovereign would either have left his country or former dominions with adequate wealth or be in a position to redeem valuables against cash if necessary, an assumption that would before long prove very wide of the mark. At Curzon's behest, the British legation in Budapest approached Horthy with a view to providing an allowance for their crowned king. On his behalf, Foreign Minister Count Nicholas Bánffy made it clear that any allowance would be conditional on Charles converting his act of renunciation in 1918 into a formal and unqualified abdication. A similar response came from the Czech authorities in Prague.

At the end of August, the Swiss federal government relaxed their previous restriction and agreed the emperor could stay there with no new time limit, but with the proviso that they would maintain more control over his movements. He had given his word to inform the Swiss parliament forty-eight hours before leaving for any other place of exile. However, in the light of his refusal to assent to a binding abdication, he regarded Hungary as home, not exile, and unbeknown to anyone else, he was planning a second return.

In June, two months earlier, the legitimists in Hungary, sensing that the government was taking no real action to bring Charles back, launched a major offensive against Horthy and Bethlen, with the aim of creating favourable conditions for Charles' return. In response, Horthy and Bethlen began secret discussions with legitimist leaders in early August, and the government made tentative preparations for Charles' return. At the end of the month, the Hungarian minister in Paris informed leaders at the French foreign ministry that his return was unavoidable due to public opinion. On 21 October, after reaching agreement with the legitimist leader Andrassy, Bethlen made an ill-timed speech to moderate legitimist aristocrats, declaring that the exercise of royal power was not just a right but a necessity; that Charles' declaration of November 1918, forfeiting participation in the conduct of state affairs, was made under duress and therefore invalid; and that he would begin negotiations with the Great Powers at a suitable time to persuade them to support a restoration. He also denounced attempts to restore Charles by force.

The previous day, after dictating his will, Charles flew from Dübendorf airport, landing surreptitiously in western Hungary. The legitimist officers had assured him that on his entry into Budapest, no sort of opposition was to be expected, and a restoration would be welcomed. Not having been warned that some of Hungary's most prominent legitimists had no knowledge of the plan, he thought this was the long-awaited cry for help from the Hungarian nation, believing that the people needed him. Considering himself under no obligation to consult Horthy, whose cabinet Charles maintained was without legitimacy, he named six members of what he intended to be his provisional government.

On the afternoon of 21 October, while Bethlen was speaking, a group of armoured trains was being prepared by troops led by Major Gyulai Ostenburg, one of Charles's most faithful supporters, in response to a message that communist agitation had broken out in Budapest and Horthy had called for Charles' help to restore order. In a stirring mass ceremony, the battalion took a traditional oath of loyalty to Charles as king of Hungary and king of Bohemia, and it left for Budapest late that morning. It stopped at each village station so the local garrison and public officials could take the oath of loyalty and groups of loyal peasants could chant 'long live the King!' as they paid homage to the royal couple.

This delay allowed Horthy to marshal his supporters again. When he was informed later that day, he was shocked that Lehár and Ostenburg had betrayed him. Bethlen presided over a cabinet meeting next morning and announced that force would be used if necessary. Claiming that Hungary would be destroyed, Horthy insisted on a declaration of loyalty from his army. Many of the senior officers preferred to reserve their own judgment, and most of those whose units were stationed along the royal armada's path found it impossible (or inexpedient) to be disloyal to Charles. The highest military officers in Budapest were reluctant to assume command of the government forces, and several refused. Furthermore, of the twelve commanders of battalions outside Budapest, only two reported that they could reach the city ready for combat by the 23rd, and the Budapest garrison was thought unreliable. The entente powers reaffirmed their opposition to a restoration while the Czechoslovak, Yugoslav, and Romanian ministers declared that such a move could lead to bloodshed.

On the morning of 23 October, Hungary seemed on the brink of civil war. Charles's army was on the outskirts of Budapest, where martial law had been declared, while Czechoslovakia was reported to be mobilising. Horthy was advised that if the legitimists launched an attack, the defence would collapse. The first indication of things to come came at 9 a.m., when legitimist General Pál Hegedűs came to Kelenföld station and was persuaded to see Horthy and Bethlen in person. The latter denounced Charles's 'mad enterprise', while Hohler, at the British legation in Budapest, informed Hegedűs that Britain would neither recognise Charles as emperor nor permit the return of a Habsburg on the throne. He warned that Budapest, if taken by royal troops, would be occupied by the Czechs within a week. Hegedűs had trusted Charles's assurances that the Great Powers backed him, but now denied any association with him and offered to broker an armistice.

After meeting the general, Horthy went with Gömbös to the station and urged the troops to hold their position. There was a small amount of firing from Charles's army and a few of the soldiers defending the government were killed. The skirmish was a surprise to both sides, particularly Charles's troops, who had assumed that any march on Budapest would be bloodless. Charles then reluctantly agreed to armistice negotiations and a truce until the next morning. He was called on to order his troops to lay down arms and turn over all war material, with his safety guaranteed if he abdicated in writing. In return, all supporters of the restoration, except agitators and ringleaders, would be pardoned. As Charles read these terms, shots rang out and a stray bullet hit the royal train; he was quickly bundled into a carriage, which began to move westward. The indignant Lehár and Ostenburg called for a fight to the last drop of blood, but Charles saw that enough was enough and he ordered the train to stop. From his window, he shouted that he forbade any more fighting as it would be senseless, and then dictated a surrender order. The government moved decisively to restore domestic order, and some prominent legitimists were arrested. Charles and Zita were placed under military custody in a monastery in Tihany. Apart from refusing to abdicate, Charles complied with every request made of him.

Despite a clear victory for Horthy, Czechoslovakia and Yugoslavia refused to demobilise the army divisions they were deploying on Hungary's borders. On 29 October, Edvard Beneš, who was prime and foreign minister of Czechoslovakia, wrote to the French government threatening mobilisation against the country within a week unless the Habsburgs declared their forfeiture of the crown or were otherwise debarred, the Little Entente, a newly-formed alliance of Czechoslovakia, Romania, and Yugoslavia, did not participate in disarming Hungary, and Hungary showed no willingness to compensate Prague for its troop mobilisation. Although Horthy initially objected, later that week, in order to forestall any threats of invasion, Bethlen informed Hohler that Hungary was placing herself entirely in the hands of the Great Powers and would conform to their decisions. He gave assurances that legislation would be passed excluding the Habsburgs, and Horthy urged his officers that all insurgents should be evacuated from western Hungary, or else he would do so himself.

On 4 November, Bethlen presented the National Assembly in Budapest with a bill that abolished the sovereign rights of King Charles. The Pragmatic Sanction of 1723, guaranteeing hereditary succession in Hungary to the Austrian ruling house, was declared invalid, and the nation now had regained the right of choosing its king. The kingdom of Hungary thus theoretically remained a monarchy, leaving the way open for a Habsburg to be elected king in the future.

Meanwhile, the Swiss government had ordered Charles and his family to leave the country. Where they were to live was a subject of dispute for several days, until the French suggested the Portuguese island of Madeira. The western powers jointly proposed this solution in Lisbon and the Portuguese government accepted, after being assured that the cost of maintaining them would not be their responsibility.

On 2 November, a British gunboat, HMS *Glowworm*, left Hungarian waters with the royal family aboard. They were lodged in what was intended as a temporary basis, in a large suite of rooms at Villa Victoria, an annexe of Reid's Palace Hotel in Funchal. How much money they would require to live in Madeira was an issue, for the family had little money they could call their own. Colonel Francis Mildmay, an English Conservative MP, was particularly annoyed at how they had been treated. In a letter to Lord Cecil Harmsworth, at the Foreign Office, he pointed out that the powers who had signed the Treaty of Versailles 'banished the Emperor to this far island and then washed their hands of him, not troubling as to how he was to live'.[6] In November, an ambassadors' conference in Paris decided to grant them an annual allowance of 100,000 gold francs, or £20,000 on British money. As neither the victorious entente powers nor the defeated enemy nations, including the now separate Austria and Hungary, could be expected to contribute to the fund, it was suggested that the four 'succession states' of Poland, Czechoslovakia, Yugoslavia, and Romania should be responsible for paying it to Portugal as the administering government. They flatly refused, and the Great Powers likewise declined to offer any advance. The latter were equally averse to any funds reaching the family from private sources, as they feared that to do so might create a risk of Charles following the example of Napoleon a century earlier, leaving Madeira and attempting to regain his throne a third time.

In desperation, Charles and Zita turned to Bruno Steiner, an Austrian lawyer who had been entrusted with selling a collection of Habsburg family jewels brought out to safety in Switzerland in November 1918. He was tracked down by Zita's brother, Xavier, in a Frankfurt hotel, living under an assumed name. Astonished at being discovered, he promised to fetch the remaining items from the Frankfurt bank where they were in safe keeping the next day, and then promptly left the hotel that night under cover of darkness. A lawsuit was lodged against him, but the family neither saw him nor the jewels again.[7]

Every move by the family, no matter how innocent, was closely watched. In January 1922, Robert, the second son, needed an operation for appendicitis. While he was convalescing at a nuns' hospital at Zürich, Zita came to visit him. The allies suspected she might take the opportunity to launch another bid for the Hungarian throne, and it was reported that the former empress and queen, 'who is considered an intriguer and the real head of the Habsburg restoration movement in Europe, must be watched closely during her short stay in the country in order that the Swiss government may not be fooled for the third time by her intrigues'.[8] Every day she was at the hospital, all the nuns leaving the building had to submit to a search by police and lift their veil to prove none of them were the empress in disguise.

Charles's meagre funds were now almost exhausted, and in February 1922, his equerry, Count Joao d'Almeida, appealed to the entente powers that had brought him to Funchal against his will and who were thus obliged to provide financially for him. A reply was sent requesting details of his present resources, including all 'real and personal property'. Lengthy legal and financial negotiations would doubtless have followed, but these were forestalled when a local landowner offered to put a villa, the Quinta del Monte, at the family's disposal without charge. Situated in the hills, it would have been ideal as a summer home, but in the winter months with cold, wet, and foggy weather, it was no place for a man of his poor health. When they moved in, the house itself was damp, smelt of mildew, had no electric light, and water only on the first floor, the only fuel being green wood that smoked incessantly. Zita was expecting another child in May and calling a midwife or doctor would place a heavy burden on their dwindling funds.

On 9 March, Charles, Otto, and Adelheid took the long walk to Funchal and back to buy some toys for Charles Ludwig, whose birthday it was next day. It was warm and sunny in the town, but chilly as they returned. Charles had come without his coat and caught a cold. Five days later, he took to his bed with fever and a severe bronchial cough. As every penny had to be saved, they did not call a doctor until a week later, and by the time he was examined, one of his lungs was already affected. Zita sat constantly by his bedside, managing on very little sleep herself, while two of the children also had pneumonia and another a severe gastric infection.

On the afternoon of 30 March, his mind was wandering, and he became convinced that a group of Austrians had arrived at the villa to see him. Although Zita gently humoured him and said she would go and talk to them, he said that they had come a long way, and he tried to prop himself up against his pillows to receive them himself. He told her that he had to suffer like this, 'so my peoples can come together again.'[9] At another moment, he asked her sadly why they would not let them go home.

On the morning of 1 April, he was steadily losing ground, as she recited short prayers into his ear. Just before midday, he whispered to her, 'I love you so much.'[10] A priest came and administered Holy Communion, and softly muttering the name of Jesus, the last emperor died.

The Imperial Survivors

Empress Zita and Crown Prince Otto

The new *de jure* emperor of Austria and king of Hungary was their eldest son, Otto, aged nine. After his father had died, Zita told him that his father was now sleeping the eternal sleep, and that 'you are now Emperor and King.' Although he was now head of the House of Habsburg, Otto chose to retain the title of crown prince.

Shortly after the death of Charles, King Alfonso XIII approached the British Foreign Office via his ambassador in London. They agreed to let Zita and her seven children, with an eighth on the way, move to Spain. A warship was sent to Funchal to escort them to Madrid, and they were offered the use of Palacio Uribarren at Lekeitio in the Bay of Biscay. After staying there for nearly eight years, the family of nine moved to Ham Castle, in the village of Steenokkerseel near Brussels. The property was rented from Marquis Jean de Croix, a French nobleman, and he installed running water and central heating before they took up residence in January 1930.

Here they held a ceremony on 30 November 1930 to mark the eighteenth birthday of Crown Prince Otto. To mark the occasion, a ceremony was held on the large drawing room of the castle attended by about eighty people, including family and close relatives, household officials, and magnates from the old monarchy. They gathered as Zita, clad in the mourning dress that she had worn since the day of her husband's death and would do so until her own but this time relieved by the diamonds of the Star Cross Order, proclaimed his birthday, and that in accordance with the ancient family rulings of Habsburgs, he 'has become, in his own right, sovereign and head of that reigning house'. The man who was now *de jure* ruling emperor—until then, his mother had theoretically been regent—had just begun a degree course at Louvain University. For him, there was 'no sudden sense of responsibility', and he asked her to continue as head of the family until his studies were due to finish four years later. Although he took more of a hand in family matters after that date, to him it was 'a fifty-fifty partnership' in which she would always ask him before taking any action herself with regard to anything involving them.[1]

Under legislation passed shortly after the fall of the empire, Charles had been banned from returning to Austria again, while Otto and other male members could only return if they renounced all claims to the throne and accepted the status of private citizens. This was repealed in 1935 and the family were given back their property. That same year, Otto graduated from university with a degree in political and social sciences, after completing a thesis on 'the right, born of usage and of the peasant law of inheritance, of the indivisibility of rural land ownership in Austria'. Mindful of his status as emperor in theory, if not in practice, in 1937, he wrote that he knew the overwhelming majority of the Austrian population would like him to assume the heritage of his beloved father one day, and that they had never been given a chance to vote for or against a republic. An unremitting opponent of Fascism, he called it an 'un-Austrian movement' that promised everything to everyone, while aiming for the most ruthless exploitation and subjugation of the Austrian people.

He enjoyed considerable public support in Austria, and during the years before the Second World War, over 1,600 municipalities in the country named him an honorary citizen. He was generally thought to be more popular than his mother. According to American journalist John Gunther, in a book published the previous year, a monarchical restoration would have been more likely as long as the return of Otto did not automatically mean the return of his mother as well, 'to say nothing of hundreds of assorted and impoverished Habsburg cousins and aunts, who would flock to Vienna'. Even more of an obstacle, he noted, would be the opposition of Czechoslovakia and Yugoslavia, the states most likely to fear that their people might want to rejoin a recreated monarchy.[2]

After the *Anschluss* or German annexation of Austria into Germany on 12 March 1938, which he called 'a dreadful day' in his diary, Otto was sentenced to death by the Nazi regime, with orders that he should be executed immediately if caught. His personal property and that of the House of Habsburg were confiscated and not returned after the war. The so-called Habsburg Law relating to the expulsion and takeover of the assets of the house that had been repealed was reintroduced by the Nazis, while the leaders of the Austrian legitimist movement, Otto's supporters, were arrested and several were executed. While he was unable to save everybody, he still played a major role in helping around 15,000 Austrians, many Jewish, to flee the country at the beginning of the Second World War.

With the German invasion of Belgium on 10 May 1940, Zita and the family became war refugees, left France, and fled to Portugal. The American government granted them exit visas on 9 July, they sailed to New York later that month, and later settled in Quebec. Otto also left Europe for the United States, and from 1940 to 1944, he lived in in Washington, DC. In 1941, Hitler personally revoked the citizenship of the whole family, who were now stateless. Throughout the rest of the war years, Otto and his brothers were in regular contact with President Franklin D. Roosevelt and the federal government, and he persuaded the Americans with some success to halt or at least restrict the bombardment of Vienna and other Austrian cities. Robert became the Habsburg representative in London, while Charles Ludwig and Felix joined the American army, and Rudolf smuggled himself into Austria in the final days of the war to help organise the resistance.

In the summer of 1943, Rear-Admiral Lord Louis Mountbatten visited Zita in Quebec. To her astonishment, he informed her that an idea was being aired on London that after the war, Otto might be offered the crown of a truncated Germany.[3] As she herself was by far the most prestigious living link with the old Europe, as well as the woman who would in effect be the Queen Mother, he was interested to hear her views. When Otto was told, he felt sure it was the idea of Winston Churchill, whom he knew to be seeking a post-war solution to Germany's problems 'on a monarchical basis'. He believed the duke of Brunswick, son-in-law of Emperor William II, who had died in exile in Holland two years earlier, was also being considered as a logical choice as head of the Guelph line that had provided the Hanoverian Kings of England, and a natural choice. Zita was unconvinced by the idea.

Later that year, at a conference at Teheran, Churchill met Roosevelt and Joseph Stalin, the Russian leader, and suggested the concept of a Danubian regional grouping to offset the influence of an isolated Prussia after the war. He believed that Bavaria, Austria, and Hungary should form part of a broad peaceful confederation. Otto feared that Austria was in danger of becoming a Soviet satellite state, something a Danube federation that was effectively a restoration of Austria-Hungary would have prevented. It was opposed by Stalin, who insisted that Austria and Hungary should remain separate states, and Roosevelt, who thought post-war Germany should be split into five separate zones in addition to another two controlled by the United Nations. With this, any lingering thoughts, remote as they were, that King Otto of the Habsburg dynasty might rule or at least reign somewhere in Europe finally withered and died.[4]

Empress Zita celebrated her fifty-third birthday on the first day of peace, 9 May 1945, and she spent the next two years touring the United States and Canada, raising funds for war-ravaged Austria and Hungary. After returning regularly to Europe for the weddings of her children, she moved back permanently to Luxembourg in 1952, so she could look after her mother, Maria Antonia, until her death at the age of ninety-six in 1959. She then went to live at Zizers, Graubünden, in Switzerland, ironically in the same country that had once demanded the departure of her husband and herself from its borders.

Otto also returned to Europe at the end of the war, and he lived for some years in France and Spain. Still effectively stateless, in 1946, he was issued with a passport of the Principality of Monaco, thanks to the intervention of Charles de Gaulle, President of France. In May 1951, he married Princess Regina of Saxe-Meiningen. She was closely related to two royal dynasties outside Germany, as a second cousin of Queen Beatrix of the Netherlands and a great-great granddaughter of Princess Feodora of Leiningen, half-sister of Queen Victoria of England. They lived at the Kaiservilla, in Pöcking, Bavaria, and had two sons and five daughters. In May 1956, he was at last recognised as an Austrian citizen by the provincial government of Lower Austria, on the condition that he accept the name Dr Otto Habsburg-Lothringen. This only entitled him to a passport valid in every country but Austria. He had already submitted a written statement in February 1958, undertaking to renounce for himself and his family all privileges formerly entitled to them as members of the House of Habsburg. This did not satisfy the requirements of the Habsburg Law, stating that Otto and the other descendants of Charles could only return to Austria if they relinquished all royal claims and accepted the status of private citizens.

In a declaration dated 31 May 1961, Otto accordingly renounced all claims to the Austrian throne and proclaimed himself 'a loyal citizen of the republic', a move made only after much hesitation and for purely practical reasons. Interviewed in 2007 on the occasion of his approaching ninety-fifth birthday, he admitted he had done so under duress and not by choice. Nevertheless, it was sufficient for the Austrian administrative court to issue him and his wife a Certified Proof of Citizenship on 20 July 1965. Despite opposition from the socialists to the heir of the deposed dynasty being welcomed back, after the People's Party won a majority in the national election in June 1966, he was finally given an Austrian passport and could thus visit his home country again four months later for the first time in forty-eight years.

Zita spent her final years quietly with her family. The lifting of restrictions on the Habsburgs entering Austria had initially applied only to those born after 10 April 1919, thus preventing her from attending the funeral of her daughter, Adelheid, in 1972. A further easing allowed her, like her eldest son, to return to a very different Austria after an absence of several decades.

In a series of interviews published in March 1983 with the *Kronenzeitung*, a Viennese tabloid newspaper, she asserted that the deaths of Crown Prince Rudolf and Mary Vetsera at Mayerling were not a suicide pact, but murder by French agents after he had uncovered a conspiracy to overthrow Emperor Francis Joseph. If he had murdered his mistress and then killed himself, she insisted, he would certainly not have been granted a Christian burial. It overlooked the fact that he had been granted a dispensation after death as he was supposedly insane at the time, although any communications between emperor and Pope at the time on the subject had long since been missing, presumably destroyed. When a friend asked her whether this could be proved, she dictated a reply to confirm that no proofs could be found, but stood firm by her statement that the Vatican would never have granted a Christian burial for a person guilty of such deeds, and it had done so because he had been murdered. No evidence supporting her claim was discovered, and a belief existed that she intended to see the stain of disgrace and suicide on the Habsburgs wiped away in order to promote the beatification of Emperor Charles for his valiant efforts to bring about an early end to the First World War. Even her family regarded her pronouncements as misguided, not to say embarrassing. Foremost among them was Otto, who gently refuted her allegations in the press. Nonetheless, Charles was beatified by the Catholic Church at a ceremony conducted by Pope John Paul II in October 2004.

Now in her nineties, Zita's remarkable health was at last beginning to fail. She developed inoperable cataracts in both eyes and became almost blind. Her last big family gathering took place at Zizers, in 1987, when her children and grandchildren joined her to celebrate her ninety-fifth birthday. There would be no more major parties or celebrations during her lifetime, for during the summer of 1988, she developed pneumonia, and later that year, she became bedridden.

Early in the new year of 1989, she told the family that the end could not be far off. They came to her bedside and took turns keeping vigil until she died on 14 March, aged ninety-six. Her funeral was held in Vienna on 1 April, and the government allowed it to take place on Austrian soil on condition that that the cost was borne by the Habsburgs themselves. Her body was carried to the imperial crypt under the Capuchin Church in the same funeral coach she had walked behind during the funeral of Emperor Francis Joseph in 1916. She had asked that her heart could stay behind at Muri Abbey, in Switzerland, where the emperor's heart had rested for decades, so that in death, she and her husband would remain by each other's side. When the procession of mourners arrived at the gates of the Imperial Crypt, the herald who knocked on the door introduced her as 'Zita, Her Majesty the Empress and Queen'. It was a fitting farewell to the woman who had indeed been the last empress in Europe.

Austria had to repeal much legislation violating human rights, notably a ban on members of the Habsburg family entering Austria, before being admitted into the European Union in 1995. After a report by the Organisation for Security and Co-operation in Europe (OSCE) criticised the prohibition against members of the Habsburg family running for the Austrian presidency, this provision was also withdrawn in June 2011 by the Austrian parliament. The law still remains in force but is considered largely obsolete, with the exception of the confiscation of the family's property in force since 1938.

After the end of the war, Otto became an ardent supporter of a united Europe. From 1973 to 2004, he was president of the International Pan-European Union, and between 1979 until 1999, he served as a Member of the European Parliament for the Christian Social Union of Bavaria party. At one session of the body in 1988, he was involved in an altercation with the Reverend Ian Paisley, a fiercely anti-Catholic representative from Northern Ireland. Pope John Paul II had just begun an address to the parliament when Paisley began shouting and held up a poster reading 'Pope John Paul II Antichrist'. Otto snatched Paisley's banner and, with the help of other members, ejected him from the chamber.

Otto's wife, Regina, died in February 2010, aged eighty-five, at their home in Pöcking, Bavaria. Surviving her by seventeen months, he died at the age of ninety-eight on 4 July 2011, also at home. Had the Austro-Hungarian Empire still been in existence, after succeeding his father to the throne, he would theoretically have reigned for a remarkable eighty-nine years. In accordance with Habsburg family tradition, his body was buried in the family crypt in Vienna, and his heart in a monastery in Pannonhalma, Hungary. Although the eldest of the family, he had outlived all of his siblings except one, his brother, Felix, who passed away two months later at the age of ninety-five.

Archduchesses Gisela and Valerie; Crown Princess Stephanie and Archduchess Elizabeth

The two surviving children of Emperor Francis Joseph enjoyed relatively quiet lives during the years left to them after their father died. Gisela and Leopold had two sons and two daughters. She was deeply involved in various social and political issues and founded charities to support the poor, blind, and deaf, taking an active role herself. Because of her tireless work and patronage of several institutions, she was known as 'the Good Angel from Vienna' and was patron for a number of institutions. During the First World War, she ran a military hospital in her home while Leopold served as a field marshal on the Eastern Front. When Charles had to renounce the throne and leave his former empire, she and Leopold remained in Austria as private citizens and she took part in elections for the Weimar national assembly early in 1919, the first to be held in Germany at which women above the age of twenty were allowed to vote. She and Leopold celebrated their golden wedding anniversary in 1923. He died in 1930, and she died on 27 July 1932, at the age of seventy-six.

Like Gisela, Valerie threw herself wholeheartedly into charity work during the First World War and became known as the 'Angel of Waldsee'. In 1900, she had become a patron of the Red Cross, for which she founded hospitals and raised large sums of money, and she was of several other similar organisations. During the war, she created a hospital barracks in the castle itself and helped to care for the wounded. A lifelong devout Catholic, she also spent much time supporting religious charities. During the last years of his life, she helped Gisela to look after their father. In her spare time, she enjoyed writing plays, poetry, and painting, mostly flowers. With her passion for the theatre, she was a keen supporter of the Burgtheater in Vienna, and she was often seen attending new productions.

Between 1892 and 1911, she gave birth to six daughters, of whom the youngest lived for only a few hours, and four sons. Her marriage to Francis Salvator was happy at first, but less so with time. He had various affairs, including one with the Viennese dancer Stephanie Richter. In 1914, she gave birth to his son, Francis Joseph, and he acknowledged the child as his. Though deeply hurt by his infidelity, she faced it stoically, confiding her true feelings only in her journal.

After the war, like her sister, she accepted the end of the Habsburg era without demur, and signed the necessary documents, renouncing all rights toward the same for herself and her descendants. She and her husband were also allowed to keep their home and possessions and lead private lives. Almost since her mother's assassination, she had accepted that the dynasty's days were numbered. At the start of the new century, she had recorded in her diary her 'perhaps highly treasonable lack of belief in Austria's survival and its only salvation in the house of Habsburg'. After her father's reign, 'let come what is most likely to bring about new and better conditions.'[5]

In the summer of 1924, she fell ill with lymphoma. Gisela visited her during the last days and found her well aware of the severity of her condition. She was fully aware of and totally resigned to dying, even almost 'joyfully anticipating her impending departure' to the extent that it seemed as if recovery would be a disappointment. She died on 6 September, aged fifty-six, and was buried in a crypt behind the high altar at the parish church in Sindelburg, Austria. Several thousand people followed her coffin to its resting place. Her widower morganatically married Baroness Melanie von Riesenfels at Vienna on 28 April 1934, and died on 20 April 1939, almost five years later.

Crown Princess Stephanie, who became Countess Lónyay, and her second husband settled in his castle, Orosvár-Rusovce, and later Archabbey, Hungary. She was always determined that her side of the story during her unhappy life in Vienna should be heard. With the aid of ghost-writers, she published her memoirs, issued in Germany in 1935 as *Ich sollte Kaiserin werden* and in England two years later as *I was to be Empress*. Some thought them too frank, and when her daughter, Elizabeth, led a successful campaign to have the book banned in Austria, Stephanie responded by cutting her out of her will. She and the count lived in Austria for a while, but at the end of the Second World War, they fled to Pannonhalma, Hungary, after the advance of the Soviet army. She died there on 23 August 1945 and he survived her by less than a year.

Elizabeth, who had married Prince Otto von Windischgrätz in 1902, had three sons and a daughter. Like her husband, she had several extra-marital affairs, and they obtained a judicial separation in 1924. Due to legal complexities, they were unable to divorce until 1948, after which she married Leopold Petznek, a social democratic member of the Austrian *Landtag*. He died in 1956 and she on 16 March 1963.

The Hohenberg Family

After the assassination of their parents, Sophie, Maximilian, and Ernest, the children recognised as the first orphans of the First World War, were initially taken into the care of their maternal aunt and uncle, Marie and Prince Jaroslav von Nostitz, their father's close friend and shooting partner, and they were subsequently raised by their step-grandmother, Archduchess Maria Theresa.

During the trial of the men accused of both murders at Sarajevo, the only defendant to express remorse was Nedeljko Čabrinović, who apologised to their children. Princess Sophie and her brothers were told about Čabrinović's apology and wrote to him, saying they had heard about his expression of contrition, and his conscience could be at peace because they forgave him for his role in what had happened. Sophie and Max signed it, but Ernest refused. It was delivered personally to Čabrinović in his cell by the Jesuit Father Anton Puntigam, who had given the last rites to their parents. On 23 January 1916, the children were told that Čabrinović had died.

When Charles came to the throne in November 1916, he was anxious to make amends for what the Hohenberg children had suffered. Among the earliest actions of his reign, once he had dismissed Montenuovo from service, was to approve a new coat of arms for the Princely House of Hohenberg, a distinction Francis Joseph had refused to sanction a year earlier. Charles not only approved the new coat of arms, but also raised Maximilian from the rank of prince to duke and established the House of Hohenberg as part of the empire's hereditary peerage. He also eliminated the annual payment they received from the imperial treasury in exchange for a grant of two income-producing estates, the old hunting lodges of Radmer and Eisenerz, and their surrounding forests of timber and game. It was a far-seeing move designed to ensure that, no matter what the fortunes of imperial Austria might be in the future, the three children would not be financially dependent on them. After the war, their properties in Czechoslovakia, including Konopiste and Chlumetz, were confiscated by the Czechoslovak government. They then moved to Vienna and Artstetten Castle.

In September 1920, Sophie married Count Frederick von Nostitz-Rieneck, and they had three sons and a daughter. Her husband died in 1973 and they were predeceased by their two elder sons, Erwein having died in a Soviet prisoner of war camp in 1949 and Francis four years earlier while fighting on the Eastern Front.

The elder son, Maximilian, Duke von Hohenberg, had been excluded from succession to the Austro-Hungarian throne, to which his father was heir presumptive at the time of his death, and also from inheritance of any of his father's dynastic titles, income, and properties, although not from his personal estate nor from his mother's property.

Although Sophie had been raised from princess to duchess of Hohenberg by Emperor Francis Joseph in 1909, Maximilian did not inherit a title on her death in 1914. Anxious to try and make amends, on 31 August 1917, Emperor Charles granted him the dukedom on a hereditary basis, simultaneously raising him from Serene Highness to Highness. If rumours were to be believed, he might have been given a more prestigious post as well. Six years earlier, it had been rumoured in France that Germany was planning to install him as imperial governor of Alsace-Lorraine at a later date. After the initial story had circulated, no more was heard of the idea.

Maximilian graduated with a law degree from the University of Graz in 1926. Later that year, he married Countess Maria of Waldburg, and they had six sons. They lived in Vienna, and he divided his time between working as a lawyer and managing the family estates. Not being a true Habsburg, he was neither banished nor his properties confiscated under Austria's law of exile passed in April 1919. His brother, Ernest, who had inherited his father's love of outdoor life and took a particular interest in forestry, married Marie-Thérèse Wood in May 1936, and they had two sons.

In 1938, after the *Anschluss*, both brothers were arrested by the Gestapo after making anti-Nazi statements, and their properties in Austria were confiscated by Nazi authorities. They were deported to Dachau concentration camp where they were chiefly employed in cleaning the latrines, which they did cheerfully and maintained good relations with fellow prisoners. Maximilian was released after six months, while Ernest was transferred to other concentration camps, released in 1943 and then compelled to stay at Artstetten Castle; the *Reich* authorities also expropriated the family's other properties in Austria, but they were returned in 1945 after the liberation of Austria. The residents of Artstetten elected Maximilian as mayor, with the concurrence of the Soviet occupation authorities, and he served two five-year terms. Yet both had suffered physically from their years of imprisonment and never enjoyed good health afterwards. Ernest died at Graz in March 1954, aged forty-nine, and Maximilian at Vienna in January 1962 at the age of fifty-nine. Both were buried at Artstetten Castle. Sophie outlived her brothers and died in October 1990 at Thannhausen, aged eighty-nine.

Endnotes

Chapter 1

1. Morton, F., *A Nervous Splendour* (Little, Brown, 1979), p. 41.
2. Crankshaw, E., *The Fall of the House of Habsburg* (Longmans, 1963), p. 14; Taylor, A. J. P., *The Habsburg Monarchy 1809–1918* (Hamish Hamilton, 1948), p. 22.
3. Taylor, *op. cit.*, p. 46.
4. Ashley, E., *The Life of H.J. Temple, Viscount Palmerston, 1846–65*, 2 vols (Bentley, 1876), Vol. I, p. 103.
5. Marek, G., *The Eagles Die* (Hart-Davis, McGibbon, 1975), p. 39.
6. Haslip, J., *Imperial Adventurer* (Weidenfeld & Nicolson, 1971), p. 15.
7. Brook-Shepherd, G., *Royal Sunset* (Weidenfeld & Nicolson, 1987), p. 118.
8. Redlich, J., *Emperor Francis Joseph of Austria* (Macmillan, 1929), p. 14.
9. Taylor, *op. cit.*, p. 47.
10. Margutti, Baron von, *The Emperor Francis Joseph and his Times* (Hutchinson, 1921), p. 3.
11. Redlich, *op. cit.*, p. 31.
12. Crankshaw, *op. cit.*, p. 15.

Chapter 2

1. Palmer, A., *Twilight of the Habsburgs* (Weidenfeld & Nicolson, 1994), p. 48.
2. Redlich, J., *Emperor Francis Joseph of Austria* (Macmillan, 1929), pp. 32-3.
3. Marek, G., *The Eagles Die* (Hart-Davis, McGibbon, 1975), p. 68.
4. Haslip, *The Lonely Empress* (Weidenfeld & Nicolson, 1965), p. 33.
5. Listowel, J., *A Habsburg Tragedy* (Ascent, 1978), p. 44.
6. Van der Kiste, J., *Emperor Francis Joseph* (Sutton, 2005), p. 21.
7. Tschuppik, K., *The Empress Elizabeth of Austria* (Constable, 1930), p. 23.
8. Palmer, *op. cit.*, p. 78.
9. Redlich, *op. cit.*, p. 142.
10. Crankshaw, E., *The Fall of the House of Habsburg* (Longmans, 1963), p. 131.
11. Corti, E. C. C., *Elizabeth, Empress of Austria* (Thornton Butterworth, 1936), p. 73.
12. Haslip, *op. cit.*, p. 118.
13. Crankshaw, *op. cit.*, p. 164.
14. Marek, *op. cit.*, p. 126.
15. Redlich, *op. cit.*, p. 281.

Chapter 3

1. Margutti, Baron von, *The Emperor Francis Joseph and his Times* (Hutchinson, 1921), p. 63.
2. Barkeley, R., *The Road to Mayerling* (Macmillan, 1958), p. 11.
3. Crankshaw, E., *The Fall of the House of Habsburg* (Longmans, 1963), p. 181.
4. Haslip, *The Lonely Empress* (Weidenfeld & Nicolson, 1965), p. 147.
5. Corti, E. C. C., *The English Empress* (Cassell, 1957), p. 99.
6. Van der Kiste, J., *Emperor Francis Joseph* (Sutton, 2005), p. 79.
7. Corti, E. C. C., *Elizabeth, Empress of Austria* (Thornton Butterworth, 1936), pp. 142-3.
8. Hyde, H. M., *Mexican Empire* (Macmillan, 1946), pp. 291-2.
9. Palmer, A., *Twilight of the Habsburgs* (Weidenfeld & Nicolson, 1994), p. 161.
10. Corti, *Elizabeth, op. cit.*, p. 111.
11. Magnus, P., *King Edward the Seventh* (John Murray, 1964), p. 101.
12. Corti, *Elizabeth, op. cit.,* p. 184.

Chapter 4

1. Clark, R. W., *Freud* (Weidenfeld & Nicolson, 1980), pp. 32-3.
2. Haslip, J., *The Lonely Empress* (Weidenfeld & Nicolson, 1965), p. 250.
3. *Ibid.*, p. 257.
4. Palmer, A., *Twilight of the Habsburgs* (Weidenfeld & Nicolson, 1994), p. 189.
5. Louise of Belgium, Princess, *My Own Affairs* (Cassell, 1921), p. 97.
6. Mitis, O., *The Life of the Crown Prince Rudolph of Habsburg* (Skeffington, 1930), pp. 26-7.
7. *Ibid.*, pp. 198-9.
8. Barkeley, R., *The Road to Mayerling* (Macmillan, 1958), p. 74.
9. Listowel, J., *A Habsburg Tragedy* (Ascent, 1978), p. 121.
10. Margutti, Baron von, *The Emperor Francis Joseph and his Times* (Hutchinson, 1921), p. 83.
11. Stephanie of Belgium, Princess, *I was to be Empress* (Ivor Nicholson & Watson, 1937), p. 94.
12. Mitis, *op. cit.,* p. 68.
13. Corti, E. C. C., *Elizabeth, Empress of Austria* (Thornton Butterworth, 1936), p. 244.
14. Margutti, *op. cit.,* p. 89.
15. Röhl, J., *Young Wilhelm* (Cambridge University Press, 1998), p. 467.
16. Stephanie, *op. cit.,* pp. 112-3.
17. *Ibid.*, p. 255.
18. Listowel, *op. cit.,* p. 91.
19. Stephanie, *op. cit.,* p. 146.
20. Corti, *Elizabeth, op. cit.*, p. 290.
21. Palmer, *op. cit.,* p. 235.
22. Haslip, *The Lonely Empress, op. cit.,* p. 354.
23. Stephanie, *op. cit.,* p. 258.
24. *Ibid.*, p. 37.
25. King, G., and Wilson, P., *Twilight of Empire* (St Martin's, 2017), p. 91.

Chapter 5

1. Stephanie of Belgium, Princess, *I was to be Empress* (Ivor Nicholson & Watson, 1937), p. 239.
2. Haslip, *The Lonely Empress* (Weidenfeld & Nicolson, 1965), p. 383.
3. King, G., and Wilson, P., *Twilight of Empire* (St Martin's, 2017), p. 95.
4. Corti, E. C. C., *Elizabeth, Empress of Austria* (Thornton Butterworth, 1936), p. 310.
5. Stephanie, *op. cit.,* p. 245.
6. Listowel, J., *A Habsburg Tragedy* (Ascent, 1978), p. 212.
7. Larisch, M., *My Past* (Eveleigh Nash, 1913), pp. 286-8.
8. Paget, Lady W., *Embassies of Other Days*, 2 vols. (Hutchinson, 1923), Vol. II, p. 465.
9. *Ibid.*, pp. 465-6.
10. Listowel, J., *A Habsburg Tragedy* (Ascent, 1978), p. 215.
11. Stephanie, *op. cit.,* pp. 246-7.
12. Haslip, *op. cit..,* p. 404.

13. Röhl, J., *Wilhelm II: The Kaiser's Personal Monarchy* (Cambridge University Press, 2004), p. 129.
14. Margutti, Baron von, *The Emperor Francis Joseph and his Times* (Hutchinson, 1921), p. 98.
15. *Ibid.*, p. 74.
16. King and Wilson, *op. cit.*, p. 146.
17. Corti, *Elizabeth, op. cit.*, p. 323.
18. Margutti, *op. cit.*, p. 74.
19. Haslip, J., *The Emperor and the Actress* (Weidenfeld & Nicolson, 1982), p. 109.

Chapter 6

1. Paget, Lady W., *Embassies of Other Days,* 2 vols. (Hutchinson, 1923), Vol. II, p. 494.
2. Haslip, J., *The Lonely Empress* (Weidenfeld & Nicolson, 1965), p. 412.
3. Haslip, J., *The Emperor and the Actress* (Weidenfeld & Nicolson, 1982), p. 124.
4. Pakula, H., *The Last Romantic* (Weidenfeld & Nicolson, 1985), p. 74.
5. Redlich, J., *Emperor Francis Joseph of Austria* (Macmillan, 1929), p. 448.
6. Paget, *op. cit.*, Vol. II, pp. 557-8.
7. Haslip, *The Lonely Empress, op. cit.*, p. 427.
8. Haslip, *The Emperor and the Actress, op. cit.*, p. 125.
9. Victoria, Queen, *The Letters of Queen Victoria, 3rd Series,* 3 vols. (John Murray, 1930–2), Vol. III, p. 36.
10. Corti, E. C. C., *Elizabeth, Empress of Austria* (Thornton Butterworth, 1936), p. 362.
11. *Ibid.*, p. 365.
12. *Ibid.*, p. 367.
13. *Ibid.*, p. 368.
14. Tschudi, C., *Elizabeth, Empress of Austria and Queen of Hungary* (Swan Sonnenschein, 1901), p. 245.
15. Corti, *Elizabeth, Empress, op. cit.*, p. 384.
16. Haslip, *The Emperor and the Actress, op. cit.*, p. 225.
17. Palmer, A., *Twilight of the Habsburgs* (Weidenfeld & Nicolson, 1994), p. 292.
18. Margutti, Baron von, *The Emperor Francis Joseph and his Times* (Hutchinson, 1921), p. 35.

Chapter 7

1. Cassels, L., *The Archduke and the Assassin* (Frederick Muller, 1984), pp. 38-9.
2. King, G., and Woolmans, S., *The Assassination of the Archduke* (Macmillan, 2013), p. 54.
3. Cassels, *op. cit.*, p. 43.
4. Haslip, J., *The Emperor and the Actress* (Weidenfeld & Nicolson, 1982), p. 221.
5. Brook-Shepherd, G., *Victims at Sarajevo* (Harvill, 1984), p. 85.
6. *Ibid.*, p. 86.
7. Eisenmenger, V., *Archduke Franz Ferdinand* (Selwyn & Blount, 1928), pp. 239-40.
8. King and Woolmans, *op. cit.*, p. 80.
9. Vivian, H., *Francis Joseph and his Court* (John Lane, 1917), p. 120.
10. King and Woolmans, *op. cit.*, p. 85.
11. Ketterl, E., *The Emperor Francis Joseph I* (Skeffington, 1929), p. 84.
12. *Ibid.*, p. 27.
13. Van der Kiste, J., *Emperor Francis Joseph* (Sutton, 2005), p. 185.
14. Gore, J., *King George V* (John Murray, 1941), p. 189.
15. Pope-Hennessy, J., *Queen Mary* (Allen & Unwin, 1959), p. 385.
16. King and Woolmans, *op. cit.*, p. 107.
17. William II, *My Early Life* (Methuen, 1926), p. 230.
18. Haslip, *The Emperor and the Actress, op. cit.*, p. 197.
19. Margutti, Baron von, *The Emperor Francis Joseph and his Times* (Hutchinson, 1921), p. 221.
20. Bülow, Prince B. von, *Memoirs 1897–1903* (Putnam, 1931), p. 148.
21. Marek, G., *The Eagles Die* (Hart-Davis, McGibbon, 1975), p. 414.
22. Beller, S., *Francis Joseph* (Longman, 1996), p. 188.
23. *Ibid.*, p. 189.

Chapter 8

1. Margutti, Baron von, *The Emperor Francis Joseph and his Times* (Hutchinson, 1921), p. 154.
2. King, G., and Woolmans, S., *The Assassination of the Archduke* (Macmillan, 2013), p. 100.
3. Brook-Shepherd, G., *The Last Empress* (HarperCollins, 1991), p. 25.
4. Brook-Shepherd, G., *Victims at Sarajevo* (Harvill, 1984), p. 113.
5. King and Woolmans, *op. cit.*, p. 143.
6. *Ibid.*, pp. 159-60.
7. Brook-Shepherd, *The Last Empress, op. cit.*, p. 39; *Victims at Sarajevo, op. cit.*, p. 118.
8. Brook-Shepherd, G., *The Last Habsburg* (Weidenfeld & Nicolson, 1968), p. 25.
9. Gribble, S., *The Life of the Emperor Francis Joseph* (Eveleigh Nash, 1914), pp. 341-2.
10. Brook-Shepherd, *Victims at Sarajevo, op. cit.*, p. 212.
11. Gerard, J., *Face to Face with Kaiserism* (Doran, 1918), p. 210.
12. King and Woolmans, *op. cit.*, p. 152.
13. Brook-Shepherd, *The Last Habsburg, op. cit.*, p. 27.
14. Brook-Shepherd, *Victims at Sarajevo, op. cit.*, p. 222.
15. Pauli, H., *The Secret of Sarajevo* (Collins, 1966), p. 275.
16. Margutti, *op. cit.*, pp. 138-9.
17. Brook-Shepherd, *Victims at Sarajevo, op. cit.*, p. 256.
18. Aronson, T., *Crowns in Conflict* (John Murray, 1986), p. 75.
19. Pauli, *op. cit.*, p. 273.
20. King and Woolmans, *op. cit.*, p. 213.
21. Brook-Shepherd, *The Last Habsburg, op. cit.*, p. 3.
22. Röhl, J., *Wilhelm II: Into the Abyss of War and Exile* (Cambridge University Press, 2014), p. 1017.
23. Crankshaw, E., *The Fall of the House of Habsburg* (Longmans, 1963), p. 394.
24. *The Times*, 25 July 1914.
25. Jaszi, O., *The Dissolution of the Habsburg Monarchy* (University of Chicago Press, 1961), p. 424.
26. Crankshaw, *op. cit.*, p. 394.
27. *Ibid.*, p. 404.

Chapter 9

1. Brook-Shepherd, G., *The Last Habsburg* (Weidenfeld & Nicolson, 1968), p. 43.
2. Ketterl, E., *The Emperor Francis Joseph I* (Skeffington, 1929), pp. 103-4.
3. Brook-Shepherd, G., *The Last Empress* (HarperCollins, 1991), p. 37.
4. Russell, G., *The Emperors* (Amberley, 2014), p. 84.
5. Brook-Shepherd, *The Last Habsburg, op. cit.*, p. 29.
6. Margutti, Baron von, *The Emperor Francis Joseph and his Times* (Hutchinson, 1921), p. 362.
7. Brook-Shepherd, *The Last Habsburg, op. cit.*, p. 46.
8. Ketterl, *op. cit.*, pp. 251-2.
9. Brook-Shepherd, *The Last Empress, op. cit.*, p. 47.

Chapter 10

1. Brook-Shepherd, G., *The Last Empress* (HarperCollins, 1991), p. 46.
2. *Ibid.*, p. 55.
3. *Ibid.*, pp. 84-5.
4. Brook-Shepherd, G., *The Last Habsburg* (Weidenfeld & Nicolson, 1968), p. 74.
5. Brook-Shepherd, *The Last Empress, op. cit.*, p. 50.
6. Brook-Shepherd, *The Last Habsburg, op. cit.*, p. 77; Bogle, J., and Bogle, J., *A Heart for Europe* (Gracewing, 2000), p. 82.
7. Brook-Shepherd, *The Last Habsburg, op. cit.*, p. 60.
8. Röhl, J., *Wilhelm II: Into the Abyss of War and Exile* (Cambridge University Press, 2014), p. 1136.
9. William II, Ex-German Emperor, *My Memoirs* (Cassell, 1922), p. 267.

10. Balfour. M., *The Kaiser and his Times* (Cresset, 1964), pp. 374-5.
11. Brook-Shepherd, *The Last Habsburg, op. cit.*, pp. 149-50.
12. Brook-Shepherd, *The Last Empress, op. cit.*, p. 100.
13. Brook-Shepherd, *The Last Habsburg, op. cit.*, p. 151.
14. *Ibid.*, p. 176.
15. Brook-Shepherd, *The Last Empress, op. cit.*, p. 123; *The Last Habsburg, op. cit.*, p. 180.
16. Brook-Shepherd, *The Last Empress, op. cit.*, p. 127.
17. *Ibid.*, p. 130.
18. George, R., *Heirs of Tradition* (Carroll & Nicolson, 1949), p. 206.
19. Brook-Shepherd, *The Last Habsburg, op. cit.*, p. 214.

Chapter 11

1. *New York Times*, 16 February 1919.
2. Brook-Shepherd, G., *The Last Habsburg* (Weidenfeld & Nicolson, 1968), p. 238.
3. Brook-Shepherd, G., *The Last Empress* (HarperCollins, 1991), p. 140.
4. *Ibid.*, p. 143.
5. *Ibid.*, p. 151.
6. Bogle, J., and Bogle, J., *A Heart for Europe* (Gracewing, 2000), p. 148.
7. Brook-Shepherd, *The Last Habsburg, op. cit.*, pp. 322-4.
8. *New York Times*, 13 January 1922.
9. Wheatcroft, A., *The Habsburgs* (Viking, 1995), p. 290.
10. Brook-Shepherd, *The Last Habsburg, op. cit.*, p. 330.

Chapter 12

1. Brook-Shepherd, G., *The Last Empress* (HarperCollins, 1991), p. 232.
2. Gunther, J., *Inside Europe* (Hamish Hamilton, 1936), pp. 321-3.
3. Brook-Shepherd, *The Last Empress, op. cit*, p. 295.
4. *Ibid.*, p. 303.
5. Hamann, B., *The Reluctant Empress* (Knopf, 1986), p. 374.

Bibliography

Books

Aronson, T., *Crowns in Conflict: The Triumph and the Tragedy of European Monarchy 1910–1918* (John Murray, 1986)

Ashley, E., *The Life of H.J. Temple, Viscount Palmerston, 1846–65: With Selections from his Speeches and Correspondence*, 2 vols (Bentley, 1876)

Balfour. M., *The Kaiser and his Times* (Cresset, 1964)

Barkeley, R., *The Road to Mayerling: Life and Death of Crown Prince Rudolph of Austria* (Macmillan, 1958)

Beller, S., *Francis Joseph* (Longman, 1996)

Bled, J.-P., *Franz Joseph* (Blackwell, 1992)

Bogle, J., and Bogle, J., *A Heart for Europe: The Lives of Emperor Charles and Empress Zita of Austria-Hungary* (Gracewing, 2000)

Brook-Shepherd, G., *The Last Empress: The Life and Times of Zita of Austria-Hungary* (HarperCollins, 1991); *The Last Habsburg* (Weidenfeld & Nicolson, 1968); *Royal Sunset: The Dynasties of Europe and the Great War* (Weidenfeld & Nicolson, 1987); *Victims at Sarajevo: The Romance and Tragedy of Franz Ferdinand and Sophie* (Harvill, 1984)

Bülow, Prince B. von, *Memoirs 1897–1903* (Putnam, 1931)

Cassels, L., *The Archduke and the Assassin: Sarajevo, June 28th 1914* (Frederick Muller, 1984); *Clash of Generations: A Habsburg Family Drama in the Nineteenth Century* (John Murray, 1973)

Clark, R. W., *Freud, the Man and the Cause* (Weidenfeld & Nicolson, 1980)

Corti, E. C. C., *Elizabeth, Empress of Austria* (Thornton Butterworth, 1936); *The English Empress: A Study in the Relations between Queen Victoria and her Eldest Daughter, Empress Frederick of Germany* (Cassell, 1957)

Crankshaw, E., *The Fall of the House of Habsburg* (Longmans, 1963)

Eisenmenger, V., *Archduke Franz Ferdinand* (Selwyn & Blount, 1928)

George, R., *Heirs of Tradition: Tributes of a New Zealander* (Carroll & Nicolson, 1949)

Gerard, J., *Face to Face with Kaiserism* (Doran, 1918)

Gore, J., *King George V: A Personal Memoir* (John Murray, 1941)

Gribble, S., *The Life of the Emperor Francis Joseph* (Eveleigh Nash, 1914)

Gunther, J., *Inside Europe* (Hamish Hamilton, 1936)

Hamann, B., *The Reluctant Empress: A Biography of Elizabeth, Empress of Austria* (Knopf, 1986)

Haslip, J., *The Emperor and the Actress: The Love Story of Emperor Franz Josef and Katherina Schratt* (Weidenfeld & Nicolson, 1982); *Imperial Adventurer: Emperor Maximilian of Mexico* (Weidenfeld & Nicolson, 1971); *The Lonely Empress: A Biography of Elizabeth of Austria* (Weidenfeld & Nicolson, 1965)

Hyde, H. M., *Mexican Empire: The History of Maximilian and Carlota of Mexico* (Macmillan, 1946)

Jaszi, O., *The Dissolution of the Habsburg Monarchy* (University of Chicago Press, 1961)

Ketterl, E., *The Emperor Francis Joseph I: An Intimate Study* (Skeffington, 1929)

King, G., and Wilson, P., *Twilight of Empire: The Tragedy at Mayerling and the End of the Habsburgs* (St Martin's, 2017)

King, G., and Woolmans, S., *The Assassination of the Archduke: Sarajevo 1914 and the Murder that Changed the World* (Macmillan, 2013)

Larisch, M., *My Past* (Eveleigh Nash, 1913)

Listowel, J., *A Habsburg Tragedy: Crown Prince Rudolf* (Ascent, 1978)

Louise of Belgium, Princess, *My Own Affairs* (Cassell, 1921)

Magnus, P., *King Edward the Seventh* (John Murray, 1964)

Marek, G., *The Eagles Die: Franz Joseph, Elisabeth, and their Austria* (Hart-Davis, McGibbon, 1975)

Margutti, Baron von, *The Emperor Francis Joseph and his Times* (Hutchinson, 1921)

Mitis, O., *The Life of the Crown Prince Rudolph of Habsburg: With Letters and Documents found amongst his Effects* (Skeffington, 1930)

Morton, F., *A Nervous Splendour: Vienna, 1888–1889* (Little, Brown, 1979)

Paget, Lady W., *Embassies of Other Days*, 2 vols. (Hutchinson, 1923)

Pakula, H., *The Last Romantic: A Biography of Marie, Queen of Roumania* (Weidenfeld & Nicolson, 1985)

Palmer, A., *Twilight of the Habsburgs: The Life and Times of Emperor Francis Joseph* (Weidenfeld & Nicolson, 1994)

Pauli, H., *The Secret of Sarajevo: The Story of Franz Ferdinand and Sophie* (Collins, 1966)

Pope-Hennessy, J., *Queen Mary, 1867–1953* (Allen & Unwin, 1959)

Redlich, J., *Emperor Francis Joseph of Austria: A Biography* (Macmillan, 1929)

Röhl, J., *Young Wilhelm: The Kaiser's Early Life, 1859–1888* (Cambridge University Press, 1998); *Wilhelm II: The Kaiser's Personal Monarchy, 1888–1900* (Cambridge University Press, 2004); *Wilhelm II: Into the Abyss of War and Exile, 1900–1941* (Cambridge University Press, 2014)

Russell, G., *The Emperors: How Europe's Rulers were Destroyed by the First World War* (Amberley, 2014)

Stephanie of Belgium, Princess, *I was to be Empress* (Ivor Nicholson & Watson, 1937)

Taylor, A. J. P., *The Habsburg Monarchy 1809–1918: A History of the Austrian Empire and Austria-Hungary* (Hamish Hamilton, 1948)

Tschudi, C., *Elizabeth, Empress of Austria and Queen of Hungary* (Swan Sonnenschein, 1901)

Tschuppik, K., *The Empress Elizabeth of Austria* (Constable, 1930)

Van der Kiste, J., *Emperor Francis Joseph: Life, Death and the Fall of the Habsburg Empire* (Sutton, 2005); *Windsor and Habsburg: The British and Austrian Reigning Houses, 1848–1922* (Sutton, 1987)

Victoria, Queen, *The Letters of Queen Victoria, 3rd Series: A Selection from Her Majesty's Correspondence and Journal Between the Years 1886 and 1901*, ed. G. E. Buckle, 3 vols. (John Murray, 1930–2)

Vivian, H., *Francis Joseph and his Court* (John Lane, 1917)

Vovk, J. C., *Imperial Requiem: Four Royal Women and the Fall of the Age of Empires* (iUniverse, 2012)

Wheatcroft, A., *The Habsburgs: Embodying Empire* (Viking, 1995)

William II, Ex-German Emperor, *My Early Life* (Methuen, 1926); *My Memoirs: 1878–1918* (Cassell, 1922)

Journals and Newspapers

New York Times
Royalty Digest
The Times

Index